Apartheid

Published by the United Nations
Educational, Scientific and Cultural Organization
7, Place de Fontenoy, 75700 Paris
First edition 1967
Second edition 1972
Third impression 1973
Printed by Offset-Aubin, Poitiers
ISBN 92-3-100980-X

Apartheid

Its effects on
    education, science, culture and information

Second edition, revised and enlarged

Unesco   Paris 1972

Preface to the first edition

The racial policies of the Government of the Union, now the Republic of South Africa have been before the United Nations since the first session of the General Assembly in 1946. India, in that year, brought before the Assembly a complaint that the Government of South Africa had enacted legislation which discriminated against South Africans of Indian origin. Since then the racial policies of the Government of South Africa have been under consideration by both the General Assembly and the Security Council. Resolutions passed by the General Assembly reflect the mounting concern of world opinion about the racial situation within South Africa and the frustration occasioned by the refusal of the government to respond to the repeated appeals by the United Nations that its racial policies should be brought into conformity with the United Nations Charter. Resolution 395 (V) of the General Assembly, 2 December 1950, states that 'a policy of "racial segregation" (apartheid) is necessarily based on doctrines of racial discrimination'. In 1954, the Assembly 'invited' the Government of South Africa to reconsider its position in the light of the principles of the Charter. In 1955, the Assembly 'expressed its concern' about the policies of the South African Government. In 1957, it 'appealed' to the government to revise its policy and resolution 1375 (XIV), 17 November 1959, reminded it that 'government policies which accentuate or seek to preserve racial discrimination are prejudicial to international harmony', noted 'with concern that the policy of apartheid is still being pursued' and 'expressed its opposition to the continuance or preservation of racial discrimination in any part of the world; . . .'.

In August 1963, the Security Council recommended that the sale and shipment of all arms, ammunition and military vehicles to South Africa should stop. This followed a more comprehensive resolution, 1761 (XVII), adopted by the General Assembly in November 1962, which asked Member States to take specific measures, such as breaking off diplomatic relations with the Government of the Republic of South Africa or refraining from establishing such relations and the boycott of all South African goods. These recommendations were not, however, mandatory. At the same session, the General Assembly also established a special committee which would keep the situation in South Africa under review between sessions of the Assembly and would submit reports to this Assembly and to the Security Council.

In resolution 1978 (XVIII), 16 December 1963, the General Assembly 'invites the Specialized Agencies and all Member States to give to the Special Committee their assistance and co-operation in the fulfilment of its mandate'. In conformity with this resolution, the United Nations Special Committee on the Policies of Apartheid of the Government of the Republic of South Africa, through the Secretary-General of the United Nations, on 20 April 1965, requested Unesco 'to prepare a study on the effects of apartheid in the fields of education, science and culture'. This request was accepted by the Executive Board of Unesco, meeting at its seventieth session, when it 'authorized' the Director-General to 'prepare the study requested of Unesco by the Special Committee on the Policies of Apartheid of the Government of the Republic of South Africa . . .'.[1] The decision of the Executive Board was in conformity with Unesco's responsibilities in the fields of racial discrimination as inscribed in its Constitution.

This report on the 'Effects of the Policy of Apartheid in the Fields of Education, Science, Culture and the Dissemination of Information[2] in South Africa' was therefore undertaken by the Unesco Secretariat for submission to the United Nations Special Committee on the Policies of Apartheid of the Government of the Republic of South Africa.

Its object is to confront the policies and practices of the Government of the Republic of South Africa in the fields of education, science, culture and the dissemination of information with a number of international norms of conduct to which Unesco is legally and morally dedicated:

---

1. United Nations Educational, Scientific and Cultural Organization, 70 Ex. Decisions, Paris, 4 June 1965.
2. It was considered that the report should cover all the fields of competence of the Organization, and consequently it includes an appraisal of the effects of the policy of apartheid on the dissemination of information, as well as on education, science and culture.

The Constitution of Unesco:

'Article 1
The purpose of the Organization is to contribute to peace and security by promoting collaboration among the nations through education, science and culture in order to further universal respect for justice, for the rule of law and for the human rights and fundamental freedoms which are affirmed for the peoples of the world, without distinction of race, sex, language or religion.'

The United Nations Charter:

'Article 1
The purposes of the United Nations are:

. . . .
3. To achieve international co-operation . . . in promoting and encouraging respect for human rights and for fundamental freedoms for all without distinction as to race, sex, language or religion.

'Article 55
. . . the United Nations shall promote:
. . . c. universal respect for, and observance of, human rights and fundamental freedoms for all without distinction as to race, sex, language or religion.'

The Universal Declaration of Human Rights (1948):

'Article 1
All human beings are born free and equal in dignity and rights.

'Article 2
Everyone is entitled to all the rights and freedoms set forth in this Declaration, without distinction of any kind, such as race, colour, sex, language, religion, political or other opinion, national or social origin, property, birth or other status.'
[Other articles will be quoted in the relevant chapters of this study.]

The United Nations Declaration on the Elimination of all Forms of Racial Discrimination (1963-65)

The Unesco Convention and Recommendations against Discrimination in Education (1960)

The Unesco Declaration of the Principle of International Cultural Co-operation (4 November 1966)

Lastly, in so far as the biological aspects of race have a bearing on the questions dealt with in this report, *The Proposals on the Biological Aspects of Race*, adopted in Moscow (1964) under the auspices of Unesco, which stated:

'The peoples of the world today appear to possess equal biological potentialities for obtaining any civilizational level. Differences in the achievements of different peoples must be attributed solely to their cultural history. . . . Neither in the field of hereditary potentialities concerning the overall intelligence and the capacity for cultural development nor in that of physical traits, is there any justification for the concept of "inferior" and "superior" races. . . .'

The sources used for the preparation of this report have been various official texts (laws, regulations, parliamentary debates, etc.) of the Government of the Republic of South Africa, and reports from other organizations of the United Nations System (Special Committee of the United Nations on the Policies of Apartheid and the International Labour Organisation). Various publications relevant to apartheid and published by scientific and research institutions both in South Africa and outside have also been utilized, as well as information published in the press, and some unpublished information emanating from personalities—scientists and university people having a direct knowledge of the conditions in which the policy of apartheid is applied in South Africa and whose competence and objectivity, in the judgement of the Secretariat, may not be doubted.

In one specific field—that of the consequences of the policy of apartheid on culture, the opinions of South African authors on the conditions of writing and on the problems of creative literature in a society governed by apartheid have been quoted.

In the preparation of the report, the Secretariat was able to obtain the assistance of Professor Folke Schmidt, University of Stockholm (Sweden) (Chief Consultant); J. P. Clark, Nigerian poet and playwright, University of Lagos; Professor P. Sherlock, Vice-Chancellor of the University of the West Indies, Mona (Jamaica); and Professor F. Terrou, Institut Français de Presse, Paris, consultants, respectively, in the fields of culture, education and information. However, views expressed in this report do not necessarily reflect their opinion; they commit only the Secretariat of Unesco.

Although South Africa withdrew from Unesco in 1955,[1] the Director-General proposed through the Secretary-General of the United Nations that Professor Folke Schmidt (Sweden), employed by Unesco as Chief Consultant during the preparation of this report, be granted a visa to visit the Republic of South Africa in order to collect data and to check all official source material. This request was not accepted by the South African Government.

This report was submitted to the Secretary-General of the United Nations on 30 December 1966 and transmitted by the latter to the chairman of the United Nations Special Committee on the Policies of Apartheid of the Government of the Republic of South Africa on 11 January 1967. On 6 February 1967 the Secretary-General of the United Nations communicated to the Director-General of Unesco a copy of a letter dated 3 February 1967 from the acting chairman of the Special Committee in which transmittal of the report was acknowledged on behalf of the Special Committee and reference made to a statement to the press issued on 18 January 1967 by its chairman which reads as follows:

'A special study by the Unesco Secretariat on "the effects of the policy of apartheid on education, culture and information" has been submitted to the Special Committee on the Policies of Apartheid of the Government of the Republic of South Africa and made public today. This study has been prepared in response to a request made by the Special Committee in April 1965 in discharge of its mandate to review the various aspects of the policies of apartheid.

'On behalf of the Special Committee, I wish to congratulate and express our great appreciation to the Director-General and the Secretariat of Unesco for preparing such a comprehensive and authoritative study.

'This well-documented study shows, through undisputable facts and figures, the fraudulence of the so-called policy of "separate development", advertised by the peddlers of apartheid and their apologists.

'It shows how the apartheid régime has deliberately depressed the educational standards of the non-whites, who constitute the great

---

1. On 5 April 1955, it gave notice of its withdrawal from the Organization, the reason given being 'the interference in South African racial problems by means of Unesco publications which are being advertised and distributed in the Union by the South African Institute of Race Relations'.—Report by the Director-General on the Activities of the Organization, presented to the Executive Board at its 42nd session March-November 1955.

majority of the sons and daughters of the land, and has proved to be an enemy of culture and of civilization.

'It shows clearly that a racist régime can never be trusted with its promises of ensuring the satisfaction of even the material and cultural needs of its subjects.

'This study deserves to be widely disseminated all around the world and studied by all those concerned with the progress of education, science, culture and information. The Special Committee will lend its full co-operation to Unesco towards this end and hopes that governments, non-governmental organizations and information media will give the contents of the study the widest circulation.

'It is to be earnestly hoped that this study will encourage governments, organizations, foundations and individuals to consider ways and means to provide assistance to the victims of the inhuman system of racial discrimination. The United Nations Trust Fund for South Africa and the United Nations Education and Training Programme for South Africans, as well as non-governmental funds like the International Defence and Aid Fund and the Southern Africa Education Fund, deserve greater support.

'But above all, it is to be hoped that the study will encourage more energetic and concerted efforts by world public opinion to promote decisive action for the elimination of apartheid which is recognized by the United Nations and Unesco as constituting a crime against humanity and a threat to international peace and security.'

In this report, the term 'white' is used for people of European stock. The term 'African' replaces the word 'Bantu' which is at present used by the South African Government to designate people of African stock, except in direct quotations where, if the word 'Bantu' was originally used, it is retained. The term 'Asian' is used for people of Chinese or Indian descent, and 'Coloured' for those of mixed European and African or Asian background. The use of these terms 'white', 'African', 'Asian' and 'Coloured', has been unavoidable because of the nature of apartheid itself. However, the Secretariat rejects the concepts of race and of ethnic group relations that such terms imply.

Preface to the second edition

At the request of the United Nations Commission on Human Rights, and the Special Committee on the Policies of Apartheid of the Government of the Republic of South Africa, the original book has been revised to bring the material up to date. It is published to mark the International Year Against Racial Discrimination, 1971.

The policies of apartheid have continued to be of increasing concern to the United Nations and its Specialized Agencies. The reason for this is stated in the following extract from the report of the Special Committee on the Policies of Apartheid of the Republic of South Africa, S/9939, 18 September 1970, paras. 102, 104-6 :

'In resolution 2506 B (XXIV) adopted on 21 November 1969 on the question of the policies of *apartheid* of the Government of the Republic of South Africa, the General Assembly noted with concern that the Government of South Africa had continued to intensify and extend beyond the borders of South Africa its inhuman and aggressive policies of apartheid and that those policies had resulted in violent conflict. It expressed the conviction that the policies and actions of the Government of the Republic of South Africa were contrary to the obligations of a Member State and constituted a grave threat to international peace and security.'

The Special Committee notes that by continuing to apply its repressive legislation designed to suppress demands for social, economic and political changes accepted elsewhere in the world as normal, the South African Government has shown its determination to close all avenues of peaceful change in the country.

The South African Government has not only continued to persecute the opponents of its policies, but it has pursued the widest and severest application of the measures of racial separation and segregation, thus heightening racial bitterness and increasing the danger of violent conflict inside South Africa.

The threat of a violent racial conflict is all the more serious since, in view of the rejection by the South African Government of the peaceful means advocated by the United Nations for an equitable settlement of the situation, the oppressed people of South Africa and their liberation movements are now convinced that their inalienable rights and freedoms recognized in the United Nations Charter and the Universal Declaration of Human Rights can be achieved only through armed struggle and underground activities.

Contents

Introduction

South Africa, a society in which Africans, Asians and Europeans co-exist in the same territory, has been the result of a long history going back to the first European settlement in the Cape of Good Hope in 1652. It is a history not only of prolonged contact (some of it friendly) between these groups of people, but also a history of conflict over land and cattle at first, then over industrial opportunities when towns grew up. There were also conflicts between the Boers, descendants of the first Dutch settlers, and the English-speaking South Africans—conflicts which terminated in the Boer War and the defeat of the Dutch-speaking Afrikaners by the English colonizers. About the mid-twentieth century then, the ingredients of the present alarming South African situation were all present—the rivalry between the Afrikaner and the English-speaking South Africans which split the white population into two main groups, the suspicion and fear which most of the white group felt for Africans who were numerically stronger, against whom they had fought a series of wars and whom they had traditionally treated as a source of cheap labour. There was also the Coloured group formed from a mixture of white, Hottentot and Malay elements and an Asian group brought to South Africa in the nineteenth century as labour for the new sugar plantations in Natal.

At the end of the Second World War there was another factor on the South African scene. White supremacy, threatened occasionally over the 300 years of white settlement, was challenged by the emergence of independent States in Africa and Asia. On the political front the struggle for independence was a struggle for 'one man-one vote', and had direct consequences for South African whites, who, in framing the Constitution of 1910, had resisted any effective participation of non-whites in the political process. There was another challenge; in all countries there arose a new demand for the implementation of 'human rights', a demand encouraged by the

United Nations Universal Declaration of Human Rights of 1948. In South Africa this meant a demand for equality of opportunity in the social and economic front and was thus a direct threat to white privileges.

The National Party came to power in 1948 on an appeal which rested almost entirely on its promise to safeguard and, if necessary, strengthen 'white supremacy'. In its public statements the government identified this political, economic and social policy with the ideology of 'apartheid', which was described in the 1947 election manifesto of the National Party as follows:

'In general terms our policy envisages segregating the most important ethnic groups and sub-groups in their own areas where every group will be enabled to develop into a self-sufficient unit. We endorse the general principle of territorial segregation of the Bantu and the Whites . . . the Bantu in the urban areas should be regarded as migratory citizens not entitled to political or social rights equal to those of the Whites. The process of detribalization should be arrested . . . .'

From the beginning there were two co-existing concepts of apartheid. One was that the races—subdivided into tribes—should be completely segregated into self-sufficient territories. The other was that apartheid was not to mean complete territorial segregation but a more rigid enforcement of non-white social, economic and political inferiority. From 1948 to 1970, the South African Government has moved in both directions. On 4 December 1963, the then Prime Minister, Dr. H. F. Verwoerd stated that '. . . we shall be able to prove that it is only by creating separate nations that discrimination will in fact disappear in the long run'. It is certain that some idealistic white South Africans hoped that the incipient conflict in the South African situation would be resolved by apartheid. Further, many hoped that while the political and economic aspirations of the African majority—and the Coloured and Asian minorities—would be met by 'separate development', the privileges of a white South Africa would be guaranteed.

The creation of Bantustans—'black homelands'—from the scattered reserves and the establishment of the Transkei in 1963 as an example of a semi-autonomous state, are steps in this 'separate development'. It is not necessary here to go into the government's case for independent Bantustans—or the case against it. It is sufficient to note the report of the United Nations Special Committee on the Policies of Apartheid of the Government of the Republic of South Africa, 13 September 1963:

'These moves are engineered by a government in which the African people concerned have no voice and are aimed at the separation of the races and the denial of rights to the African population in six-sevenths of the territory of the Republic of South Africa in return for promises of self-government for the Africans in scattered reserves which account for one-seventh of the territory. These reserves contain less than two-fifths of the African population of the Republic, while many of the Africans in the rest of the country are largely detribalized and have little attachment to the reserves. . . . The creation of Bantustans may, therefore, be regarded as designed to reinforce white supremacy in the Republic by strengthening the position of tribal chiefs, dividing the African people through the offer of opportunities for a limited number of Africans and deceiving public opinion.'

The Transkei experiment has been followed by the setting up of the 'Territorial Authorities' in other 'homelands' as a step towards the establishment of limited self-government on the Transkei model.[1]

Since separation or apartheid is the ideological and legal basis for the inequalities in access to education and to culture, and interferes with scientific development and freedom of information, it would be useful to examine briefly at this point the legislation which enforces separation. Legislation affecting particular fields of Unesco's competence will be analysed in detail in the relevant chapter.

One important step in any attempted separation of the races was the enforced removal of people of differing races who had lived closely together.

The Population Registration Act of 1950 with its later amendments provided for the classification of the South African population into three main groups: white, Coloured and African—the Asians constituting a sub-group in the Coloured group. This classification was fundamental to the whole government policy of 'separateness' for each race.

1. The 'Nations of the Republic' and their population were given in the South Africa yearbook of 1970 as: Xhosa, 3,134,265; European descended, 3,067,638; Zulu, 2,788,415; Coloured, 1,488,267; Bapedi, 1,188,859; Sotho, 1,156,436; Tswana, 886,240; Shangaan, 518,775; Asians, 477,414; 'smaller Bantu national units', 1,134,819.—*State of South Africa Yearbook, 1970: Economic, Financial and Statistical Yearbook of the Republic of South Africa*, p. 67, Johannesburg, 1970.

As from 1 August 1966 it became compulsory for all citizens of the Republic over 16 years of age to possess identity cards and to produce these at the request of an authorized person. The racial group of the holder is on this card.

Control of the freedom of movement of Africans has been achieved through the 'pass laws'. A system of pass laws was in effect before the National Party came to power; however, these laws varied from province to province. Some classes of Africans were exempted from carrying them, and in the Cape, while they existed in theory, they were in practice no longer required.

The Natives (Abolition of Passes and Co-ordination of Documents) Act of 1952 repealed previous laws. Henceforth all Africans were required to possess a 'reference book' which contains detailed information about the holder, including a space for efflux and influx control endorsements. Failure to produce the 'reference book' on demand is a criminal offence, punishable by a fine of not more than the equivalent of U.S.$28 or imprisonment for not longer than one month. Between 1 January and 30 June 1963, 162,182 Africans had been prosecuted for failing to register or to produce these documents.[1]

In 1967-68, Africans had been prosecuted for pass law offences on an average of 1,900 per day.[2]

The Natives (Urban Areas) Consolidation Act of 1945 and its amendments of 1952, 1956 and 1957, together with the Bantu Laws Amendment Act No. 42 of 1964, provided for the compulsory residence in location, native villages or hostels of Africans within an urban area. It regulated the entry of Africans into the areas and the place of their settlement. The presence of an African in a prescribed area for more than seventy-two hours is subject to severe restrictions. To take up work he must get permission from a labour bureau and to visit the area permission must be sought from a labour officer. Some Africans are exempted from these restrictions, for example, those continuously resident in the area since birth (who must provide

1. *Annual Report of the Commissioner of the South African Police*, for the year ended 30 June 1964.
2. *Annual Report of the Commissioner of the South African Police*, for the year ended 1968.

Law infringement (relating to pass laws, African taxation, etc.)	Number committed for trial
Bantu reception depot regulations, rules and regulations relating to Bantu residential areas, mission stations, and Bantu reserves	157 807
Foreign Africans entering urban areas	17 245
Registration and production of documents by Africans	352 517
Bantu (Urban Areas) Consolidation Act not specified elsewhere	142 727
Masters' and Servants Acts and Bantu Labour Regulation Act	23 365
Bantu tax	243 437

proof that they are entitled to be there). But even Africans who qualify to remain in a prescribed area may be deemed 'idle' or 'undesirable' and then be ordered out of the area, forfeiting their residential rights. Moreover, there seems to be some confusion as to what the exemptions are and to whom they apply.

The Group Areas Act has been followed by a list of Group Areas Declarations—setting aside areas for the exclusive occupation of one or other population group. This Act has been implemented in spite of repeated resolutions by the General Assembly: resolutions 395 (V) of 2 December 1950, 551 (VI) of 12 January 1952, 615 (VII) of 5 December 1952, and 719 (VII) of 11 November 1953.

The proclamations issued in October 1963 involved, in Durban alone, the eviction of nearly 10,000 families, the great majority of them Indians. In 1964 the declarations were designed to resettle virtually all of the 38,000 Indians on the Rand.

Eviction orders are not confined to situations in which there may be a degree, however small, of mixed residential districts; the orders were framed to force non-whites out of the town centres and to resettle them on the outskirts. Thus, the joint ministerial statement of February 1966 declared District Six—one of the oldest sections of Cape Town—which had been populated by Coloured residents for over 300 years, as a white area. A Coloured population of over 20,000 were to be forced to move.

The Group Areas Amendment Act No. 69 of 1969 extended the scope of certain provisions that previously applied in group areas only. They now apply in virtually the whole country with the exception of African areas.

If a racially disqualified person acquires property by inheritance, this property must be sold within a year to a person who is qualified to own it, unless exemption is granted. This Act tightens the former provisions which had made it possible for the State President by proclamation to define an area and, after a year had elapsed, to declare that buildings or premises may be used for a specific purpose only. It will now be possible to issue the proclamation with regard to an entire area, rather than to individual buildings or premises.

Up to September 1968, 58,999 Coloured families, 35,172 Indian families, 784 Chinese families and 656 white families had become disqualified to remain in their homes;[1] 23,587 Coloured families,

1. *House of Assembly Debates (Hansard)*, Vol. 1, 7 February 1968, Cols. 303, 312.

17,723 Indian families and 497 white families had been resettled to that date.

In spite of the ideology of apartheid, in spite of the uprooting of thousands of families, the complete separation of peoples into tribal and ethnic groupings in South Africa has proved impossible. The closely integrated economic structure, the location of all the major industries, all the mineral wealth, all the important harbour facilities and all the best arable land in that part of South Africa which was outside the reserves in white ownership meant that Africans—as well as Coloured persons and Asians—remain dependent on the town and farming complex of white South Africa for a livelihood. Even the government's attempt to encourage African-owned small-scale industries in the Transkei has come up against the relative poverty of the area, the comparative lack of natural resources and the lack of accumulated capital. For good or ill, white and non-white South Africa remain economically interdependent. If the non-whites need the job opportunities at present available in white South Africa, white South Africa could not maintain its present industrial and agricultural production—nor the present high standard of living—without non-white labour. In fact, whatever the stated policy of the government, there has been an increasing number of Africans admitted to urban areas.

Table 1 gives the number of Africans admitted to the main urban areas and the number endorsed out during 1964 and for the first three months of 1965.

Between 1962 and 1964 the African population of Johannesburg increased from 609,100 to 706,389; the number of African men employed in Durban increased from 74,500 in 1946 to 136,000 in 1965. In the Western Cape, the number of Africans employed by local authorities, the provincial administration, public service departments, agriculture and industry increased from 1963 to 1964 by 7.5 per cent (from almost 77,000 to a little under 83,000) and increasing numbers were being recruited for employment through the labour bureaux in the Transkei.[1] In the Rand the African population exceeds the white by more than 500,000.[2]

1. *Second Special Report of the Director-General on the Application of the Declaration Concerning the Policy of Apartheid of the Republic of South Africa*, p. 11, Geneva, ILO, 1966.
2. *A Survey of Race Relations in South Africa, 1966*, p. 168, Johannesburg, South African Institute of Race Relations, 1967. (Further footnote references to this work are given, together with the relevant year, in the abridged form: *A Survey of Race Relations . . . .*)

TABLE 1. Numbers of Africans admitted to and endorsed from main urban areas in 1964 and first three months of 1965

Year	Admitted		Endorsed out	
	Men	Women	Men	Women
1964	156 352	18 747	84 258	13 983
First 3 months of 1965	44 409	5 133	19 159	3 855

Source: House of Assembly Debates (Hansard), Vol. 12, 1965, Col. 4430. Quoted from *A Survey of Race Relations in South Africa, 1965*, p. 155, Johannesburg, South African Institute of Race Relations, 1966.

The main push of apartheid has been therefore in the direction of more rigid racial discrimination, with growing inequalities in opportunities (see Tables 2, 3, 4, 5 and 6).

TABLE 2. Population by racial group

Group	1946	1951	1960[1]	1970[2]
Africans	7 830 559	8 360 083	10 927 922	14 893 000
Whites	2 372 004	2 641 689	3 088 492	3 779 000
Coloured persons	928 062	1 103 016	1 509 258	1 996 000
Asians	285 260	366 664	477 125	614 000

1. *State of South Africa Yearbook*, 1971: *Economic, Financial and Statistical Yearbook of the Republic of South Africa*, p. 11, Johannesburg, 1971.
2. Preliminary census results 1970 (unpublished officially), an estimated total of 21,172,000.

TABLE 3. Population of South Africa by racial groups: distribution

	Africans	Whites
Percentage of population	67.9	19.2
Percentage of cash income monthly	18.8	73.3
Average monthly income per head (in Rand)[1]	7	95

1. Paper prepared by W. Langschmidt, managing director of market research in Africa, quoted in the *Rand Daily Mail*, 11 March and 26 April 1968. 1 Rand = U.S. $1.40.

TABLE 4. Population of South Africa by racial groups: average monthly salaries (in Rand)[1]

	Africans	Coloured persons	Asians	Whites
Mining	18[2]	62	76	297
Wholesale trade	47.6	170.5	94.4	244.6
Retail trade	37.5	51.4	18.9	129.7
Banking	52.6	55.8	72.2	204.7
Building societies	49.2	76.5	106.7	226.8
Public services	36.1	100.3	127.0	211.4
Provincial adminis- trations	31.9	49.2	66.9	198.1
Local authorities	38.0	71.0	48.9	230.2
Tax rate income by R.500	5.26	—	—	—

1. Statistics for mining, wholesale trade, retail trade, banking and building societies taken from a news release of the Department of Statistics, 30 September 1969, published in *A Survey of Race Relations in South Africa, 1969*, p. 107, Johannesburg, South African Institute of Race Relations, 1970; those for public services, provincial administrations and local authorities taken from a news release of the Department of Statistics, 15 July 1969, published in *A Survey of Race Relations . . . , 1969*, p. 108.
2. To this should be added for Africans free accommodation, food, recreation, medical care and certains items of clothing. Estimates of the value of these varies. According to the *South African Journal of Economics*, March 1966, in gold mining the monthly cost to the mines was approximately R.7.30 while it was approximately R.12.90 value to the Africans. *Star* (Johannesburg), 11 September 1968, calculated it as R.7.50 value to the Africans.

TABLE 5. Population of South Africa by racial groups: old age and blind pensions and disability grants (in Rand)

	Africans	Coloured persons and Asians	Whites
Free income permitted	21	96	192
Basic pension	21	72	336
Bonus	—	—	48
Extra allowance	30	108	—
Total pension	51	180	384

Source: A Survey of Race Relations in South Africa, 1968, p. 285, Johannesburg, South African Institute of Race Relations, 1969.

TABLE 6. Population of South Africa by racial groups: sickness and infant mortality rates

	Africans	Coloured persons	Asians	Whites
Tuberculosis rate per 100,000				
For 1966	446.5	484.9	203.8	35.67[1]
For 1967	460.7	436.5	204.9	34.91[1]
Infant mortality rate under 1 year old per 1,000 live births for 1965	No figures given	136.1	56.1	29.21[2]
Kwashiorkor rate per 100,000 for 1965[3]	980	410	40	Negligible

1. *Journal of the S. A. Natal Tuberculosis Association*, here quoted from *A Survey of Race Relations in South Africa, 1968*, p. 275, Johannesburg, South African Institute of Race Relations, 1969.
2. Estimates in mid-1966. *Statistical Yearbook 1966*, Table C32, compiled by the Department of Statistics, Pretoria, South Africa.
3. *A Survey of Race Relations in South Africa, 1965*, p. 276.

As it could be expected, the policy of apartheid has given rise to opposition. There have been protests, demonstrations and riots from the non-whites, while among whites opposition to the government's policy has ranged from criticism to more political involvement.

A minority can hardly succeed in preserving its absolute supremacy in all spheres without the use of force. It is therefore not surprising that the implementation of the policy of apartheid has been accompanied by an abuse of police power, a disregard for the integrity of the individual and by the censorship of the press.

The real or imagined fear of counter-violence has led those in power to a multiplication of procedures aimed at strengthening the system of apartheid by destroying opposition.

Again and again during the post-war period, attention has been called to the situation in South Africa with regard to civil rights.[1] One need only briefly draw attention to the 90-day detention clause

1. See in particular the report of the International Commission of Jurists, *South Africa and the Rules of Law*, 1960; *Report of the United Nations Special Committee on the Policies of Apartheid of the Government of the Republic of South Africa*, 10 December 1964 (A/5825/Add.1) and 16 August 1965 (S/6005); and later reports including *Repressive Legislation of the Republic of South Africa* (ST/PSCA/SER.A 7).

in the General Law Amendment Act of 1963, which, when it was withdrawn on 11 January 1965, was in fact replaced by the 180-day detention measure of the Criminal Procedure Amendment Act No. 96 of 1965. Under this Act, the Attorney General may issue a warrant for arrest and detention for a maximum of six months (180 days) of a person who is likely to give evidence for the State in any criminal proceedings with respect to certain offences, as long as that detention is deemed to be in the interest of such person or of the administration of justice.[1]

The International Commission of Jurists observed:

'This must be one of the most extraordinary powers that have ever been granted outside a period of emergency. It authorizes the detention of an innocent person against whom no allegations are made and no suspicion even exists; it authorizes detention in the absolute discretion of the Attorney General. It denies the detainees access to a lawyer without special permission; and it precludes the courts from examining the validity of the detention even within the already very wide powers of the Act. It further authorizes the subjection of the detained witness to solitary confinement for a period of six months and, with the object, *inter alia* of excluding "tampering with or intimidation" of any person, places him in a situation where he is in the almost uncontrolled power of the police who also have an interest in the evidence he may give.'[2]

Section 22(1) of the General Law Amendment Act of 1966 provides for the detention of suspected terrorists for interrogation for periods of up to fourteen days. This may be extended by a judge of the Supreme Court on an application from the Commissioner of Police.

The Terrorism Act (No. 83 of 1967) was framed to take into account the end of the policy of non-violence as the only method of opposing apartheid. African leaders in exile had announced that change would come only through force and the Organization of African Unity had approved of a policy of recruiting and training South Africans as freedom fighters. Section 2 of the Terrorism Act defines terrorism. Under this section '... a person shall be guilty of terrorism if he with intent to endanger the maintenance of law and order in the Republic

1. See A. S. Mathews and R. C. Albino, 'The Permanence of the Temporary: An Examination of the 90 and 180 Days Detention Laws', *South African Law Journal, 1966,* p. 16 ff.
2. *Bulletin of the International Commission of Jurists,* Geneva, September 1966. Here quoted from *Report of the United Nations Special Committee on the Policies of Apartheid of the Government of the Republic of South Africa,* p. 121, October 1966 (A/6486).

or any portion thereof, in the Republic or elsewhere, commits any act or attempts to commit . . . any act, or if he conspires with another to commit or to aid or procure the commission of any act . . . inciting instigating, commanding, aiding, advising, encouraging, or procuring another to commit any act in South Africa or elsewhere constitutes terrorism'.

Subsection (1)(b) of the Act defines as a form of terrorism, undergoing any training inside or outside of South Africa which could be useful to any person intending to endanger the maintenance of law and order. Aiding, advising, encouraging or procuring another to undergo such training is also terrorism.

'Training' is not defined. 'Could be' and 'any person' indicates the wide scope of this section.

The third alternative form of terrorism is the possessing of 'any explosives, ammunition, fire-arm or weapon' unless the possessor can prove beyond a reasonable doubt that he did not intend using such explosives, ammunition, fire-arm or weapon to commit any act likely to have any of the results referred to in Subsection (2) of the Terrorism Act anywhere in South Africa.

'Weapon' is not defined. Mere 'possession' places the burden of proof on the accused, whether that possession is legal or illegal.

Section 6 extends the provisions already contained in the 90- and 180-days laws. It empowers a lieutenant-colonel or any higher-ranking police official to arrest any person whom he believes to be a terrorist or to have withheld information about other terrorists or about offences under the Act and to have him detained anywhere in South Africa without any time limit whatsoever. The detainee shall be held for interrogation until the Commissioner of Police 'is satisfied' that he 'has satisfactorily replied to all questions at the said interrogation or that no useful purpose will be served by his detention' or until the Minister of Justice orders his release.

Subsection (5) forbids any court to pronounce upon the validity of any action taken under this section or to order the release of any detainee. Subsection (6) provides that any person detained under the Act shall be held in solitary confinement. No one except police and/or prison officials shall have access to the detainees. No one is entitled to obtain information about any detainee or to find out what information was obtained from him. Persons accused of terrorism shall be tried summarily and terrorism trials shall be by a Supreme Court judge sitting alone, without jury or assessors. Most provisions of the

Act are retroactive to 27 June 1962. Section 3 (harbouring terrorists) and 6 (detention) are not retroactive.

The numbers detained under the Terrorism Act have not been disclosed. There has been disquieting evidence of torture of political detainees,[1] including the testimony of a world-renowned expert in forensic medicine, and between February and September 1969 seven political detainees had died in prison.[2]

There are, too, the techniques of banishing, or listing persons, and of banning.

Banishment is an action which can be taken against Africans. Section 5(1)(b) of the Native Administration Act of 1927, amended 1952 and 1956, empowers the State President, whenever he deems it expedient in the public interest, without notice, to order any tribe, portion of a tribe or individual African to move to any stated place. Banishment has been used, e.g., to remove from the reserves persons who have been active opponents of chiefs or of government measures for 'Bantu authorities', or land betterment, or the issuing of reference books to women.[3]

In addition, emergency regulations for the Transkei (Proclamations 400 and 413) provide that any persons suspected of committing an offence under the regulations of any law, or of intending to do so, or of possessing information about an offence may be arrested without warrant and held in custody until the police or prison authorities are satisfied that they have fully and truthfully answered all relevant questions put to them. The offences include: holding a meeting of more than ten Africans without special permission (church services and funerals are exempted), making any statement or performing any action likely to have the effect of interfering with the authority of the State, one of its officials, or a chief or headman, or boycotting an official meeting.

1. United Nations Commission on Human Rights, reporting to the General Assembly, February 1968. See also *Report of the Special Committee on the Policies of Apartheid of the Government of the Republic of South Africa*, p. 17, 18 September 1970 (S/9939).
2. Nicodemus Kgoathe, died 2 February 1969; Solomon Modilane, died 25 February 1969; James Lenkoe, died 10 March 1969; Michael Shivute, died 16 June 1969; Jacob Monnatgotla, died 9 September 1969; Caleb Mayekiso, died 31 May 1969; Imam Hadji Abdulla Haroun, died 27 September 1969. In two cases the magistrate's verdict was suicide and in five the verdict was natural causes. In two cases the cause given for wounds was bathroom injuries. In two cases (one of them where the verdict was suicide) the relatives of the deceased have instituted civil actions against the Prime Minister and the Minister of Police following allegations of torture made during the inquests.
3. Muriel Horrell, *Action, Reaction and Counteraction*, p. 64, Johannesburg, South African Institute of Race Relations, 1963. See also *A Survey of Race Relations in South Africa, 1965*, p. 52, Johannesburg, South African Institute of Race Relations, 1966.

The person held in custody under these regulations may not consult with a legal adviser unless with the consent of the Minister of Bantu Administration and Development.[1]

Between January and April 1966, a total of sixty-two Transkeians were detained by the South African authorities.[2] During 1968, thirty-two persons in the Transkei were detained by the South African authorities.[3]

Under the Suppression of Communism Act of 1950, amended in 1962, a person might be listed as a member or active supporter of the Communist Party of South Africa (banned in 1950) or of any other organization deemed unlawful (as the African National Congress, the Pan-African Congress and the African Resistance Movement). In 1962 a list of 437 names of persons, 129 whites and 308 non-whites, was published in the government *Gazette*.[4] Since then some have been removed from the list, others have been added. Although, strictly speaking, the publication of the names has no direct legal consequences, the Minister of Justice is empowered to take certain actions against a listed person. It should be mentioned that the same actions might be directed against certain other categories, too, such as persons convicted of actions deemed to have furthered the aims of communism.

In addition to 'listing', banning orders of the most varying character might be served. Thus, a person might be prohibited from becoming or being a member of specified organizations or organizations of a specified nature. Further, a person may be prohibited from attending gatherings of any kind, including social gatherings. Such prohibitions are rather frequent. With certain exceptions it is an offence to record, publish, or disseminate any speech, utterance or writing made anywhere at any time by a person under such ban.

In addition a banning order may imply that the person concerned is prohibited from absenting himself from any stated place or area, he may be confined to a town or a suburb, he may be confined to house arrest for a certain number of hours, and public holidays. It

1. *A Survey of Race Relations . . . , 1965*, p. 52.
2. *Report of the United Nations Special Committee on the Policies of Apartheid of the Government of the Republic of South Africa*, October 1966 (A/6486), quoted from the Chief Minister of the Transkei in a reply to a question in the Legislative Assembly reported in *World* (Johannesburg), 8 June 1966.
3. Of these twenty-seven were released without charges having been laid against them, having been detained for periods ranging from 2 to 125 days. Five were charged after having been detained from 96 to 102 days. Of these, one was acquitted, three convicted and one case withdrawn. At the end of 1968, sixteen Transkeians were in detention.—*House of Assembly Debates (Hansard)*, Vol. 14, Col. 5816.
4. *Annual Survey of South African Law*, 1962, p. 53, University of the Witwatersrand, South Africa.

is sometimes required that the person shall remain at home 24 hours each day.[1]

The publication of particulars in the *Gazette* contains the date of delivery of notice and the date on which notice expires. The period varies, often it is one or two years, and sometimes five years.

It has been calculated that in 1969, 355 banning orders under the Suppression of Communism Act were in force against persons in South Africa.[2]

While Unesco is not directly concerned with the economic and political aspects of apartheid in the Republic of South Africa, the policy of apartheid has consequences for education, science, culture and the dissemination of information—consequences which follow logically from the philosophical concept of man as conceived by the ideology of apartheid, from the economic inequality which the policy creates and reinforces, and from the political situation which severely curtails freedom for all South Africans, and in particular for the non-white South Africans who form the majority of the country's population.

In conformity with the ideal of 'separateness', Africans, Asians, Coloured persons, and whites are educated as independent groups within the population, the 'separateness' emphasized by the administrative structure of education, by methods of finance, by differences in syllabus, and by different levels of achievement deliberately imposed to fit in with different expectations in employment. Ultimately education is geared for the effective preparation of the Africans for their future occupations as unskilled labourers. Higher training is intended only for the small number of persons who can be employed in skilled work in African 'homelands' or African 'development schemes.'

The result of racial discrimination in education and in the pattern of employment is seen clearly in the field of science. South Africa is facing a chronic shortage of top-level manpower in science and technology as well as in management. The shortage cannot be remedied by relying on the white population alone. Moreover, the general repressive atmosphere is inimical to the development of a spirit of free inquiry and has led to the loss to South Africa of some scien-

1. *House of Assembly Debates (Hansard)*, 28 January 1964, Cols. 405-6.
2. *A Survey of Race Relations . . . , 1969*, p. 41.

tists of great eminence, particularly in the field of the social sciences. The political atmosphere has also affected recruitment of staff, particularly from universities in the United Kingdom.

'Separate development' in the field of culture has reduced to a minimum all contacts between whites and non-whites that are not purely of an economic nature. As in all other fields, 'separate development' is in fact synonymous with 'inequality of access', but, moreover, cultural apartness, as opposed to cultural interaction for which Unesco stands, has limited the creative possibilities of all South Africans.

That policy cannot be separated from principle is illustrated in Part IV, 'Information'. Whilst the South African Government in its statements continues to uphold the right to freedom of information, the need to enforce the policy of apartheid has affected the relevant legislation and its application, the action taken denying in fact the principle of freedom of information.

I. Education

'1. Everyone has the right to education. Education shall be free, at least in the elementary and fundamental stages. Elementary education shall be compulsory. Technical and professional education shall be made generally available and higher education shall be equally accessible to all on the basis of merit.
'2. Education shall be directed to the full development of the human personality and to the strengthening of respect for human rights and fundamental freedoms. It shall promote understanding, tolerance and friendship among all nations, racial or religious groups, and shall further the activities of the United Nations for the maintenance of peace.
'3. Parents have a prior right to choose the kind of education that shall be given to their children.'

Article 26 of the Universal Declaration of Human Rights

' . . . the term "discrimination" includes any distinction, exclusion, limitation or preference which, being based on race, colour, sex, language, religion, political or other opinion, national or social origin, economic condition or birth, has the purpose or effect of nullifying or impairing equality of treatment in education and in particular:
(a) of depriving any person or group of persons of access to education of any type or at any level;
(b) of limiting any person or group of persons to education of an inferior standard.'

Article 1, Unesco Convention against Discrimination in Education

1   Aims and objects

An inquiry into the effects of the policy of apartheid in the field of South African education of necessity begins with an examination of the basic objectives of the Government of South Africa. What does the government seek from education? How does its purpose compare with that generally accepted by other societies of the world?

In 1945, three years before the Nationalists came to power, two statements were made in the House of Assembly by members who were prominent in the National Party:

'As has been correctly stated here, education is the key to the creation of the proper relationship between European and non-European in South Africa. . . . Put native education on a sound basis and half the racial questions are solved. . . . I say that there should be reform of the whole educational system and it must be based on the culture and background and the whole life of the native himself in his tribe. . . . This whole (present) policy is also a danger for our own Western civilization.'[1]

'We should not give the natives an academic education, as some people are too prone to do. If we do this we shall later be burdened with a number of academically trained Europeans and non-Europeans, and who is going to do the manual labour in the country? . . . I am in thorough agreement with the view that we should so conduct our schools that the native who attends those schools will know that to a great extent he must be the labourer in the country.'[2]

An important influence in defining the objectives of education in South Africa was the concept of Christian National Education,

1. M. D. C. de Wet Net, in: *House of Assembly Debates (Hansard)*, Vol. 52, 2 April 1945, Cols. 4494-9.
2. J. N. le Roux, ibid., Col. 4527.

outlined by the Institute of Christian National Education for the Federation of Afrikaner Cultural Organizations (FAK)[1]. The Christian National Education policy was published in a pamphlet issued by FAK in 1960; it stated:

'In full preservation of the essential unity of history we believe that God . . . has willed separate nations and peoples, and has given to each nation and people its special calling and tasks and gifts. . . . We believe that next to the mother tongue, the national history of the people is the means of cultivating love of one's own. . . .'[2]

Christian National Education did not have the support of all white South Africans. English-speaking teachers associations, NUSAS, the English-speaking press and some Afrikaners opposed it. They claimed that it overemphasizes the differences between peoples and could, by encouraging unilingualism and by developing divergent conceptions of history, dangerously divide Afrikaans-speaking from English-speaking South Africans. Moreover they mistrusted the Christian National Education opinion that subjects like science and history should be presented in the light of fixed belief.[3] Even among those who supported it, there were some who saw Christian National Education not as a method of denying equal rights for Africans in accordance with a pre-destined pre-ordained plan, but rather as a way of guaranteeing the Afrikaner heritage against the influence of the English-speaking South African on the one hand, and on the other, guaranteeing the same separateness—together with intensified missionary endeavour—for all groups within South Africa. They believed that equality both in education and in cultural rights could come about only through separateness. They pointed to the concept of 'negritude' and the 'African personality' in other parts of Africa. In South Africa they felt that the uniqueness of the African tradition could be fostered best by strengthening, or the reconstructing where this was necessary,

1. Christian National Education which first appeared in the Netherlands in 1860 was in Afrikaner circles in South Africa seen as early as 1876 as a means of restoring the Church's influence over the youth and as protecting them against the domination of English culture. It was from the start linked with the protection of the Dutch heritage and the Dutch language, and was a reaction to the tendency for public schools to use English as the medium of instruction. See T. R. H. Davenport, *The Afrikaner Bond, 1880-1911*, p. 30-3, Cape Town, London and New York, Oxford University Press, 1966.
2. Quoted from F. E. Auerbach, *The Power of Prejudice in South African Education*, p. 112, Cape Town and Amsterdam, 1965.
3. See also Gwendolen M. Carter, *The Politics of Inequality in South Africa since 1948*, 2nd ed., p. 261-6, London, Thames & Hudson, 1959.

of old tribal loyalties and the reinforcing of the mother tongue which they saw as one of the basic necessities for separateness, while permeating the whole with the Christian principles of the Dutch Reformed Church. Both in the Transvaal and in the Orange Free State, Christian National Education has been adopted. It has had an important influence in certain sections of the Cape Province while in Natal the Provincial Council has refused to accept it. The principles of Christian National Education are important not only because they have been accepted by some provinces within the Republic of South Africa, but because the interlocking interests within Afrikaner society ensure that there are close ties between the Institute of Christian National Education, the Federation of Afrikaaner Cultural Organizations and influential members of the Nationalist Party.

What the Africans want from education has been summed up as a quest 'for integration into the democratic structure and institutions of the country. To them one of the most effective ways of achieving this is by education—an education essentially in no way different from or inferior to, that of other sections of the community'.[1]

2 Primary and secondary schools: administration

African schools: the Bantu Education Act

Until 1953 African schools were, with regard to administration and controls, of four types: private schools run by religious communities,

---

1. D. G. S. M'Timkulu in 'The African and Education', *Race Relations Journal*, Vol. 16, No. 3, 1949. Quoted from Muriel Horrell, *A Decade of Bantu Education*, p. 157, Johannesburg, South African Institute of Race Relations, 1964.

etc., which could, if they wished, apply for official recognition and State aid; subsidized mission schools founded by church organizations, subsidized by the State and whose syllabus was prescribed by the provincial education departments; government schools run by an education department; community or tribal schools, where the communities or tribes assumed the responsibility for the maintenance of the school.

The administrative control over African schools had become very complex. Each Provincial Council legislated for its own area—in the Cape the Education Department dealt with the education of all children but in all other provinces there were departments of native education—the control was shared with church authorities, while Parliament voted funds for African education. In an attempt to achieve greater co-ordination a Union Advisory Board for Native Education was set up in 1945, and in 1949 it had two African members: Professor Z. K. Matthews and Dr. J. S. Joroko.

In 1949, the South African Government appointed a committee which had as part of its mandate:

'(a) The formulation of the principles and aims of education for Natives as an independent race, in which their past and present, their inherent racial qualities, their distinctive characteristics and aptitude, and their needs under ever-changing social conditions are taken into consideration.

'(b) The extent to which the existing primary, secondary and vocational educational system for Natives and the training of Native teachers should be modified in respect of the content and form of syllabuses, in order to conform to the proposed principles and aims, and to prepare Natives more effectively for their future ocupations.'

The main proposals of this committee, known as the Eiselen Commission, were embodied in the Bantu Education Act of 1953, and as amended in 1954, 1956, 1959 and 1961. This Act, which affected the African population, represented the first major application of the official policy of apartheid to education.

The Bantu Education Act of 1953 provided for the direct control of African schools by the Ministry of Bantu Affairs[1] and not by the

---

1. The former Department of Native Affairs became the Ministry of Bantu Affairs, which itself subsequently became the Department of Bantu Administration.

provincial governments. The aim was to introduce a system of African education closely co-ordinated with other aspects of African development, which could not be achieved with the existing system of divided control.

The Minister of Native Affairs introducing the bill said:

'Education must train and teach people in accordance with their opportunities in life according to the sphere in which they live. . . . Good racial relations cannot exist when the education is given under the control of people who create wrong expectations on the part of the Native himself. . . . Native education should be controlled in such a way that it should be in accordance with the policy of the State . . . racial relations cannot improve if the result of native education is the creation of frustated people.'[1]

The Bantu Education Act, then, was not only to regulate the system of African education so that anomalies between provinces and schools should be removed, it was to control it in accord with the policy of the State.

The Bantu Education Act transferred administration of African schools from the provincial authorities to the Department of Native Affairs. The minister, acting under wide powers, withdrew grants as from 1957 to private schools for Africans. Private organizations were given the choice of relinquishing control of primary or secondary schools and selling or letting the building to the department or retaining the schools as private, unaided institutions. But even in the latter case they would have to accept departmental syllabuses and regulations regarding appointment of teachers, admission of students and media of instruction. One of the arguments against the former system was the lack of consultation between school principals and Africans. In the new system some responsibility was to be delegated from the Central Government to 'Bantu' authorities and local councils as far as control over primary schools was concerned, and when no such authorities existed school boards were to be created. However, unlike white school boards, the members of these school committees were to be subject to the approval of the Secretary for Bantu Education himself, and subsidies from the Central Government could be withdrawn on a month's notice without any reason given for this

1. *Housse of Assembly Debates (Hansard)*, Vol. 83, 17 September 1953, Col. 3575.

withdrawal.[1] Moreover the Union's Advisory Board for Native Education had had in 1949 two African members. This board was responsible for advising on important policy decisions as far as African education was concerned. These policy decisions were now being taken by the Department of Bantu Administration so that African participation at this level had been effectively abolished.[2]

The result was that all mission and church schools, other than those maintained by the Catholic Church[3] and the Seventh-Day Adventists, were transferred to the Department of Bantu Administration, or were forced to close.[4]

In line with the theory of separate development along tribal units, African education is to be decentralized from the Department of Bantu Education to Bantu Territorial Authorities. There will be five regional organizations in white areas and six in the reserves.

Control will, however, be maintained by the department. It will be responsible for the education of Africans in white areas, for the professional control and guidance of the territorial education departments. It will prescribe the syllabus, determine educational methods, control inspectors, administer examinations and issue certificates.

Secondary-school control was to remain vested in the principal or in a special committee while schools on farms, mines or factory property could be managed by the owner of the property or his representative.

Coloureds

The Coloured Peoples Education Act of 1963 provided that the control, until then vested in the provinces, of the education for Coloured persons should be vested in a Division of Education within the Department for Coloured Affairs. After this Act, no one could manage a private school at which more than fourteen Coloured pupils were enrolled unless the school was registered with the department.

1. *House of Assembly Debates (Hansard)*, Vol. 89, 13 June 1955, p. 19, Col. 7663; Government Notice No. 841 of 22 April 1955.
2. In reply to a question in the House of Assembly, the Minister of Bantu Education stated that of the twenty-eight higher administrative posts, eighty higher professional posts and forty-two administrative posts on the salary scale R.2,280 ($\times$ 120)-2,760 in his department, none were occupied by Africans.—*House of Assembly Debates (Hansard)*, 9 April 1965, Cols. 4084-5.
3. The Catholic Church set about establishing a £1 million fund to finance their schools.—Horrel, op. cit., p. 26.
4. The then Bishop of Johannesburg, the Rt. Rev. Ambrose Reeves, decided that he could not cooperate with the government even to the extent of leasing buildings to the Department of Bantu Affairs. Schools under his control were either handed over to the owners to run, or closed.— (Horrell, op. cit., p. 29).

The Act provided not only for the transfer of schools, but for the control of conditions of service for the teachers, one condition of service being that teachers could not belong to any organization to which the minister, in a notice in the *Gazette*, declared that they should not belong. An Education Council for Coloured Persons would act in an advisory capacity.

Asians

The Indians' Education Act of 1965 also provided for the control of education for Indians to be vested in the Central Government under the Department of Indian Affairs. The Act had provisions similar to the Coloured Peoples Act of 1963, the minister being empowered to establish an Indian Education Advisory Council, school committees, etc., he could recognize associations of Indian teachers, and it defined what could be considered misconduct on the part of teachers.[1]

These two Acts, the Coloured Peoples Act of 1963 and the Indians' Education Act of 1965, would seem, therefore, to follow the pattern of the Bantu Education Act of 1953, and to provide the legal basis for a control of education in line with the government's policy of 'separate development'.

Whites

Until 1967 education for whites was administered under the South Africa Act (1909), Article 88; primary and secondary education for white pupils had been administered in the provinces by the Provincial Council. With the exception of Natal, each school had a local committee elected by parents, whose chief function was the selection of teachers, subject to the final approval of the department. In Natal, the Provincial Department controlled everything and there were no parent committees. With a view to co-ordinating the work of the provinces the government instituted in 1935 an Inter-provincial Consultative Committee.

The National Education Policy Act No. 39 of 1967 provides that, after consultation with the Provincial Administration and the National Advisory Education Council, the Minister of Education, Arts

---

1. *House of Assembly Debates (Hansard)*, Vol. 13, 20 April 1965, Cols. 4434-6; 21 April 1965, Cols. 4554, 4556; 28 April 1965, Cols. 4926, 4967, 5015.

and Science may determine the policy which is to be pursued in res pect of education in schools. Private unsubsidized schools were no affected, and aided private schools were not affected by some provi sions of the Act. The National Advisory Education Council had beer set up in 1962. All members are appointed by the government. They are selected from the minister's department, from the provinces or because they have special competence in the field of education.

The new Act provided for an advisory committee in addition to the council. This consists of the heads of provincial education department and the Secretary for Education, Arts and Science, who is the chairman.

The general policy of white education was laid down in the Act:

(a) the education shall have a Christian character, but the religious convictions of the parents and pupils shall be respected in regard to religious instruction and ceremonies;

(b) education shall have a broad national character;

(c) the mother tongue, if it be English or Afrikaans, shall be the medium of instruction;

(d) requirements as to compulsory education, and the limits relating to school age, shall be uniform;

(e) education (including books and stationery) shall be provided free of charge to full-time pupils in State or provincial-controlled schools whose parents live in the Republic or are South African citizens;

(f) education shall be provided in accordance with the ability and aptitude of and interest shown by the pupil, and the needs of the country, and in this regard appropriate guidance shall be furnished to pupils;

(g) there will be national co-ordination of syllabuses, courses, exam ination standards and research and planning, regard being had to the advisability of maintaining such diversity as circum stances may require;

(h) parents will be given a place in the system through parent teachers' associations, school committees, etc.;

(i) when planning, consideration will be given to suggestions and recommendations of officially recognized teachers' associations;

(j) conditions of service and salary scales of teachers will be uniform.

The minister explained what was meant by "Christian" and "national" according to this Act:[1]

1. *House of Assembly Debates (Hansard)*, Vol. 5, 22 February 1967, Col. 2011.

'My interpretation of the Christian character of education, is that education shall build on the basis of the traditional Western culture and view of life which recognize the validity of the biblical principles, norms and values; by national, it is understood that education shall build on the ideal of the national development of all citizens of South Africa, in order that our identity and way of life shall be preserved, and in order that the South African nation may constantly appreciate its task as part of Western civilization.'

The bill, when introduced, was criticized on the grounds that it conferred extremely wide powers on the minister, removed effective control from the provinces, removed parental choice as to the language of instruction and decreased the functions of the National Advisory Education Council. It was rejected by the Natal Provincial Executive Committee.

In May 1968 a new Division of National Education was established under the minister for the administration of the Act and a permanent interdepartmental committee was established to co-ordinate the country's educational policy for all racial groups. Government Notice R809 of 16 May 1969 complemented the Act. It made mother-tongue instruction compulsory for all pupils admitted to governmental and government-subsidized schools, up to and including Standard 8.

Ninety-two per cent of European pupils receiving primary and secondary education attend State schools.[1] The remainder attend private schools, mainly run by church bodies.

1. *World Survey of Education*, Vol. I: *Handbook of Educational Organization and Statistics*; p. 612-13, Paris, Unesco, 1955.

3 Primary and secondary schools: finance

Africans

Financing African education was introduced by Act No. 5 of 1921. The costs were to be met partly by taxation levied on Africans and partly by funds drawn from general revenue. The Act debarred the Provincial Councils from imposing special direct taxation on Africans except under certain conditions. That is, it was provided that every province should expend annually on the education of 'natives' a sum not less than its expenditure on such education during the financial year 1921/22, that the Governor-General might, from time to time, make grants to any province for the extension and improvement of educational facilities among 'natives', and that such grants should be made out of the revenues derived from 'the direct taxation of the persons, lands, habitations or incomes of natives'.[1]

This Act which became important in the Nationalist argument in favour of financing African education mainly from additional African taxation would seem to lay the precedent that the cost of extensions in African education should be carried by the African himself.

A second Act, No. 41 of 1925 (Native Taxation and Development Act) had changed the taxation of Africans from the provinces to the Central Government, and the provisions of funds for Africans' education became the responsibility of the Central Government.

Both the principles, that further expansion of African education should be financially borne by Africans, and that African educational policy was the responsibility of the Central Government, were included in the Bantu Education Act of 1959 and the budgetary provisions which accompanied it.

It is true that the money available from the general tax levied upon the Africans increased from £233,348 in 1926/27 to £459,831 in

---

1. Union of South Africa, *Report of the Commission on Native Education, 1949-51*, p. 36 (the Eiselen report).

1944.[1] However, in order to permit expansion of African education the principle of having a ceiling on the contributions from the general revenue was abolished in 1945.

After the introduction of the Bantu Education Act of 1953 the government reverted to an earlier position that there should be a ceiling to the contributions from the general revenues. From the fiscal year 1955/56 when the Bantu Education Account came into operation there has been transferred from Revenue Account a fixed annual amount of R.13 million. To this was added a sum for university colleges (R.1.5 million for 1969/70).

The Minister of Native Affairs in pegging the subsidy for African education said:

'I think it is a wise thing to do in the interest of the country and its finances, but also because Bantu education can only be guided along sound lines when we build up this principle that while the European is prepared to make heavy contributions to native education, the native community will have to shoulder their share of the responsibility for this development in future.'[2]

In order to meet the increasing cost in African education the Native Taxation and Development Act (No. 41 of 1925) was amended in 1958 so that the basic general tax for which only African men were eligible could be raised from R.2 to R.3.50. From 1959 and 1960 this basic figure was increased according to the proportion of the taxable incomes of individual taxpayers while in 1960 African women, who had not before paid the general tax became liable if their income exceeded R.360 per annum.

As from 1 March 1970, the basic general tax payable by male African adults is decreased from R.3.50 to R.2.50 a year. Instead the rates of the additional general tax will rise more steeply with increases in income. No rebates or deductions whatsoever will be allowed, and husbands and wives will be taxed separately. But taxes and the right of extra taxation by territorial authorities remain the same.

Government Notice No. 251 of 22 February 1957, as amended by R217 and R218 of 21 February 1964, stated the regulations for school funds in 'Bantu' community schools. These funds were to be derived from bazaars, concerts, etc. In addition there were

1. Horrell, op. cit., p. 31. £1 = R.2.
2. Minister of Native Affairs, *House of Assembly Debates (Hansard)*, 3 June 1954, Col. 6211.

to be 'voluntary' contributions from pupils ranging from 10 cents in lower primary to R.6 for students in vocational or technical schools or classes.[1] (See also page 56, 'School Fees and Textbook Supplies'.) School boards were also required to raise part of the money toward capital costs of higher and post-primary schools. Moreover, when schools are erected in the new African urban townships, the costs of the lower primary schools may be included in the loans for housing schemes, and Section 36 of the Natives Laws Amendment Act No. 36 of 1957 empowered the Minister of Native Affairs to take into consideration the costs of providing educational services when deciding upon rentals in African townships or hostels. During the six-year period, 1955/56 to 1960/61, the National Housing lent R.1,177,556 to local authorities for building lower primary class-rooms.[2] African tenants were expected to gradually repay these loans through rents.

In 1969 local authorities were informed by the Department of Bantu Administration that the R for R subsidy for school buildings would be discontinued as from after 31 March. The school levy of not more than 20 cents per month payable by all African heads of families was to be introduced 'without delay'.

In practice, the fixing of the levy at no more than 20 cents per month meant that there was a ceiling to how much an urban African council could recuperate for initial capital expenditure from rents collected from tenants and lodgers.

The annual grant from the Consolidated Revenue Fund for African education was fixed at R.13 million.[3] The South African Institute of Race Relations, working out the purchasing power of this amount against the retail price index, concluded that R.13 million in 1963 would purchase in 1965 only the equivalent of R.10.8 million.[4]

1. Horrell, op. cit., p. 16. Those exempted from this tax are: '(a) Any Bantu who satisfies the receiver [of 'Bantu' tax—usually the Bantu Affairs Commissioner] that he is indigent and is prevented from working by reason of age, chronic disease or other sufficient cause or that he is in necessitous circumstances and is prevented by causes not within his own control from earning sufficient to enable him to pay the tax; (b) Every Bantu who satisfies the receiver that he has attained the age of 65 years; and (c) any Bantu who satisfies the receiver that in consequence of his regular attendance at an educational institution approved by the Bantu Affairs Commission he has been precluded from earning wages which would enable him to pay the tax.' See 'Bantu Taxation in the Republic of South Africa', *Bantu Education Journal* (official organ of the Department of Bantu Education, Pretoria, Republic of South Africa), March 1969, p. 35.
2. Horrell, op. cit., p. 15.
3. See page 49 for increase in this figure for 1970/71.
4. *Secondary Education for Africans*, p. 12, Johannesburg, South African Institute of Race Relations (RR. 96/65).

In Table 7 the revenue for 1955/56 (the first year of operation of the Bantu Education Account) is compared with that for 1960/61 and with estimates of revenue from the same sources in 1963/64.

The increase in the total income available for African education between 1955/56 and 1969/70 was due to an increase in African taxation, to a greater percentage of the African general tax—four-fifths until 1961 and five-fifths afterwards—which was allocated to African education, and to loans from the General Loan Account. (See Table 8.)

The Bantu Education Account has also become increasingly in debt to the Loan Account for capital sums advanced for buying mission properties, building departmental schools, and for erecting

TABLE 7. Comparison of revenues for 1955/56 and 1960/61 with estimates of 1963/64 (in Rand)

Item	1955/56	1960/61	1963/64
Fixed statutory appropriation from general revenue	13 000 000	13 000 000	13 000 000
Four-fifths of African general tax (and five-fifths in 1963/64)	3 932 566	5 459 033	7 800 000
Miscellaneous receipts (boarding fees, etc.)	121 278	665 508	730 000
TOTAL	17 053 844	19 124 541	21 530 000

Source: Muriel Horrell, *A Decade of Bantu Education*, p. 34, Johannesburg, South African Institute of Race Relations, 1964.

TABLE 8. Estimates of revenue for 1969/70 (in Rand)

Item	Estimated revenue
Statutory appropriation from Consolidated Revenue Account	13 000 000
Appropriation for university colleges	1 500 000
Proceeds of African general tax	10 500 000
Miscellaneous receipts (boarding fees, etc.)	1 016 000
Interest-free advance from Loan Account	13 510 000
TOTAL	39 526 000

Source: *A Survey of Race Relations in South Africa, 1969*, p. 183, Johannesburg, South African Institute of Race Relations, 1970.

TABLE 9. Relationship between net national income and education

Year	Net national income (millions of Rand)	Total expenditure on education (thousands of Rand)	Expenditure on Bantu schools (thousands of Rand)	Total expenditure on education as percentage of net national income	Expenditure on Bantu schools as percentage of net national income
1953/54	2 833	113 418	16 032	4.0	0.57
1958/59	3 710	149 189	18 458	4.02	0.50 (0.4975)
1961/62	4 622	188 390	19 207	4.07	0.42
1963/64	5 651	...	22 352	...	0.42 (0.39554)

... = Data not available.

Source: *Secondary Education for Africans*, p. 12, Johannesburg, South African Institute of Race Relations (RR.96/65). The figures in parentheses are Unesco calculations.

university college buildings. The net debt by 31 March 1969 was calculated as R.11 million.[1]

The Transkei's budget is separate from the Bantu Education Authority and is voted for by the Transkei territorial authority; R.6,627,000 was voted for the year 1969/70.

Other territorial authorities, e.g. Ciskei and Tswana have been allocated R.5,150,000 from the South African Bantu Trust Fund. This amount may be augmented by the authorities from other sources.

The relationship between net national income and education can be seen from Table 9. It relates South Africa's net national income to total educational expenditure and to expenditure on African schools.

While expenditure on education in general had risen in proportion to the net national income, the percentage spent on African schools was decreasing.

The Minister for Bantu Education explained how increased enrolment was handled without a corresponding rise in expenditure. It was done by:

1. The introduction of double session in the Sub-standards, that is, the first two years of schooling. In 1958, 45.6 per cent of the children were in these standards.

1. *A Survey of Race Relations . . . 1969*, p. 183.

2. The policy of appointing as far as possible women teachers for the lower primary classes. The majority are teachers with Standard 6 plus three years of teacher training whose starting salary was £10 13s. 4d. per month.
3. The grading of farm schools into junior and senior schools with a corresponding saving on salaries since teachers in junior schools are paid a very small salary.
4. The conversion of school feeding funds for the expansion of educational facilities, where requested by the school boards. This last was already being done. In 1966 school feeding was estimated to cost £35,000. In 1954, it was £628,000.[1] This is particularly serious in view of the high rate of malnutrition among Africans.

'Several surveys among African school-children revealed that 60 to 70 per cent were recognizably malnourished; 50 per cent needed nursing and medical attention, and almost 10 per cent required hospitalisation for diseases directly or indirectly attributable to malnutrition.'[2]

Du Plessis, Withman and Fellington found that 86 per cent of African children in one school were undernourished as judged by weight. Potgeitee *et al.* consider that since 75-85 per cent of African families in Pretoria have an income lower than the minimum needed for basic expenses, 80 per cent of school-going children from African households in Pretoria suffer from malnutrition or undernutrition. Figures in the reserves are higher than in the townships.

In 1968 it was estimated that Africans in urban areas had paid R.340,000 in the form of additions to their rentals for erecting of lower primary schools. Schools boards and committees had raised R.535,000 towards the erection, maintenance and running costs of schools and R.2 million for the salaries of privately paid teachers.[3] To this should be added the proceeds of the general tax, repayments of loans, and schools fees.

1. *House of Assembly Debates (Hansard)*, Vol. 1, 1965, Col. 3867.
2. *African Taxation: Its Relation to African Social Services*, p. 27, Johannesburg, South African Institute of Race Relations, 1960 (Fact Paper No. 4). In 1943 the government introduced a school feeding scheme for African children on the same basis as for children of all racial groups. See Horrell, op. cit., p. 154.
3. *House of Assembly Debates (Hansard)*, Vol. 10, 15 April 1969, Col. 3960; Vol. 18, 13 June 1969, Col. 7954.

Rough estimates as to the amount contributed by Africans to the costs of educating their children during the year 1960/61 give the following figures: R.5,459,033 in direct taxation; R.114,225 advanced towards the erection of schools (this sum includes amounts added to the rentals of houses in urban areas); R.200,000 contributed towards the salaries of teachers; R.2,860,632 on school requisites, fees, etc.; in all, R.8,633,890.[1]

The extent to which Africans must go to raise money for education is demonstrated by the campaign of the African educational body, the Association for the Educational and Cultural Advancement of the African People (ASSECA). In May 1970 it started a campaign to raise R.1 million by a voluntary levy of 10 cents from every African man and woman.

The lack of finance available for African education was not by chance. Even if the government's policy that Africans should pay for their education were accepted, the government estimate of the African contribution to the gross national product was R.1,085 million. Mrs. Helen Suzman, in a private motion, pointed out that if the ratio of 4 per cent of this gross product to be spent on education were applied consistently, the government contribution to African education would be R.44 million and not R.13 million.

The government reply left no doubt as to the reason for the pegged subsidy:

'Africans were to be trained only insofar as the economies of the African community could absorb them, they were not to be trained to serve an integrated South African community.'[2]

By 1970-71 it was increasingly obvious that the money available for African education was inadequate even within the discriminatory situation of 'separateness'. In spite of increased African taxation, indebtedness to the Loan Account had risen to R.33 million by 1970. For the budgetary period 1970/71 the government broke the 'pegging' rule in African education for the first time in sixteen years.

The 'Bantu' education vote has been increased from R.13 million to R.17 million, an increase of R.4 million. The Institute of Race Relations, commenting on this, pointed out that 'whether this amount in real terms is greater than it was sixteen years ago, is however open

1. Horrell, op. cit., p. 161.
2. *House of Assembly Debates (Hansard)*, Vol. 5, 21 February 1967, Cols. 1669, 1675, 1682, 1683.

o doubt, as the Rand is worth about half of what it was at that ime'.[1] There has been a drop of about R.1.3 million in the amount o be collected through taxation for the Bantu Education Account, eaving a net increase of R.2.7 million that is available for African education for 1970-71.

The Estimated Revenue for 1970-71 (in Rand) is:[2]

Fixed amounts for the Consolidated Revenue Account including R.1.5 million for universities	14 500 000
African taxation	11 000 000
Fees	1 000 000
Balance carried forward from 1969-70	1 182 000
Special Contribution from the Consolidated Revenue Account	17 500 000
TOTAL	45 182 000

This arrangement is only temporary, since the ministry hopes that by March 1972 a more 'satisfactory'[2] method of African taxation will have been introduced.

Coloureds

Coloured education continued to be financed partly from the Consolidated Revenue Fund and partly from provincial taxation. For the year 1966 it amounted to R.23,640,500 of which R.501,000 had gone to the University of the Western Cape, and R.2,000 to Fort Hare for Coloured students still attending classes there.[3]

In the budget speech of 21 February 1963, however, the Minister of Coloured Affairs said that Coloured people would to an increasing extent be able to make a direct contribution to their education and to the costs connected with it.[4] This, in fact, was already being done. The Indian community alone had contributed over R.2 million to building their own schools during the period 1937-65. Indian teachers had given 3-6 per cent of their basic salaries for a two-year period.[5]

1. *Race Relations News*, Vol. 32, No. 9, September 1970.
2. *A Survey of Race Relations . . . 1970*, p. 202-3.
3. Quoted in *A Survey of Race Relations . . . 1965*, p. 258.
4. *House of Assembly Debates (Hansard)*, Vol. 15, 21 February 1963, Cols. 1739-45, 2193-204, 3997-8.
5. Stanley G. Osler, address to the Teachers' Educational and Professional Association, Cape Town, 28 June 1965.

Estimates of expenditure for Coloured pupils for 1969/70 were R.41,993,700. This does not give the complete picture since the salaries of senior administrative personnel whose time is not entirely devoted to education are included in the budget and certain substantial administrative expenses.

Indians

Estimates for Indian education for the year 1969/70 was R.20,348,100. It does not include the expenditure in the Cape nor the salaries of officials of the ministry who do not devote all their time to education, general administrative costs and contributions to pension funds.

Some questions are posed by these estimates. The first is the high cost of the maintenance of 'separate' universities (see Table 10). Of the R.39,506,000 for African education, R.2,746,000 goes to the maintenance of African universities. Of the R.20,348,100 for Indian education R.3,510,000 goes for the capital cost of the university and another R.1,360,000 for administrative costs: a total of R.4,870,000, or more than 20 per cent.

TABLE 10. Estimates of educational expenditure for the year 1969/70 (in Rand)

Item	Estimated expenditure
Africans	
Salaries, wages and allowances:	
administrative staff	5 000 000
General administration	934 100
Supplies, services and maintenance of buildings	720 000
Bursaries and loans to pupils	110 000
Examination expenses	230 000
Subsidies to schools	22 313 900
Financial assistance to community	
schools for capital expenses	50 000
Maintenance of university colleges	2 746 000
Provision for retirement benefits	1 781 000
Redemption of loans from Loan Account	471 000
Grant-in-aid to the South African Trust	
Fund towards educational services by	
territorial authorities	5 150 000
	39 506 000

Item	Estimated expenditure
Coloureds	
Salaries of educational personnel at head and regional offices	687 800
School buildings and additions to schools (Loan Account)	6 637 300
Primary, secondary and high schools teacher training	32 382 200
Departmental technical schools	193 900
Assistance to State-aided vocational schools	23 500
Assistance to State-aided special schools	476 900
Assistance to continuation classes	14 100
University College of the Western Cape	802 000
Bursaries and loans to students	706 000
Grants-in-aid to educational and sports organizations	70 000
	41 993 700
Indians	
Salaries of staff of Division of Education	420 000
Salaries of staff of primary and high schools and teacher-training colleges	10 865 600
Erection of school buildings	1 514 350
Maintenance of nursery, primary, high and teacher-training schools	2 099 000
Assistance to M. L. Sultan Technical College	539 500
Assistance to State-aided special schools	37 500
University College:	
Capital costs	3 510 000
Administrative costs	1 360 000
Bursary for students	1 550
Bibles for schools	600
	20 348 100

Source: A Survey of Race Relations in South Africa, 1969, p. 183, 197, 102, Johannesburg, South African Institute of Race Relations, 1970.

The next is the cost of separate administrative staff. In African education all salaries except those of the minister and the deputy minister are charged to the Bantu Education Account, and R.5,150,000 is for grants-in-aid towards the 'territorial' authorities.

Not only is the money available for African education insufficient but the cost of the apartheid structure has decreased the efficiency with which the money may be used.

Whites

White primary and secondary education is financed by provincial taxation and partly by a subsidy from the Central Government (see Table 11). The general subsidy from the Central Government amounts to about 50 per cent of the total provincial expenditure, to which is added a special subsidy for three provinces: the Cape, Natal and the Orange Free State.

While this represents provincial expenditure, the total budget allotted to white education is difficult to establish.

The Secretary for Bantu Education, Dr. H. J. van Zyl was reported as estimating that if the unit costs currently applicable to whites were to be applied to African education, the latter would amount to R.400 million per year.[1]

TABLE 11. Provincial expenditure on education (in thousand Rand)

Year[1]	Cape	Natal	Transvaal	Orange Free State
1960	41 968	13 651	33 919	8 835
1961	43 903	14 403	37 031	9 227
1962	45 127	14 893	40 004	9 650
1963	46 248	15 509	42 482	10 174
1964	51 246	18 163	46 910	11 197
1965	35 451	18 732	48 180	11 781

1. Year ending 31 March.
Source: State of South Africa Yearbook, 1966, p. 96.

1. *A Survey of Race Relations . . . 1969*, p. 206.

TABLE 12. *Per capita* expenditure on African pupils, 1953-61

Year	Amount (Rand)	Enrolment	Cost per pupil (Rand)
1953/54	16 032 494	938 211	17.08
1955	15 769 550	1 005 774	15.68
1956	17 277 660	1 090 601	15.88
1957	18 036 350	1 143 328	15.78
1958	17 990 126	1 259 413	14.28
1959	18 457 830	1 308 596	14.10
1959/60	19 473 200	1 411 157	13.80
1960/61	18 852 514	1 513 571	12.46

Source: M. Horrell, *A Decade of Bantu Education*, p. 41, Johannesburg, South African Institute of Race Relations, 1964, from estimates given by F. J. de Villiers, then Secretary for Bantu Education.

Some comparative figures

Table 12 gives the *per capita* expenditure on African pupils over the period 1953-61 in State and State-aided schools. This includes amounts spent on redemption of loans, but excludes expenditure on the maintenance of university colleges and capital expenditure on the Loan Account.

Per capita expenditure in 1967 was approximately R.11.50 for pupils in primary classes and R.52.58 for pupils in secondary classes.[1] In 1968 it was R.11.50 in primary classes and R.52.58 in secondary classes,[2] and in 1969 R.13.55 and R.55 respectively.[3]

Muriel Horrell calculated that the total *per capita* expenditure had risen from R.12.39 in 1966/67 to R.15.55 in 1967/68, but it was still below the 1953/54 level[4] (see Table 12).

Table 13 shows comparative unit costs of education in 1962, here reproduced with explanations from Stanley Osler's address to the Teachers' Educational and Professional Association, Cape Town, 1965. It should be noted that while the centralized character of African education permits a single over-all figure for African education to be relevant, in the case of Coloureds, Indians and whites, *per capita* expenditure varies considerably from province to province.

1. *House of Assembly Debates (Hansard)*, Vol. 11, 11 April 1967, Col. 3938.
2. ibid., Vol. 7, 19 March 1968, Cols. 2379, 2401.
3. ibid., Vol. 5, 7 March 1969, Col. 2067.
4. *A Survey of Race Relations . . . 1968*, p. 215.

TABLE 13. Comparative unit costs of education, 1962, as given by the provincial Departments of Education

Department	(1) Unit cost per pupil (Rand)	(2) Number of pupils (Sub. A-Std. X)	(3) Cost (1 × 2) (Rand)	(4) Population estimate June 1962	(5) Cost per head of Population (3 ÷ 4) (Rand)
African education[1]	12.11[2]	1 770 371	21 439 292.81	11 387 000	1.88
Coloureds and Indians					
Cape	60.65	296 360	17 974 234		
Natal	50.30	128 559	6 466 553		
Orange Free State	47.00	4 711	221 417		
Transvaal	92.88	46 253	4 295 979		
School of Industries	384.00	579	222 336		
Reformatories	461.00	933	430 113		
Technical College	88.46	2 070	183 103		
	62.14[3]	479 465	29 793 735	2 196 000	13.57
Whites Cape education	147.73	205 650	30 380 675		
Natal	150.00	70 134	10 520 100		
Orange Free State	157.00	65 092	10 219 444		
Transvaal	129.70	330 922	42 920 583		
Education, arts and science[4]	257.21	40 500	10 417 176		
	146.65[3]	712 298	104 457 978	3 182 000	32.83

Source: Stanley G. Osler, address to the Teachers' Educational and Professional Association, Cape Town, 28 June 1965, Chapter III, p. 30, 31. One does not know whether the unit costs are strictly comparable as there is no record of what items each department included. The estimate of the population for June 1962 is only an estimate. In view of this the unit costs per head of population must be treated with caution.
1. In the case of Africans the figures are over-all figures.
2. In 1953/54 was R.17.08.
3. Average.
4. Technical colleges included (full-time, part-time and post-matriculation students).

This table indicates the inequality that exists in the financing of education for the various racial groups. The estimated cost per head of population in 1965 was R.1.88 for Africans, R.13.57 for Coloureds and Indians and R.32.83 for whites. Moreover the cost per pupil for African education had declined from R.17.08 in 1953/54 to R.12.46 in 1960/61.

The government contribution as a percentage of the expenditure had also declined. It represented 34.18 per cent in 1953 and 3.7 per cent in 1969/70.

An estimated analysis of the expenditure according to racial groups for 1965/66) is shown in Table 14.

TABLE 14. Expenditure according to racial groups

Group	Total expenditure (in Rand)	Per head of population (in Rand)	Percentage of total expenditure
Africans	29 057 000	2.39	8.90
Asians	14 300 000	26.83	4.38
Coloured	30 839 000	17.71	9.45
Whites	252 259 000	74.30	77.27

Source: Calculated by Muriel Horrell in *A Survey of Race Relations in South Africa, 1967*, p. 266, Johannesburg, South African Institute of Race Relations, 1968.

4 School fees and textbook supplies

School fees: Africans

The following are details of school fees for African students (1963/64
Lower primary schools: a voluntary contribution not exceeding 1
  cents per pupil per quarter.
Higher primary schools: a voluntary contribution not exceedin
  30 cents per pupil per quarter.
Post-primary community schools: a voluntary or compulsory co
  tribution not exceeding R.1 per pupil per quarter.
Post-primary government schools: a compulsory contribution of R.
  per pupil per quarter plus a further contribution not exceedin
  R.6 per pupil per year in trade schools or per pupil taking a techn
  cal course at a post-primary school.[1]
The South Transvaal Region of the Institute of Race Relation
calculated that in 1967 such contributions in the Johannesburg are
may average R.1.70 a year in primary schools and R.6.80 a year i
post-primary schools.[2]

Since the policy of the government is to site secondary school
for Africans in rural rather than urban areas, a large percentag
of pupils wishing to continue studies after Form III, must atten
boarding schools. Fees for these range from R.55 to R.60.

School books: Africans

The value of school books supplied free to African pupils for th
year 1963 is shown in Table 15. The amount spent on textbooks wa
R.100,900 in 1967/68 and R.315,000 in 1969/70. For readers it wa
R.258,300 in 1967/68 and R.375,550 in 1969/70.[3]

Table 16 shows the costs of textbooks and writing materials (pe

1. *House of Assembly Debates (Hansard)*, 7 May 1965, Cols. 5519-21.
2. *A Survey of Race Relations . . . 1967*, p. 234.
3. *A Survey of Race Relations . . . 1970*, p. 212.

pupil) to be purchased by African parents as estimated by the Institute of Race Relations.

In 1965 they estimated that if textbooks, writing materials, school levies and examination fees (where applicable) are taken into account, it cost parents an average of R.1.42 a year to keep a child in lower primary school, R.5.02 for those in higher primary classes, R.16.50 in junior secondary classes and R.33.50 in senior secondary classes.[1]

In 1967, it was calculated that if books, uniforms and accessories were included, but boarding and transport fees omitted, it would at a conservative estimate cost African parents R.17.25 to keep a child in a lower primary school, R.28 in a higher primary school, R.48.20 in a secondary school and R.65 in a high school catering for day students.[2]

TABLE 15. Value of school books supplied free to African pupils (in Rand)

Standards	Government schools	State-aided schools	Community schools
Sub-standard A	1 079.20	10 980.99	45 635.41
Sub-standard B	832.45	6 720.52	32 388.80
Standard 1	711.30	5 316.51	28 055.10
Standard 2	556.75	3 516.10	21 931.75
Standard 3	396.41	1 863.95	17 141.86
Standard 4	312.23	1 104.45	12 650.23
Standard 5	273.48	465.99	10 316.70
Standard 6	292.18	290.49	9 334.15

Source: Minister of Bantu Education, *House of Assembly Debates (Hansard)*, 7 May 1965, Cols. 5520-1. No books are supplied free to pupils in classes above Standard 6.

TABLE 16. Cost of textbooks and writing materials (per pupil) to be purchased by African parents

Class	Rand	Class	Rand
Sub-standard A	0.57½	Standard 5	3.34
Sub-standard B	0.85½	Standard 6	3.59
Standard 1	1.02½	Form I	13.75
Standard 2	1.10	Forms II and III	22.94
Standard 3	2.51½	Forms IV and V	34.30
Standard 4	2.59		

Source: A Survey of Race Relations in South Africa, 1964, p. 277-8. Johannesburg, South African Institute of Race Relations, 1965.

1. *A Survey of Race Relations . . . 1965*, p. 245.
2. ibid., p. 235. See also 'Introduction' page 28, for African salaries.

Fees and textbooks supplies: Coloureds

As from the beginning of 1969, all textbooks and stationery are supplied free of charge.

Fees and textbooks supplies: Indians

Indian pupils receive free textbooks on loan. They must supply their own stationery.

School fees: whites

Education is free for all white children until the end of secondary school.

Books and stationery are free, but independent private schools may charge fees for sport, extra library books, film projectors, and other audio-visual aids.

The pattern of financing education for the various population groups is clear: the African population pay for the education of their children through direct and indirect taxation (including a 'general tax' which is payable by the African population alone),[1] through voluntary 'contributions' to specific educational projects, and through school fees.

Moreover, school fees for Africans increase for secondary schooling while grants for books are not payable with secondary schooling. For the individual African,[2] the cost of maintaining a child in secondary school must affect the parental decision as to whether or not the child proceeds to secondary school. This situation is unlikely to get better with time, on the contrary, unless the government contribution is appreciably increased, an expanding school population

1. Africans pay income and provincial taxes on the same basis as do members of other racial groups; however, in place of the personal tax paid by whites, Coloureds and Asians, the Africans pay a general tax. Africans are taxed for eight more years of their lives than are members of other racial groups, and while personal taxation is reduced for married men of other racial groups, African men pay general tax at a uniform rate, while an African woman is not exempt from paying the general tax when she marries. Married women of other groups are. In the lowest income groups the rate of general taxation for African men is higher than is the rate of personal taxation of other groups. In addition, Africans pay further direct taxes which are not paid by members of other racial groups: the local tax, the Transkeian General Levy, tribal levies in other areas, education tax in urban areas, hospital levy in the Orange Free State.
2. See 'Introduction', Table 4, for income rates. In Cape Town the mean average income per household in 1963 (African) was R.62.02 and the mean average expenditure was R.64.88 (higher than the mean monthly income).—*A Survey of Race Relations . . . 1964*, p. 233.

will make education at all levels increasingly expensive for the African population. The low *per capita* income of Africans highlights the economic difficulties with which they are faced, if they are to develop an efficient educational system.

5 Enrolments and syllabuses

Primary schools: Africans

The first priority in African education is mass literacy and the extension of primary education at the lowest level. In this field the present South African Government has achieved results. However, expansion of primary-school facilities can only be done within the limitations set by the lack of finance. Shortage of finance showed up in teachers' salaries, in the type of schools which could be built, in the facilities within these schools—lack of finance remains one of the main obstacles to expanding the African school system. It also affects the quality of the education given.

There is a division between lower primary (7-10 years) and higher primary (11-14 years) recommended by the Eiselen Commission.[1] The lower primary school was to concentrate on the 'tool subjects (three R's)',[2] admissions were to be voluntary although attendance was to be compulsory, promotion was to be automatic, and at the end of the lower primary school (10 years) the pupils were to be tested in order to determine whether they had made sufficient progress to continue on to the higher primary.

1. Union of South Africa, *Report of the Commission on Native Education, 1949-51*, p. 140.
2. i.e. Reading, (w)riting and (a)rithmetic.

TABLE 17. Enrolment at primary-school level[1]

Class	1955	1960	1961	1962[2]	1969
Sub-standard A	282 910	393 535	410 119	426 827	521 663
Sub-standard B	183 617	272 120	292 048	306 375	394 359
Standard 1	151 144	238 146	248 771	268 278	335 891
Standard 2	113 499	188 668	196 363	203 792	251 615
Standard 3	90 948	138 495	144 093	153 688	195 369
Standard 4	66 101	97 437	105 621	112 103	142 078
Standard 5	47 353	70 012	77 000	85 466	111 619
Standard 6	34 667	49 684	63 086	71 738	101 975
	970 239	1 452 246	1 537 101	1 628 267	2 054 569

1. Figures taken from *Bantu Education Journal*, April 1970, p. 3, 20-1; published by the Department of Bantu Education, Pretoria.
2. *Bantu Education Journal*, April 1965. Quoted in Muriel Horrell, *A Decade of Bantu Education*, p. 70, Johannesburg, South African Institute of Race Relations, 1964.

There has been a considerable increase in enrolments at the primary school level, as indicated in Table 17. In 1955 the total primary enrolment was 970,239; in 1962 it was 1,628,267. In 1969 it was 2,054,569.

However, a comparatively small number of African children pass from lower primary to higher primary.

There is a continuous drop-out and only about 40 per cent of those starting lower primary enter higher primary school. F. E. Auerbach states that from 1955 to 1967, 5.4 million African children started school. Of these 1.4 million dropped out after one year, and a further 1.3 million before they had stayed long enough to be literate in their mother tongue.[1] Of the year group which started school in 1963, 239,000 had dropped out by 1966.[2] Less go on to secondary school. The statistics up to 1969 from the *Bantu Education Journal*, April 1970, showed an all-over increase of 0.18 per cent over the 1968 figures of African pupils in Form I. If the Transkei was excluded, it was —1.40 per cent from 1968. It gave the reason for it: there was lack of accommodation at secondary level. African school boards must bear half the cost of erection of higher primary and post-primary schools.[3]

According to the Department of Bantu Education the number of pupils in double sessions in 1968 were as follows: 417,214 in

1. 'Education and Action', *Race Relations News*, June 1970.
2. *Race Relations News*, January 1969.
3. *A Survey of Race Relations . . . 1964*, p. 274.

ıb-standard A, 305,088 in Sub-standard B, 13,675 in Standard 1,
d 4,954 in Standard 2; a total of 740,931. The number of pupils
double sessions had increased by 5.1 per cent (37,942 pupils) since
•67.¹

ıllabus. The syllabus in primary schools for Africans was the following: Lower primary course: religious education, a Bantu language, English, Afrikaans, arithmetic, writing, music, arts and
crafts, gardening and environmental study.

ıgher primary course: this corresponds to the syllabus of the lower
primary course with the following exceptions. Social studies take
the place of environmental study. Added to the course are: nature
study, tree planting, soil conservation, needlework (for girls) and
woodwork and metal work (for boys).

ɔr the first two years (Sub-standards A and B) the school day is
vided into two sessions of 3 hours each, including a half-hour break.
ıe curriculum is spread over 825 minutes a week at the rate of
ʲ5 minutes a day. Of this weekly total, religious instruction and
ʲalth parades take up 205 minutes. Afrikaans, English and the
ʲrnacular have 380 minutes, arithmetic 140 minutes and writing and
ıging 100 minutes. Thus, roughly 25 per cent of the time is spent
religious intruction and health parades in the lower primary
ʲurses. A teacher is responsible for one group, usually Sub-standard
in one shift, and for another group, usually Sub-standard B, in
ıe second shift.

Children in Standards 1 and 2 (the third and the fourth year)
•llow a curriculum spread over 1,650 minutes, double the time
located to the lower standards. The school day lasts five and a
ılf hours. Religious instruction and health parades take up 300
ınutes (18 per cent), English, Afrikaans and the vernacular 610
ınutes (36 per cent), arithmetic 200 (15 per cent), environmental
ʲudies 120 minutes (8 per cent), gardening, handicrafts, needlework,
ınging and writing 420 minutes (25 per cent).

Changes were introduced in 1968. These were based on a 'core
ʲllabus' which would be in use in all schools to ensure a proper
ʲasis for the work required for matriculation. In primary schools
ıe result as from 1968 is a greater stress on language usage in English
nd Afrikaans. General science replaces nature study in Standards

Figures taken from *Bantu Education Journal*, April 1969, p. 19. These figures seem to exclude the Transkei.

5 and 6 and there are changes in the social studies syllabus. Whi
those changes do not go far enough to upset the basic structur
they do modify it and bring it closer to the general pattern of educatio
in South Africa.

There is a heavy emphasis on manual training. This is particular
true of farm schools—schools established by European farmers fo
the education of the children of African employees.

On 31 March 1964, there were 2,430 'Bantu' farm schools wit
215,997 pupils and 3,763 teachers.[1] In 1968, 223,417 pupils were i
lower primary classes in farm schools, 30,110 in higher prima
classes. No secondary schools were provided.[2]

The pupil/teacher ratio which these figures indicate as well as th
accent on manual training raises the question as to how far the
schools are intended as educational institutions which can perm
African children who attend them to proceed to higher educatio
and move out of a dependence on European farms for a livelihood.

Primary schools: Coloureds

Education is compulsory in all areas for Coloureds between the age
of 7 and 14 'where there is demand for it and accommodation pe
mits'.[4] It has been ruled as compulsory for any child who lives withi
a three-mile radius and who enrols in any class at the beginning c
the year.

In the Cape Province attendance has been made compulsory i
schools for Coloured children resident within three miles of th
schools, and as from 1 January 1964, school attendance for Coloured
in Natal was made compulsory for all pupils until completion of th
school year in which every pupil reaches the age of 16 years, c
successfully completes the prescribed course for Standard 8.[5]

Double shifts were held in sixty-five schools in Cape Province
seven in the Transvaal and three in Natal.[6] In 1969 double session
operated in 915 classes, mainly Sub-standards A and B; 30,295 pupi
were involved.[7]

The Minister of Coloured Affairs estimated the number of Coloure

1. Minister of Bantu Education, *House of Assembly Debates (Hansard)*, 9 April 1965, Cols. 4344-
2. Figures taken from *Bantu Education Journal*, April 1969, p. 18.
3. See also Chapter 8 of this section for the qualifications of teachers teaching in farm schools.
4. *A Survey of Race Relations . . . 1963*, p. 219.
5. Minister of Coloured Affairs, *House of Assembly Debates (Hansard)*, 14 May 1965, Col. 5993.
6. *House of Assembly Debates (Hansard)*, 1 June 1965, Cols. 6831-2.
7. *House of Assembly Debates (Hansard)*, Vol. 14, 16 May 1969, Col. 6014.

children in the 6-14 group who were not attending school to be: in Cape Province, 28,300; in Natal, nil (attendance is compulsory); in Transvaal, 3,181; in Orange Free State, 808; a total of 32,289.[1]

Of these 89.19 per cent were enrolled in primary schools.[2]

In 1970 80-85 per cent of coloured children were in schools, with about 98-99 per cent of those between 9 and 10 enrolled.[3]

Primary schools: Indians

Education is not compulsory for Indian children.

In 1969, 76.78 per cent of the children attending school were enrolled in primary classes.[4] In the same year double sessions operated in 589 classes of 90 schools from Class 1 to Standard 6 and it was estimated that 22,469 pupils were affected.[5]

Primary schools: whites

Education is compulsory for white children between the ages of 7 and 16 years. Compulsory education means that potential drop-outs are kept on at school until they are 16 years of age.

Secondary education: Africans

The priorities in the government's 'Bantu' education programme are mass literacy and widespread primary education—priorities which have been seriously questioned in many developing countries, since access of nationals to higher employment both in government and in industry, depends to some extent on higher formal education.

'Fifty years ago the main emphasis was on primary education, but today in many budgets much greater emphasis is given to higher education; to technical education or to adult education. . . . The tendency is to agree to regard these as investment expenditures, and to give them absolute priority while leaving the extension of

---

1. *A Survey of Race Relations . . . 1964*, p. 284.
2. Percentages calculated by Muriel Horrell from numbers given by the Minister of Coloured Affairs.— *A Survey of Race Relations . . . 1969*, p. 221.
3. Minister of Coloured Affairs, quoted in *A Survey of Race Relations . . . 1970*, p. 221.
4. *A Survey of Race Relations . . . 1969*, p. 236.
5. ibid., p. 202.

primary education to fight for its place in public expenditure with roads, health and all the other services which governments have to provide. . . . Looked at . . . primary, secondary and university education constitute a pyramid where all levels must expand in step.'[1]

In reaching conclusions about priorities in education, the Conference of African States at Addis Ababa (1961) put great emphasis on the expansion of secondary education. It noted that some African countries had unduly neglected secondary and higher education in proportion to primary education and pointed out that economic development was highly dependent on skills of the kind which are taught in institutions to students of 15 years of age or more.

'It is of the highest priority to ensure that an adequate proportion of the population receives secondary, post-primary and university education; this should be put before the goal of universal primary education if for financial reasons these two are not yet compatible.'[2]

At the subsequent Paris meeting in 1962 of ministers of education, it was decided to maintain the priority given to secondary level education on the grounds 'that it serves its many purposes, which include meeting the need for professional, agricultural and administrative personnel, as well as the entrance to higher education institutions that each country faces'.[3]

The following is the syllabus for African secondary schools in South Africa.

Junior secondary course

1st group: religious education, physical education, music and singing.
2nd group: a Bantu language (mother tongue), English, Afrikaans, social studies, arithmetic or mathematics or general mathematics, two subjects chosen from Latin or German or any other approved language, mathematics or general mathematics or arithmetic (if not already taken), a natural science (general science or physical science or biology), agriculture, woodwork, arts and crafts, homecraft, biblical studies or any other approved subject.

1. W. Arthur Lewis, *Theory of Economic Growth*, p. 185, London, Allen & Unwin, 1955.
2. *Conference of African States on the Development of Education in Africa. Addis Ababa, 15-25 May, 1961, Final Report*, p. 10, Paris, Unesco, 1962.
3. *Meeting of Ministers of Education of African Countries, Paris, 26-30 March, 1962. Final Report*, p. 32, Paris, Unesco, 1963.

A Commercial and Clerical Junior Certificate course could be taken instead of the General Junior Certificate course, in which case four optional subjects could include book-keeping, commerce, typewriting, shorthand, commercial arithmetic, a natural science, social studies, mathematics.

A Technical Junior Certificate course in which instead of general science the theory of a technical subject is given and workshop practice is given as an additional subject.

Higher secondary course

Higher primary teacher-training course. For admission, course candidates must be in possession of the Junior Certificate. The course is of two years' duration and is designed to train teachers to give instruction in the primary school.

Senior Certificate course. This course covers the work of Forms IV and V. The syllabuses do not differ from those of other South African schools. The African schools may choose either the syllabuses of the Joint Matriculation Board or those of the Department of Education, Arts and Science. At the end of the second year, one or other of these external examinations is written.

In the years before the introduction of the Bantu Education Act, the period 1943-53, the enrolment in secondary classes increased from 1.69 to 3.47 per cent of the total enrolment. In the period 1953-63 the number of those enrolled in secondary classes increased from 30,838 to 53,544, but the proportion of the total enrolment

TABLE 18. Enrolment in African schools. Total enrolment compared to enrolment in secondary classes

Year	Total enrolment	Enrolment in Forms I-V	Forms I-V as percentage of total enrolment	Enrolment in Form V	Form V as percentage of total enrolment
1928	241 775	1 071	0.44	13	0.005
1938	424 356	4 090	0.96	118	0.028
1948	749 179	18 393	2.46	528	0.070
1953	887 949	30 838	3.47	640	0.072
1958	1 338 424	41 568	3.11	938	0.070
1963	1 764 150	53 444	3.02[1]	1 040	0.059

1. Unesco calculation 3.029 per cent.
Source: Secondary Education for Africans, p. 4, Johannesburg, South African Institute of Race Relations (RR.96/65).

dropped from 3.47 to 3.02 per cent. After that there was a gradual rise and in 1969 it was 4.54 per cent of the total enrolment. (See Table 18.)

There is a wastage throughout the course. Commenting on this, the South African Institute of Race Relations pointed to the lack of adequate accommodation in schools catering for pupils from Standard 3 resulting from the fact that African school boards must bear half the costs of erection of higher primary and post-primary schools, and the shortage of departmental funds even where half the costs of building have been raised by Africans. It also pointed to the inability of many parents to afford school books and school fees, the need to send the children out to augment family incomes and the lack of adequate numbers of trained teachers for senior classes.[1]

Since a pupil would proceed from Form I to Form II, and so on, there is an appreciable drop-out between Form I and II (see Table 19).

An indication of the efficiency of teaching at the secondary school level is seen in an analysis of the results of the 1969 Junior Certificate examinations. Of the 16,389 candidates who sat, 11,100 or 67.73 per cent passed and 26.96 per cent received a third class pass,[2] which indicates a low level of attainment and eliminates the holder from continuing to the next form.

Mathematics remained a subject which few Africans took; at matriculation level in 1965, 126 full-time candidates had passed.[3]

There was very little equipment in the few science laboratories that existed; Bunsen burners, balances and microscopes were in short supply (see also Part II, 'Science'). This situation handicaps

TABLE 19. Elimination in secondary classes of African schools

Class	Year	Enrolment	Class	Year	Enrolment
Form I	1959	19 970	Form IV	1962	2 006
Form II	1960	14 105	Form V	1963	1 040
Form III	1961	10 196			

Source: Secondary Education for Africans, p. 7, Johannesburg, South African Institute of Race Relations (RR.96/65).

1. *A Survey of Race Relations . . . , 1964*, p. 275.
2. *Bantu Education Journal*, March 1968, p. 20.
3. *House of Assembly Debates (Hansard)*, 4 June 1965, Cols. 7173-4.

the African who wishes to continue to higher education in science. The Eiselen report of 1951, commenting on the fact that the subjects most favoured by Africans were those which needed a minimum of laboratory work, pointed to the shortage of funds for laboratories.[1]

There has been some improvement, but provision is still grossly inadequate. The amount set aside for equipping laboratories in existing secondary schools for 1967 and 1969 was R.135,000.

Adequacy of school facilities: secondary schools

TABLE 20. Difference in the provision of schools

Category	1962	1965	1968
Primary	7 935	8 450	9 164
Secondary	296	328	370
Other post-primary	75	72	71

Source: *Bantu Education Journal*, March 1968, p. 19.

Table 20 shows the difference in the provision of secondary schools (or divisions of schools) compared with the provision of primary schools (the Transkei is included).

Of the secondary schools only 89 continued on after Form III.[2]

The distribution of secondary pupils as between urban and rural areas in June 1968 was:[3]

Forms I-III: 34,816 in urban and 41,861 in rural areas;

Forms IV-V: 2,490 in urban and 3,072 in rural areas.

In a memorandum to the Minister for Bantu Affairs the Institute of Race Relations pointed out that:

'The number of successful matriculation candidates, particularly those who obtain a university entrance qualification, remains very low, and is unlikely to provide sufficent recruits of the educational standard required to graduate into the professions, train for senior positions in the growing civil service and fill the other positions becoming available.'[4]

1. Union of South Africa, *Report of the Commission on Native Education, 1949-51*, p. 53.
2. *Bantu Education Journal*, March 1968, p. 18.
3. Minister of Bantu Education, quoted in *A Survey of Race Relations . . . , 1969*, p. 190.
4. *A Survey of Race Relations . . . , 1964*, p. 277.

School examinations: end of secondary school

TABLE 21. Matriculation and Senior Certificate results for 1968 (these figures include the Transkei and Namibia)

	Number	Percentage
Number of schools writing examinations	85	—
Number of candidates	2 289	—
Number of candidates who passed with matriculation exemption:		
First class	66	2.8
Second class	679	29.7
Third class	30	1.3
TOTAL	775	33.8
Number of candidates who obtained a school-leaving certificate:		
Second class	322	14.1
Third class	169	7.4
TOTAL	491	21.5
Total number successful	1 266	55.3

Source: Bantu Education Journal, March 1969, p. 10, 11. The school-leaving certificate is a lower level than matriculation exemption.

Secondary education: Coloureds

A total of 53,020 Coloured pupils (approximately 10.81 per cent of the total enrolment at school age) were in secondary schools in 1969. Of these only 1,976 were in Standard 10. Of students sitting the Senior Certificate, 83 passed with first class, 1,195 passed with a second class, and 2,168 failed. Of those who passed 358 obtained the university entrance requirements.[1]

Secondary education: Indians

A total of 35,758 Indian pupils (approximately 23 per cent of the total enrolment at school age) were in secondary schools in 1968 (excluding the Cape where the figures are calculated together with

1. *House of Assembly Debates (Hansard)*, Vol. 18, 13 June 1969, Col. 7956. These figures include Indians in Cape Province.

igures for Coloured enrolment). Of these 2,692 were in Standard 10.[1]
Examination results are available only for Natal. In that province
250 qualified for university entrance.[2]

Secondary education: whites

Since schooling is compulsory from 7 to 16, the drop-out rate for
whites begins after Standard 6. The highest rate would seem to be at
Standard 9 where students may leave secondary school to work or
to go on to commercial and technical training.

Matriculation results for 1967 were:

Matriculation exemption (university entrance): first class, 4,626
(11.7 per cent); second class, 7,767 (19.6 per cent).

School-leaving certificate: first class, 1,642 (4.1 per cent); second
class, 16,242 (41.0 per cent); failures, 9,360 (23.6 per cent).

Some comparative figures

The total enrolment percentages for primary and post-primary education for Africans, Coloureds and Indians are shown in Tables 22,
23 and 24.

1. Minister of Indian Affairs, *House of Assembly Debates (Hansard)*, Vol. 2, 14 February and 17
   May, Col. 720; Vol. 16, Col. 6692.
2. *A Survey of Race Relations . . . 1969*, p. 203.

TABLE 22. Percentage distribution of African pupils in 1969 (including the Transkei)

Class	Percentage	Class	Percentage
Sub-standard A	24.48	Form I	1.65
Sub-standard B	18.04	Form II	1.36
Standard 1	15.56	Form III	0.90
Standard 2	11.69	SUB-TOTAL (Junior secondary)	3.91
SUB-TOTAL (Lower primary)	69.77		
		Form IV	0.18
Standard 3	9.18	Form V	0.11
Standard 4	6.58	SUB-TOTAL (Senior secondary)	0.29
Standard 5	5.15		
Standard 6	4.69	TOTAL (Secondary)	4.20
SUB-TOTAL (Higher primary)	25.60		
		Teacher training	0.28
TOTAL (Primary)	95.34	Vocational training	0.11
		Technical secondary	0.02
		Technical training	0.01
		SUB-TOTAL	0.42
		TOTAL (Post-primary)	4.62

Source: Bantu Education Journal, March 1969, p. 20, 21.

TABLE 23. Percentage distribution of Indian pupils in 1969 (Cape excluded)

Class	Percentage	Class	Percentage
Sub-standard A	10.1	Standard 6	8.1
Sub-standard B	9.1	Standard 7	6.3
Standard 1	12.7	Standard 8	4.3
Standard 2	12.4	Standard 9	2.6
Standard 3	12.8	Standard 10	1.7
Standard 4	10.5	TOTAL (Post-primary)	23.0
Standard 5	9.4		
TOTAL (Primary)	77.0		

Source: A Survey of Race Relations in South Africa, 1969, Johannesburg, South African Institute of Race Relations, 1970.

TABLE 24. Percentage distribution of enrolment figures of Coloured pupils (including Indians) in Cape Province

Class	Percentage	Class	Percentage
Sub-standard A	19.57	Standard 6	4.98
Sub-standard B	16.12	Standard 7	2.95
Standard 1	14.70	Standard 8	1.76
Standard 2	12.66	Standard 9	0.72
Standard 3	10.90	Standard 10	0.40
Standard 4	8.78		
Standard 5	6.46	TOTAL (Post-primary)	10.81
TOTAL (Primary)	89.19		

Source: A Survey of Race Relations in South Africa, 1969, p. 198, Johannesburg, South African Institute of Race Relations, 1970.

6   Content of textbooks

Textbooks

'First the "truth" is obviously not confined only to factual truth—which explains why such importance is attached to eliminating not merely direct counter-truths, but tendentious presentations of facts as well; deliberate errors are extremely rare, but there are cases of a more insidious form of inaccuracy, such as distortions arising from preconceived notions, concepts blindly accepted, unconscious habits of thought, and the desire of certain authors to colour the history of the past in order to justify the present. . . . Facts should not be dealt with in a subjective and emotional manner, but should be critically discussed.'[1]

'In South Africa we are in the peculiar position that the distortions which occur in our domestic history take the form which in other countries is taken in international distortions. They take the form of encouraging group pride and animosity amongst other racial and national groups which happen to be all inhabiting the same country. That makes the distortions of history in South Africa more immediately dangerous than perhaps in most other countries.'[2]

In this section analysis is attempted of textbooks used in white schools in two subjects: history and race studies.

At the outset it should be remembered that there are basically two types of white schools—the Afrikaans-medium schools and the English-medium schools. Whites, Coloureds and Asians often have the same syllabus and use the same textbooks. Africans have a different syllabus and sometimes different textbooks. Some of these books are revised or condensed versions of textbooks used in white schools.

1. *Bilateral Consultations for the Improvement of History Textbooks*, p. 41, Paris, Unesco, 1953.
2. Professor Arthur Keppel-Jones, *Bias in the Presentation of South African History*, lecture delivered at a seminar school on history teaching, Johannesburg, 1955. Quoted from Auerbach, op. cit., p. 13.

The 1949 Statement of the Institute vir Christelik Nasionale Onder-
wys (Institute of Christian National Education) (ICNO) laid down the
principles for teaching history. History was to be taught in the light of
the Divine revelation, it must be seen as the fulfilment of God's plan.
The antithesis between the Kingdom of God in Jesus Christ and
the Empire of Darkness was to be traced in history. God had willed
separate nations and peoples giving to each nation and people its
special calling and tasks and gifts. The youth could take over the
task and mission of the older generation only if in the teaching of
history they obtain a true vision of the origin of the nation and of
the nation's cultural heritage and of the contents of the sound trend
in that heritage. National history was to be, next to the mother
tongue, the great means of cultivating love of one's own.[1] History
then was to be seen as the reinforcing of Divine pre-destination,
and as an instrument for building up nationalism. How is this reflected in the history textbooks in use?

The 1948 Transvaal syllabus listed several objectives. The first was
the duty and privilege of the history teacher to inculcate in his pupils
a rational and enlightened love of country, the second was the development in the pupils of the ability to reason logically and to form
sound judgements through the study of cause and effect. History,
too, was to indicate how Western European civilization was established and how it developed in a country originally inhabited only
by native races.[2]

The syllabus was changed in 1958. The study of history was now to
show how God leads a nation to pious deeds and how a Divine plan
with a nation is carved out. . . . It was to shape nationalism as contrasted with chauvinism, and the student was to be taught that there
was a genetic connexion between the present and the past. History
was to remain a method of finding facts but it was also to be an explanation and an interpretation of the facts. Because it is an interpretation, history, while remaining objective, was not to be necessarily
neutral.[3]

The idea of a chosen people found echoes in some textbooks. The
hand of God reveals itself in the history of the Afrikaner South African. They had been planted by God as a new nation on the southern

1. ICNO Policy Statement, Article 6. Quoted from Auerbach, op. cit., p. 112.
2. *Transvaal Suggested Syllabus for Standard VII*, p. 139, Education Department, 1948.
3. Auerbach, op. cit., p. 109.

tip of Africa and had been wonderfully preserved from being wiped out.[1]

A Standard 8 guidance book underlines the differences that are presumed to exist between white and non-whites:

'The point of view of certain foreign clergymen that whites and non-whites should inter-marry and that, in the name of Christianity, is too incisive a change in the culture pattern of the non-white and the white. Such a thing can only create confusion and degeneration. All things considered the coming about and continued existence of the white Christian civilisation in spite of the mass of non-whites can be seen as nothing less than a disposition of the Almighty.'[2]

A comparison of the percentage of space given to European history gives the impression that periods of European history which accord with the concepts of nationalism are given a greater emphasis in South African textbooks than periods of inquiry or political liberalism. Thus, except for book *L*,[3] the Renaissance receives a less full treatment than the Reformation; the French Revolution in the senior textbooks and particularly in *K* is given a relatively restricted treatment. More noticeable is the difference in emphasis about South African history itself. The Great Trek gets 15 per cent of the space in *J* and 18 per cent of the space of *K* compared with 9 per cent of the space in *L*. The Founding of the Republics gets 10 per cent of the space in *J* and 14 per cent of the space in *K*, compared with 7 per cent of the space in *L*. The Orange Free State and the Basutos get 4 per cent of the space in *J*, 2 per cent of the space in *K* and is not treated at all in *L*. Kruger and Rhodes are given 7 per cent of the space in *J*, 9 per cent in *K* and 1.5 per cent of the space in *L*. The Anglo-Boer war is given 10 per cent of the space in *J*, 5.5 per cent of the space in *K* and 2.5 per cent of the space in *L*. For a complete breakdown of figures, see Tables 25, 26 and 27.

Textbooks *J* and *K* were mainly in use in Afrikaner-medium schools, textbook *L* in English-medium schools.

1. Auerbach, op. cit., p. 117.
2. Quoted here (translation from the Afrikaans) from Auerbach, op. cit., p. 118.
3. For key, see note 1 in Table 25.

TABLE 25. Percentage of text devoted to the various topics in Standard 6 textbooks (used in the Transvaal)

	J^1		K^1		L^1	
Introduction and the Cradle of Western civilization	13.0		12.0			
The heritage of Greece and Rome	16.5		8.0		23.0	
		29.5		20.0		
The chief characteristics of the Middle Ages	11.5		8.0		25.0	
Inventions and discoveries during the Renaissance	5.5		4.0			
Portuguese trade with the East	4.0		5.0		10.0	
The Dutch sail around the Cape	4.5		6.0			
		25.5		23.0		58.0
		55.0		43.0		
Foundations of Dutch settlement at the Cape	4.0		4.5		3.0	
Native races of South Africa	8.0		11.0		1.5	
The free burghers	3.0		4.0		5.0	
Exploration and discovery till 1700	3.0		4.5		3.0	
Simon van der Stel and the Huguenots	7.5		8.0		4.5	
Cape at the beginning of the eighteenth century	7.0		9.0		9.0	
Expansion 1700-79	4.0		6.5		8.0	
Influence of colonial and European wars	4.5		4.0		1.0	
1771-95	4.0		5.5		7.0	
		45.0		57.0		42.0
		100.0		100.0		100.0

Source: F. E. Auerbach, *The Power of Prejudice in South African Education*, p. 31, Cape Town and Amsterdam, 1965.

1. J = F. A. van Jaarsveld, in collaboration with J. J. van der Walt, *History for Standards 6, 7 and 8*.
   K = Dr. J. F. E. Kavinger, G. F. Robbertse and A. G. Roodt, *Histories for Standards 6, 7 and 8*.
   L = A. N. Boyce, *The Legacy of the Past: History Books for Standards 6, 7 and 8*.
   These code letters are also used in Tables 26 and 27.

Slant of text

Two myths tend to be widely believed in South Africa. The first is that the Dutch landed in an empty territory.[1] The second is that clashes with African tribes were always violent and that the early

1. See Leo Marquard, *The Peoples and Policies of South Africa*, 3rd ed., p. 3 ff, London, Cape Town and New York, Oxford University Press, 1962.

TABLE 26. Percentage of text devoted to the various topics in Standard 7 books

	J		K		L	
Renaissance	5.5		3.5		15.0	
Reformation	9.0		12.0		12.0	
Eighty Years' War	7.0		3.5		5.0	
Rise of France, Russia and Prussia	16.5		10.0		15.0	
Industrial Revolution in England	5.5		4.0		12.0	
		43.5		33.0		59.0
First British occupation	3.0		7.0		4.5	
Batavian Republic	3.0		5.0		2.0	
Second British occupation 1806-34	14.0		14.5		15.0	
The Great Trek	15.0		18.0		9.0	
The Founding of the Republics	10.0		14.0		7.0	
The Orange Free State and the Basutos	4.0		2.0		—	
Sir George Grey	3.5		2.5		—	
Progress in the Cape Colony until 1854	—		—		3.5	
		52.5		63.0		41.0
Civics	4.0		4.0		—	
		4.0		4.0		—
		100.0		100.0		100.0

Source: F. E. Auerbach, *The Power of Prejudice in South African Education*, Cape Town and Amsterdam, 1965.

history of white settlement was marked by the massacre of innocent unsuspecting whites by the Africans.[1] Early travellers had very different tales to tell:

'On Sunday the 26th of November (1497) the fleet reached the inlet termed by Da Gama the Watering Place of Sao Bras, now Mossel Bay. Here after they had been several days at anchor, a number of Hottentots appeared, some—men and women—riding on pack oxen. They were very friendly. . . . Afterwards more arrived, bringing a few sheep, which were obtained in barter.'[2]

'Others will say that the natives are brutal and cannibals, from whom no good can be expected . . . we of the Haerlem testify otherwise, as the natives came with all friendliness to trade with us at the fort . . .

1. I. D. MacCrone, *Race Attitudes in South Africa*, p. 260, Johannesburg, Witwatersrand University Press, 1965.
2. G. M. Theal, *Belangrike Historiche Documenten*, Vol. 1, p. 56-7. Quoted from MacCrone, op. cit., p. 11.

TABLE 27. Percentage of text devoted to the various topics in Standard 8 textbooks

	J		K		L	
French Revolution	12.5		8.5		10	
Napoleon	11		4.5		16	
Congresses	2.5		2		10	
1815-48	8		4		—	
		34		19		36
Africa after 1939	12		25.5		15	
		12		25.5		15
Introduction and Diamonds	7		4.5		13.5[1]	
Carnarvon's federation policy and consequences	7.5		12		7	
Discovery of gold and results	5		4		9.5	
Kruger and Rhodes	7		9		1.5	
The Anglo-Boer war	10		5.5		2.5	
Factors leading to union	3		8		2.5	
The constitution	3		—[2]		3.5	
South Africa as a member of the Commonwealth	2.5		1		—	
		45		44		40
Civics: How the country is governed	3		4.5		—	
Taxation and public finance	1		2		—	
Aftermath of union (1910-39)	5		5		9	
		9		11.5		9
		100		100.0		100

1. Includes Sir George Grey and the Basuto wars.
2. Included in Civics.
Source: F. E. Auerbach, *The Power of Prejudice in South African Education*, p. 32, Cape Town and Amsterdam, 1965.

bringing cattle and sheep in numbers. . . . The killing of our people is undoubtedly caused by revenge being taken by the natives when their cattle is seized, and not because they are cannibals.'[1]

Both MacCrone and Hawaarden point to the perpetuation of the myth that unprovoked Africans attacked European farmers:

'If African peoples are presented to school children solely as engaging in unprovoked attacks on White farmers—and this is the picture which most South African textbooks and teachers present in both

1. Leendert Jansz and N. Proot in their 'Remonstrance to the Council of Seventeen on July 26, 1949'. Quoted from MacCrone, op. cit., p. 15.

primary and secondary schools—then though the facts of individual attack may be correct, the total impact of the students and the picture they form of past events, is untrue. It omits the attacks by Europeans, the provocation suffered by the Africans, the loss of their lands, the courage and chivalry with which the Ama-Xhosa fought in defending their country from invasion.'[1]

Land tenure and its relationship to frontier clashes between the whites and the Africans was one of the key aspects of early South African history. Auerbach found that in the Transvaal no junior book explains land tenure, though two mention it, and only one senior book deals with it. He further goes on to say:

'Thus, unless teachers are aware that nearly all textbooks perpetuate errors which historians have corrected by diligent research . . . children in many schools will regard the Xhosas as thieves and possibly murderers, and the European farmers as blameless, since many of the books employ . . . emotive words calculated to arouse feelings of hostility against the Xhosa. The children are therefore likely to identify themselves virtuously with the blameless farmers, and some, if not all, present-day Africans with the Xhosa thieves.'[2]

The subject 'race studies' has been introduced in many South African schools. Table 28 shows a content analysis of race studies textbooks in the Transvaal.

An interesting aspect of this is the high percentage of space devoted to 'Bantu tribal life and reserves', and the very small percentage of space given to 'Bantu in urban areas', this in spite of the growing urbanization of Africans. However, the textbooks point to the 'problems' created by an African urban population. For Bruwer[3] while the African farm labourer and mineworkers present only minor problems the urban African is organized into political ways of thinking and by strikes and boycotts could exert a powerful influence on the South African economy. Moreover, African urbanization would lead to economic integration, would lower the working morale of the whites, and also lay on the whites a heavy and uplifting task. For Hudson[4] the problem was that increased African urbanization would lead to social assimilation.[5]

1. Eleanor Hawaarden, *Prejudice in the Classroom*, p. 41, Johannesburg, 1966.
2. Auerbach, op. cit., p. 97.
3. See Table 28.
4. See Table 28.
5. Auerbach, op. cit., p. 120-1.

TABLE 28. Content analysis of race studies textbooks

Syllabus topic	Hudson et al.[1] Standards 6-8	Bruwer et al.[1] Standards 6-8	Becker et al.[1] Standards 6 and 7	Becker et al.[1] Standards 6-8[2]
Races of the world and of Africa	6	11	13	6.5
Bushmen and Hottentots	12	15	25	12.5
Coloured people	10	12	9	9
Indians	9	9.5	9	8
Bantu tribal life and reserves	38	29.5	44	32
Contact with and employment by Whites; administration of Bantu	15	16		17
Bantu in urban areas; their administration; missions and education	9	6		12
Traditional standpoint on administration of non-Europeans	1	1		3

. Hudson, van Tonder et al., *Race Studies for Standards 6, 7 and 8*, Nasionale Pers.
Bruwer et al., *Race Studies. Standards 6, 7 and 8*, J. H. B. Voortrekkerpers, 1958, 1959.
P. L. W. Becker, *The Peoples of South Africa (Standards 6 and 7)*, Dagbreek Book Store, 1958 and 1960.
2. The book by Becker et al. appeared in 1964; the revised analysis is therefore included here.
Source: F. E. Auerbach, *The Power of Prejudice in South African Education*, p. 120, Cape Town and Amsterdam, 1965.

7 Mother-tongue instruction

African schools

In discussing mother tongue, it is well to note that in South Africa, Afrikaans and English are the only official languages, and that Bantu languages are not used as a medium in government, industry, commerce and finance. This point was made by H. Holmes, Vice Rector of the Johannesburg College of Education:

'Africans object to the use of the vernacular as a medium of instruc tion—they want English. The Africans' objections are two-fold—one irrational, the other more to the point. Africans claim to know their own languages and therefore see no need to use them at school. This attitude of the intelligentsia has probably robbed Africans of good literary works, there is far too little for the educated African to read in his own language. His second objection, the real one, is that unless he knows a European language, and preferably English, all doors to progress will be closed to him. Language to him must be functiona in a world of industry and commerce. It also makes him inter national.'[1]

Under the old system in South Africa, it was generally the practice to use the mother tongue as the medium of instruction during the first four or five years of schooling. There was, after this period, a gradual change to the use of one of the official languages—for his torical reasons usually English—so that during the last two years of primary education at least, African pupils were taught in an offi cial language.

The Bantu Education Act of 1953 'empowers the Minister to pre scribe the medium of instruction in Government Bantu Schools'. As a result instruction in the 'mother tongue' is now used throughout the primary school. In addition, the African is required to learn two official languages: Afrikaans and English. One official language is generally introduced as a subject during the child's first year at school and the other six months later.

One of the arguments against the use of a Bantu language through out the primary-school course was that the language, fashioned to the needs of a peasant community, put a limit to the wider education needed today. This gap in vocabulary was recognized by the South African Government itself. Departmental committees were established to prepare glossaries for the seven main Bantu languages. Lists of terms to be used in primary-school subjects were circulated to schools, and lists of terms for secondary-school subjects are now being pre pared.

1. *The Bantu at School*, paper given by H. Holmes at a symposium on South Africa, Maraisburg Rotary Club, Roodepoort, June 1962.

The significant factor in mother-tongue instruction—as in other aspects of African education—is that the choice of what language to be taught and for how long, was not the choice of the Africans themselves.[1]

The problem of the choice of the medium of instruction, at the primary level, does not of course exist only in South Africa. It is a worldwide problem. It should, however, be underlined that it presents itself in completely different terms outside South Africa, because it is not viewed from the angle of a discriminatory policy. In South Africa, however, the policy of apartheid has had recourse to the choice of the mother tongue as the main medium of instruction at the primary level (beyond which, it has been shown, the vast majority of African children do not pursue their studies) in order to reinforce the linguistic, social and cultural isolation of the African population within the country as well as from the world at large.[2]

One important problem in the system of teaching foreign languages in African schools is the lack of properly trained staff. Effective language teaching depends on the proficiency of the teachers in the language concerned. In most schools at present, the same overworked teacher teaches both Afrikaans and English. Under such conditions, it is to be questioned whether pupils, at the end of their school life, graduate with more than a rudimentary knowledge of English and Afrikaans.[3]

However, the Minister of Bantu Education declared that the department has supplied radio sets to higher primary and post-primary schools, and broadcast special programmes (in the official languages). At the beginning of 1964, 500 of these sets had been distributed and a further 1,500 were planned for distribution before the end of the year.[4] There has been a further increase since then.

---

1. See also *Education for South Africa. The 1961 Education Panel. First Report*, p. 56, Johannesburg, Witwatersrand University Press, 1963: 'The decision as to how fast and in what direction a culture shall change, what its attitude should be to other languages, for example, is a decision belonging to the bearers of the culture alone. In our opinion, therefore, White-inspired attempts to insist upon the preservation of Bantu languages are as misplaced as White attempts to eliminate such languages would be. The decision as to how Bantu languages as a medium of culture and learning shall develop belongs to the Bantu; or, to be more accurate, the decision as to each particular language belongs to those whose language it is.'
2. See Part III, Chapter 4.
3. The South African Institute of Race Relations commented: 'The net result of the 1946 syllabus . . . has been that Africans have, increasingly, found difficulty in expressing themselves coherently in either of the official languages.'—*A Survey of Race Relations . . . 1966*, p. 237-8.
4. *House of Assembly Debates (Hansard)*, Cols. 6348 ff. Quoted from Horrell, op. cit.

The new higher primary syllabus makes provision for radio lessons of half an hour a day, and Radio Bantu broadcasts language and other lessons. One problem is the lack of literature available in African languages. This would be less serious if African writers were writing more in their home languages. Although a great percentage of books produced in Bantu languages are textbooks, well-known African writers, are, for a variety of reasons (see Part III), writing in English, or if writing in their mother tongue, are writing manuscripts that are never published, so that the literature available to the adult African trained in his own language remains limited.

White schools

As from 1970, mother-tongue instruction became compulsory in government and government-subsidized schools, up to and including Standard 8 (until then, it was compulsory only in the Orange Free State and in the Transvaal where Christian National Education had been put into practice). This ensures that Afrikaans-speaking and English-speaking children are educated apart, and that contacts between them (except in private schools) are limited to out-of-school activities.

The language load in white schools is less than in African schools, and there is some flexibility in the choice as to when the second language, English or Afrikaans, is introduced.

Teachers in primary and secondary schools

Teacher training: Africans

Africans may qualify as teachers by taking the Primary Teacher's Certificate involving two years of professional training after the Junior Certificate at the end of Form III. This is the most common teachers' qualification. At the end of 1967 the numbers of African teachers who qualified were: Lower Primary Certificate, 126; Higher Primary Certificate, 2,043; Secondary Teachers Diploma, 64; University Education Diploma (non-graduate), 6; University Education Diploma, 24.[1]

Of the twenty-four training schools for African teachers in 1970 only four offered the JSTC—a two-year course for which the entrance qualification is the Senior Certificate. The others offered a two-year course for which the entrance qualification is the Junior Certificate. For the latter preference was given to applicants with a first- or second-class pass.[2] This suggests that some students accepted for training had received only a third-class Junior Certificate pass. The third-class Junior Certificate pass—an inferior pass introduced in 1963—does not qualify the successful candidate for admission to the next form.

Teachers in African schools

The Eiselen report, which was published in 1951, found the position of African teachers in secondary schools to be unsatisfactory. The breakdown of African teachers holding qualifications was 18.6 per cent without matriculation, 41.4 per cent without degree, 2.2 per cent with degree but without teacher's diploma, and 37.8 per cent with degree plus diploma.[3]

1. *Bantu Education Journal*, March 1968 and *A Survey of Race Relations ... 1969*, p. 225.
2. *Bantu Education Journal*, October 1969, p. 28, 29.
3. Union of South Africa, *Report of the Commission on Native Education, 1949-51*, p. 81.

By 1967 only 17.46 per cent had a degree and professional qualifications and 4.60 per cent had a degree only. If being a graduate is taken as being of a particular professional level the standard had deteriorated since 1961. This is partly offset by the higher percentage of teachers with some training or with matriculation exemptions; 1.23 per cent had not matriculated and had no professional qualifications in 1967, 48.73 per cent had 'lesser professional qualifications' which were neither a degree nor a secondary teachers' diploma.[1]

The Institute of Race Relations, commenting on the figures in 1966, pointed out that in the category 'neither degree nor professional qualifications', there may be teachers who have merely a Standard 6 certificate.

The pupil-teacher ratio has been deteriorating. In 1955 the over-all ratio was 46.1; in 1963, it was 55 pupils per teacher in lower primary classes, 50 in higher primary classes and 50 in post-primary classes. In 1967 it was an over-all figure of 58.5.

About 96 per cent of these were employed at primary community schools or farm schools.

While the number of pupils in secondary and training schools together had more than doubled between 1949 and 1963, the number of teachers had increased by barely 15 per cent.[2]

The problems of finance for African schools and the effect that this has on the salaries and the recruitment of teachers have already been discussed.

Salaries

One-fifth of all African teachers are privately paid by school boards and parents.[1]

Teacher training: Coloureds

Coloureds may qualify as teachers by taking the Primary Teachers Certificate. At the end of 1968 the number of Coloured teachers who qualified were: Lower Primary Teachers Certificate, 399; Primary Teachers Certificate, 224; specialist one-year courses for trained

1. *A Survey of Race Relations . . . 1969*, p. 195.
2. *Secondary Education for Africans*, op. cit., p. 8.

eachers, 150; Teachers' Diploma, 24; Lower Secondary Teachers Diploma, 19; University Education Diploma, 13.[1]

Teachers in Coloured schools

In 1968, 22.9 per cent of teachers in Coloured schools had degrees and professional qualifications, 2.3 per cent had degrees only, 71.1 per cent had professional qualifications without a degree, 3.5 per cent had matriculation with professional qualifications and 0.2 per cent had not matriculated and were not professionally trained.[2]

Teacher training: whites

Since 1928 the teacher training for European students in South Africa is post-matriculation. Most of the institutions offer a course of two years for women, with the option of a third year's specialized course. Men usually take a three-year course. Secondary teachers are trained at universities. The Lower Secondary Teachers Diploma is obtained after three years' post-matriculation study, the course being partly academic and partly professional. The lowest post-graduate certificate obtainable is the Secondary Teachers Diploma.[3] An amendment to the National Education Act, if passed, would transfer all teacher-

TABLE 29. Comparative pupil-teacher ratio

Year	White	Coloured and Indian	African
1946	24	38	45
1951	25	30	46
1956	23	34	49
1963	23	31	58

Sources: Statistical Yearbook, 1964, Table E9, p. 12, 15, 17; Statistical Yearbook, 1965, p. 414-15. 422-3, 428-9, 434-5 (both compiled by the Department of Statistics, Pretoria); Education and the South African Economy. The 1961 Educational Panel, Second Report, p. 57, Johannesburg, Witwatersrand University Press, 1966.

---

1. *A Survey of Race Relations . . . 1969*, p. 200.
2. The percentage of teachers in Coloured schools differs from the percentage of Coloured teachers. This would indicate a high percentage of white teachers in Coloured schools. Percentages taken from *A Survey of Race Relations . . . 1969*, p. 199.
3. International Court of Justice, *South West Africa Cases (Ethiopia and Liberia v. the Republic of South Africa)*. Counter-memorial filed by the Government of the Republic of South Africa, Vol. VII, 1963, p. 184.

TABLE 30. Percentage of teachers with degrees by race

Qualification	African	Coloured	Asian	White
Degree plus professional qualifications	1.95			
Degree only	0.05			
Bachelor's degree		3.50	9.65	27.92
Master's degree		0.13	0.15	3.01
Doctor's degree		0.03	0.07	0.41

Source: Stanley G. Osler, *Pyramids and Peoples*, p. 17, South Africa, 20 October 1964 (mimeo.).

training institutions for whites to universities and would replace the three-year post-matriculation course (two years in the case of women with a third year option for specialized training) with a four-year course. University graduates would be required to take at least a one-year course. The Minister of National Education would be able to permit three-year courses—but only for primary school teachers.

9   School libraries

'The school library is an organic, vital and functional part of the education structure existing for the quality teaching and quality education of the whole child as a creative, informed, intelligent, integrated and abundant personality in a world of new dimensions and changes.'[1]

1. 'Programme for Future Library Development in the Republic of South Africa, Article 4.1.3.1', as adopted by the National Conference, Pretoria, 5 and 6 November 1962, published in *South African Libraries*, Vol. 30, no. 1, January 1963, p. 94.

For children who could normally not be provided with books at home, the school library can be their introduction to the world of literature which lies outside the school syllabus. An examination of the school-library service for one area in South Africa illustrates that the importance of school libraries is recognized by library authorities and by librarians, but it also illustrates that libraries are geared not to the population as a whole, but mainly to the white section.

The Transvaal Education Department Library Service runs an education library and a schools' library service. In 1962 the education library had a collection of approximately 200,000 volumes, 600 periodicals and 5,000 pictures to serve teachers and officials of the education department throughout the province.

The school library had four full-time school-library advisers who visited schools in the province, and vacation courses in school librarianship were offered to school librarians.

Each new school was given a grant for the purchase of basic material, while after this there were free annual allocations based on enrolment, and an R.1 to R.2 subsidy.

There was a rebinding scheme which in 1962 handled 100,000 books per year. Standards for library buildings had been drawn up and each new school was automatically provided with a spaciously equipped library, while when old schools were being repaired extensively a library and library workroom were automatically attached. Guides for book selection and book lists were circulated and a special book classification had been adapted for the service. Two professional associations brought together school librarians: the Transvaal School Library Association and the School and Children's Library section of the Southern Transvaal Branch of the South African Library Association. However, this service was in the main restricted to schools for white children although Coloured and Indian schools were given some grants for the purchase of books and were permitted a quota of books for central rebinding.

Provincial authorities did not provide libraries for African schools, for while Coloured and Indian schools were still governed by the provincial education department and so had theoretically the same financing arrangements as white schools, the Bantu Education Act had placed African schools under the care of the Department of Bantu Education, and so African school libraries were no longer the responsibility of the provincial authorities.

D. M. Turner, F.S.A.L.A., reported in an article[1] with regard to school libraries that:

'little progress seems to have been made . . . on the whole libraries in non-White schools are poor or entirely absent and children who wish to read use such public library facilities as are available to them.'

This gap is particularly serious when one considers the economic situation in many non-white homes which makes book buying financially difficult. The gap must also be seen in terms of demand. In the estimates for 1963-64 R.2,800 was allowed for school libraries in African schools. The department subsidized the purchase of school-library books on a half-cost basis, the other half to be met from school funds. The maximum subsidy was $2\frac{1}{2}$ cents per pupils for Standards 1 and 2, and 5 cents per pupil in the high grades. No primary school however could receive more than R.20 a year, and no post-primary school more than R.50. There were regulations laid down as to the selection of books. The number of books were to be divided equally between the 'Bantu' language, Afrikaans and English, they were to be chosen from a particular list of 1,198 recommended books, and the subsidy would be paid only if circuit inspectors were given the right of inspection of existing stocks, to ensure that unsuitable literature was not being provided for school reading.[2]

In 1967-68 R.8,500 was set aside for school libraries and in 1969-70 R.9,300. The Institute of Race Relations calculated that the 1967-68 allocation of R.8,500 would provide R.32.50 for each school library even if only post-primary schools benefit.[3]

There are other problems besides lack of money to buy books. An article in *Bantu Education Journal*, December 1969, gave extracts from a speech by C. D. Zombi, Inanda Seminary, Natal, in which he explained:

'Many teachers are kept away from founding and administering school libraries because of the technical problems involved, like: lack of storage if a centralised library is to be established; heavy teaching load on teachers so that even those who would volunteer to be teacher-librarians feel that this would reduce their efficiency; the

1. D. M. Turner, 'School Libraries in South Africa: 1952-1962', *South African Libraries*, Vol. 30, No. 4, April 1963.
2. *A Survey of Race Relations . . . 1963*, p. 255.
3. *A Survey of Race Relations . . . 1967*, p. 243.

ack of library buildings and equipment due to meagre finances; lack of qualified personnel to run the school libraries; recent changes in syllabuses calling upon teachers to undergo intensive training, while at the same time they are expected to prepare pupils for external examinations. This hardly leaves time for teachers to attend to, what may be called, side issues.'[1]

Johannesburg Public Libraries reported that the majority of their present non-European readers were children. Of the total circulation of the non-European services 70 per cent were children's books.[2]

At the Graaf-Reinet section of the Cape Province libraries non-European membership in 1958 showed 75 per cent to be children.[3]

The 1967-68 membership statistics in the Johannesburg non-white libraries showed a juvenile membership of 19,693 as against an adult membership of 3,084.[4]

10 Technical and vocational education

Technical education: Africans

The Eiselen Commission found that in 1949 vocational and technical training of Africans was being given in a variety of institutions. Besides technical classes in primary schools there were industrial or handicraft centres in some towns, and industrial departments attached to mission schools. The Union Department of Education,

1. *Bantu Education Journal,* December 1969, p. 11.
2. Johannesburg Public Library, *Annual Report, 1963-64,* p. 10.
3. Province of the Cape of Good Hope, *Report of the Director of Library Services for the Years 1958 and 1959,* p. 27.
4. *Race Relations News,* May 1970.

Arts and Science had opened a school for African artisans at Zwelitsha to train African building operatives for building schemes in African areas, and the department subsidized vocational training given by provincial governments.[1]

There was no uniformity in the duration of courses given, and the commission commented on the slow growth of industrial education of a really vocational nature.[2]

The Eiselen Commission suggested an expansion of technical education. In its tentative scheme for educational development the commission mentions as one of its objectives the training in 'vocational and polytechnical schools [of] all those who can be absorbed by the development plan or the present Bantu society'. The commission gives figures for the next ten years, during which period the number of places in 'industrial' schools available, 2,170 in 1949, should be raised to 6,000.

The Vocational Education Act of 1958 and its amendments of 1959 (valid for vocational education for all races) and 1961 continued in the field of African vocational and technical training the centralization in administration and financial control which was the policy in other spheres of African education.

It is difficult to give a clear view of the actual situation with regard to technical and vocational training. To an extent private industry trains Africans in specific jobs. The following data give, however, a general idea of what kind of training is offered by the Bantu Education Department.

Technical schools. Boys who have obtained a continuation pass in standard 6 (i.e. first- or second-class pass) may apply for admission to one of the technical schools conducted by the Bantu Education Department at Bloemfontein, Port Elizabeth; St. John's College, Transkei (Umtata); Amanzimtoti (south of Durban); Edendale (Pietermaritzburg); Jalsulani (Johannesburg); Umlagi; Durban and Vlakfontein (Pretoria).

They take a three-year course leading to a junior certificate (technical) examination.

At Vlakfontein they may go on for two years after the Technical Junior Certificate to take the Technical Senior Certificate. The subjects available include building construction, carpentry, joinery,

1. Union of South Africa, *Report of the Commission on Native Education, 1949-51*, p. 36.
2. ibid.

plumbing and sheet-metal work, electrotechnics, training as general or motor mechanics, leatherwork and tailoring.

At the Vlakfontein Technical School courses are also available in drawing and draughtsmanship, radiotechnics and (with the assistance of the Swiss Government) watchmaking and repairing.

As far as the Technical Junior Certificate is concerned, it would appear that the Technical Junior Certificate course is not adequate to produce competent tradesmen, and that the boys need at least a year's further specialized training in their trades.

Combined enrolment figures for 1968 were 626. Of these 160 were being trained as motor mechanics, 89 as electricians, 84 in building construction, 77 in woodwork and 60 as 'radiotricians'.[1]

As access to courses, both at trade schools and technical schools, depends on a standard 6 certificate, the number of Africans who can take advantage of these courses is small (see Part I, Chapter 5, Enrolment and Syllabuses'). In spite of this there has had to be a restriction on the intake because of lack of schools and facilities. At the Vlakfontein Technical High School near Pretoria, entrance has been restricted to a first-class standard 6 pass, owing to lack of facilities.'[2]

The fees are high, particularly when compared with the average African income. At Vlakfontein Technical High School they were: Form I, R.22; Form II, R.30; Form III, R.18; Form IV, R.35; and Form V, R.20. To this must be added R.4 a year for materials.

One of the problems is employment after training. The availability of this depends on the area concerned, the working of job reservation practices and the racial make-up of the population. Where Indian and Coloured labour are available, as in Natal, trained Africans may find it difficult to find employment since they are last in the order of preference for employment.

Trade schools. Departmental trade and vocational schools are situated mainly in African reserves. This is deliberate. The Minister of Bantu Education explained this policy:

'I can only say that the intention is in the first place to concentrate vocational training mainly in the Bantu areas, in order to meet the

1. *Bantu Education Journal,* September 1968, p. 11.
2. *Bantu* (Pretoria), May 1967, p. 24.

need which exists for people with vocational training to assist in the development of the Bantu communities themselves.'[1]

There are thirteen trade schools in the Republic including the Transkei. Included in these are five secondary schools that provide trade school courses.

In line with departmental policy they are situated mainly in rural areas. There are ten vocational schools for girls at which dressmaking and home-management are taught. Two- or three-year courses (depending on the trade) are provided at the institutions for boys while one- or two-year courses are provided for girls.

The courses for boys include carpentry, bricklaying, plastering, general and motor mechanics, cabinet-making, plumbing, electricians' work and house wiring, leatherwork, upholstery and tailoring. On completion of their courses, boys receive a School Certificate in Vocational Training, which is recognized by the government for employment as qualified tradesmen—but only in the reserves.

Boys who have qualified in one of the four building trades, however, may seek employment under an urban local authority or with the Department of Bantu Administration and Development on a housing scheme for Africans. After they have gained at least one year's further practical experience, they may enter for trade tests and, if successful, are registered by the Department of Labour as skilled workers under the Bantu Building Workers' Act. They are then qualified to work on building projects in urban African townships as well as in the reserves.

In 1967, thirty boys who had completed the two years' theoretical study at trade school were the first group to be chosen for training as fully qualified motor mechanics. At the end of the course they could apply for loans from the Bantu Investment Corporation to enable them to open garages and service depots in the reserves. The government has debarred Africans from opening garages in urban African townships. The theoretical training is inadequate to enable the boys to enter for the National Technical Certificate (NTC).

The Duke Vocational Training Centre run by the Johannesburg Municipality without a government subsidy does provide training for the NTC. In 1967, 313 Africans had qualified for the School Certificate in Vocational Training, 84 had obtained the NTC I and 15 the NTC II.

1. *House of Assembly Debates (Hansard)*, 17 June 1959, Col. 8314.

TABLE 31. African enrolment in vocational and technical classes

Year	Number of places recommended by Eiselen Commission	Actual African enrolment in vocational and technical classes
1949	2 170	—
1955	4 000	2 237
1957	4 900	2 952
1959	6 000	1 379
1963	—	2 035

Source: Secondary Education for Africans, p. 9, Johannesburg, South African Institute of Race Relations (RR.97/65).

The criticism of the technical and vocational training of Africans is principally a criticism of its aim. As expressed by the Eiselen Commission, those Africans shall have access to training who can be absorbed by the 'Bantu society'. Africans have limited access to qualified jobs outside the reserves and African townships.

The Native Building Workers' Act authorized the training of skilled African builders for work on buildings occupied by members of their own racial groups, and prohibited the employment of Africans on any other building work in urban areas unless special exemption is granted.

It is open to doubt whether the actual training facilities are sufficient even for the limited purpose of work in African areas, since the actual numbers of places in technical and vocational schools fall short of those envisaged in the Eiselen report.

Table 31 compares recommendations of the Eiselen Commission with actual enrolments.

Technical education: Coloured students

There are State technical and vocational schools at Belleville, Athlone, Port Elizabeth, Kimberley, Johannesburg and Durban, and State-aided schools at Stellenbosch, Wittebome, Kirkwood, Aliwall North, Cradock, Flagstaff and Port Elizabeth.

Enrolment figures for 1968/69 were: State schools, 1,198 full-time (713 part-time); State-aided schools, 1,035 full-time; Peninsula Technical College, 1967/68, 68 full-time (320 part-time).[1]

1. *A Survey of Race Relations . . . 1969*, p. 208.

Technical education: Indians

The main centre for technical education is the M. L. Sultan Technical College, subsidized by the government. This is now an Advanced Technical College under the terms of the Advanced Technical Education Act (for Indians) No. 12 of 1968.

One of the results of this Act was to abolish the existing councils and governing bodies and to establish a college council half of whose members are appointed by the Minister of Indian Affairs. The new council appoints the board of studies and makes recommendations to the Minister of Indian Affairs as to the appointment of staff members.

The minister may decide on conditions of service, salaries and leave as well as the courses of study that should be offered. Subsidies may be withheld if the council does not comply with the terms under which they are granted.

As from 1968 full-time secondary students at the colleges were sent to secondary schools and as from 1971 day classes in commerce and homecraft will be dropped.

Courses leading to national diplomas in accounting, auditing and public administration have been added.

Technical and vocational training for whites

As a result of the passing of the Vocational Act in 1955, the South African Education Department completely reorganized vocational training for white students as well as for non-white students. Vocational education is now directly under the control of the Central Department of Education, Arts and Science. One of the aims was, in the field of white technical and vocational training, to make technical colleges free, bringing them in line with the free secondary education provided by the provinces. The larger institutions such as Pretoria, Witwatersrand, Cape and Natal technical colleges were not taken over and are at present subsidized by the government.

Vocational high schools (technical high schools, housecraft high schools and commercial high schools) concentrate upon a particular field. Commercial courses include the following subjects: first and second official languages, book-keeping, commerce, typing and short-hand.

Technical courses include first and second official languages, mathe-

...atics, physics, engineering, drawing and the scientific background
...o such trades as fitting, turning, welding, general motor-mechanics,
...c.[1]

TABLE 32. Enrolment in technical, commercial and vocational
institutions, June 1966

...stitution	Full-time	Part-time
...tate-aided technical colleges	5 200	23 917
...)epartmental technical colleges	4 610	8 569
...chools for apprentices	—	8 024
...echnical high schools	12 078	1 522
...ommercial and technical high schools	2 674	2 874
...ommercial high schools	7 615	1 034
...)omestic-science high schools	1 146	—
...tate-aided vocational schools	212	—
...ontinuation classes in commerce and technology	—	1 990

...ource: Report of the Department of Education, Arts and Science, here quoted from *A Survey of*
...ace Relations in South Africa, 1968, Johannesburg, South African Institute of Race Relations, 1969.

TABLE 33. Some comparative pass figures for the National Technical
Certificate (NTC)[1]

...TC level	Africans	Indians	Coloureds	Whites
	84	2	366	2 351
I	15	2	184	3 378
II	—	1	39	2 399
V	—	—	6	1 018
	—	—	1	640

.. The figures for African and Indian students refer to 1967, Coloureds and whites to 1968.
...ource: A Survey of Race Relations in South Africa, 1968, p. 245, 248, Johannesburg, South African
...nstitute of Race Relations, 1969. Also ibid., *1969,* p. 208, 209.

.. Information given here from *World Survey of Education,* Vol. III: *Secondary Education,* p. 1121-2,
Paris, Unesco, 1961.

11   Adult education

In 1959 the Minister of Bantu Education gave as an estimate that 80 per cent of the Africans in the 7-20 age group could be considered literate. In 1963 he gave 40-50 per cent as the general African literacy rate.[1]

Clearly then, a high percentage of the adult African population is illiterate. The estimates of the Tomlinson Report, as well as the 1951 census, indicated that this illiteracy rate is greatest in rural districts.

One could reasonably expect, then, that adult education would be used as a method of combating illiteracy and, furthermore, that there would be an attempt to establish adult classes, particularly in rural areas. Adult education is not, moreover, simply making adults literate—it can provide an opportunity for those who have left school to continue formal education in later life. This latter function would be particularly important among Africans in South Africa regardless of the literacy rate, simply because of the high number of drop-outs at both primary and secondary level.

That these aims in adult education were recognized by some groups in South Africa is reflected in a statement of the Council of the Institute of Race Relations. It pointed out in 1949 that adult education was:

'an important means of making good deficiencies in youth, closing the dangerous sociological gap between generation and generation, and opening up a fuller and more useful life for the individual.'[2]

A government report on adult education had earlier stated:

1. *House of Assembly Debates (Hansard)*, 13 March 1959, Cols. 2462 ff.; ibid., 14 May 1963, Cols. 5976 ff. Here quoted from Horrell, op. cit., p. 114-15.
2. Horrell, op. cit., p. 167.

'The concentration of large groups of non-Europeans in towns and villages, on afforestation and irrigation schemes and road construction works offers exceptional opportunities for combating illiteracy among them and at the same time strengthening their desire for further education.'[1]

The Eiselen Commission reported that the most important venture in the field of fundamental education up to 1949 was being undertaken by the South African Institute of Race Relations which was experimenting in the Laubach method of literacy.[2] Voluntary organizations and committees—African as well as European—were also engaged in adult education. It was estimated that 8,500 Africans were attending recognized subsidized schools and classes.[3]

The Johannesburg Central Committee for Non-Europeans ran classes for about 2,770 African adults, while the Cape non-European Night Schools Association ran twelve schools with an enrolment of about 1,100 Africans. Classes were also being run in Durban, Pietermaritzburg, Pretoria and Port Elizabeth and East London.[3]

In 1951 the government created a National Advisory Council for Adult Education to replace the National Council for Adult Education and the National Council for Physical Education. This was done according to a recommendation of the committee of inquiry appointed in 1943 by the Minister of Education to investigate the situation of adult education in South Africa.[4]

In 1953 the Bantu Education Act made it illegal to conduct an unregistered school and in 1955 the Native Affairs Department took over the admission of grants for African night schools and continuation classes. A regulation in 1957, revised in 1962, strengthened the provision of the Bantu Education Act (1953). All night schools and continuation classes for Africans were to be registered with the Bantu Education Department if they catered for ten or more pupils.

The new regulations (1957 and 1962)[5] included among others the provision that schools or classes in a white registration area must hold a permit from the Group Areas Board and that no pupil may be admitted unless he or she is over the age of sixteen and is an employee resident in the area, or is employed at the mine, factory

1. Union of South Africa, *Adult Education in South Africa. Report by the Committee of Enquiry appointed by the Minister of Education, South Africa, 1946*, p. 37.
2. Union of South Africa, *Report of the Commission on Native Education, 1949-51*, p. 68.
3. Horrell, op. cit., p. 112.
4. Union of South Africa, *Adult Education in South Africa . . .* p. 152.
5. Government Notices 1414 and 1415 of 13 September 1957; R26 of 5 January 1962.

or farm offering courses. The persons in control must be white, and where there are advisory boards they must consist of white members only.

In African urban residential areas, night schools were to be henceforth controlled by the school board, or by separate committees set up by the board. Private organizations conducting classes in African areas were required by 1 January 1958 to hand over control to these school boards or committees.

The school boards and committees are responsible for financing the schools and classes, although the Department of Bantu Education could, if funds were available, pay subsidies towards the cost of rent, light, water and sanitation as well as partial subsidies on teachers' salaries.

Two main issues are raised by these new regulations. The first is finance. The principle that the Africans should be mainly responsible for financing their education was to be applicable to adult education as well as to primary, secondary and university education. In 1958-59 the sum of R.46,000 was voted for grants to night schools and continuation classes for Africans. In 1960 this sum came down to R.20,000; in 1962-63 it was reduced to R.2,000; in 1963-64 it was further reduced to R.1,000; and in 1965 grants were discontinued.[1] The Africans already have to bear the major cost of an expanding primary and secondary education. In addition they were now being asked to finance completely night schools and continuation classes for adults.

The second issue concerned schools and classes for Africans in white areas. These are the areas where most Africans work. African locations and townships are far from the city centre, and travelling to them after work adds the fatigue of distance and loss of time to the fatigue of working. There are also many living-in African servants in white areas. It would seem normal to expect that adult classes for Africans could be conducted within the area in which they work. However, the Minister of Bantu Education put himself on record as being opposed 'to the existence of a large number of night schools in our white urban residential areas'.[2]

In Pretoria alone, eight schools in white suburbs were forced to close, and this pattern was repeated in other white areas.

---

1. *A Survey of Race Relations . . . in South Africa, 1965*, p. 243, Horrell, op. cit., p. 116.
2. *House of Assembly Debates (Hansard)*, Vol. 20, 17 June 1959, Col. 8313.

TABLE 34. Number and location of night schools and continuation classes

Type of school	In reserves			Outside reserves		
	Villages or towns	Mission property	Mine or factory property	Trust land	Municipal areas	Mine or factory property
Night schools	5	1	2	1	27	6
Continuation classes	1	—	—	2	5	—
Combined night schools/ continuation classes	1	—	—	—	3	—
TOTAL	7	1	2	3	35	6

Source: Bantu Education Journal, November 1969, p. 16.

The high number of Africans who leave school before reaching higher primary level (at the age of 10 years) has been indicated earlier in this report. Even if they are considered to be functionally literate at the end of this period, the difficulty of obtaining education afterwards must decrease their desire and their ability to read or write. Table 34 shows the number and the location of night schools and continuation classes in October 1969.

There is a high concentration of night schools and continuation classes in municipal areas: 35 out of 54. This reflects the relative prosperity of urban townships compared with the reserves.

There were 197 teachers (privately paid) and 3,736 students, of whom 2,230 were in lower primary classes, 1,191 in higher primary classes and only 315 in secondary classes.

The figure given in the *Bantu Education Journal* of October 1968 was 72 adult classes with 4,733 pupils and 350 teachers. This would seem to represent a considerable drop in the provision of adult education.[1]

The Committee of Enquiry into the State of Adult Education recommended in 1953:

'That for all non-Europeans who have reached the age of 14 years and who do not attend any approved day-schools, or who have

1. Figures given in October 1968 and November 1969 are both calculated by A. N. P. Lubbe, Assistant Education Planner, Department of Bantu Education.

complied with the provincial educational requirements, if and when instituted, irrespective of the standard attained by them, part-time classes be instituted on the same basis as for Europeans, wherever and whenever the demand for such classes warrants such a step. . . .'

This recommendation has not been carried out.

12   University education

Non-whites

As early as 1948, the year the National Party came to power, Dr. F. Malan, Prime Minister of South Africa, made the following statement in Parliament:

'An intolerable state has arisen here in the past few years in our university institutions, a state of affairs which gives rise to friction, to an unpleasant relationship between Europeans and non-Europeans. . . . We do not want to withhold higher education from the non-Europeans and we will take every possible step to give both the natives and the Coloured peoples university training as soon as we can, but in their own sphere; in other words in separate institutions.'[1]

The universities of Stellenbosch, Pretoria, the Orange Free State and the Potchefstroom University for Christian Higher Education did not accept non-white students. This was true also of Rhodes University except for certain post-graduate courses.

1. *House of Assembly Debates (Hansard)*, Vol. 64, 1948, Col. 219.

Cape Town and Witwatersrand accepted non-white students and were known as 'Open Universities'. In addition the University of Natal (sometimes, but not consistently, called an open university) accepted non-European students but in segregated classes, except for certain post-graduate classes.[1]

Until 1959 there was a certain amount of segregation at the open universities with regard to extra-curricular activities. At the University of Cape Town no university residences were available for non-whites, and at the University of the Witwatersrand there was a separate residence for non-whites. Segregation in regard to sporting activities was maintained either as a matter of definite university policy or at any rate in actual practice.[2]

At the open universities, meals were served in communal restaurants but, on the other hand, non-whites were not admitted to university dances or balls.[3] A justification was attempted in the following manner:

'The open universities believe that the advantages enjoyed by their non-White students under the policy of academic non-segregation far outweigh any disadvantages resulting from social segregation, which involves *inter alia* the exclusion of non-Whites from certain sporting and social activities.'[4]

By the introduction of the Extension of University Education Act, 1959, the government proposed to replace attendance of non-whites at the open universities with ethnic group institutions—each group, African, Asian and Coloured, having its own university, while for the Africans the group would again be divided according to tribal divisions. The aim of the government was that as separate universities for non-whites became available, the white universities would be prohibited from admitting non-whites.[5]

The University College at Durban was to be reserved for Indians, the University of the Western Cape for Coloureds, the medical faculty of the University of Natal for Indians, Coloureds and Africans, the former University College at Fort Hare for Khosa-speaking people,

---

1. *Report of the Commission of Enquiry on Separate Training Facilities for Non-Europeans at Universities 1953-54*, p. 4 (the Holloway report).
2. ibid., p. 19.
3. ibid., p. 20.
4. A. Van der Sandt Centlives, 'University Apartheid in the Union of South Africa', *Apartheid, the Threat to South Africa's Universities*, p. 33.
5. M. J. H. Viljoen, Minister of Education, *Star* (Johannesburg), 22 November 1956.

the University College at Ngoye for Zulu- and Swazi-speaking and
the University College of the North for Solto, Bendoa and Sanga.

The new course was not taken without opposition from academic
quarters. The Holloway Commission of Enquiry on Separate Training Facilities for Non-Europeans at Universities stated in its report
of 1954 that in evidence submitted to the commission it was repeatedly represented that the application of segregation in regard to
university training would be incompatible with the concept of academic freedom.[1] Professor E. G. Malherbe, himself a member of the
Holloway Commission, wrote in 1957 that:

'the proposed legislation is a deviation from the age-old university
tradition which has so far been maintained throughout the history of
South African universities, the tradition by which the universities
themselves, and not an external authority, determine the conditions
of admission to their classes.'[2]

Both the Council of the University of Cape Town[3] and the Council
of the University of the Witwatersrand[4] passed resolutions opposing
legislative enforcement of academic segregation on racial grounds,
and pointed to the impossibility of providing equal but separate
facilities.[5]

They also expressed the belief that the policy of academic non-
segregation provided the conditions under which the pursuit of
truth could best be furthered and that academic non-segregation
promoted interracial harmony and understanding.

Kenneth Kirkwood reported that even in the Afrikaans-medium
universities of Pretoria, Stellenbosch, Potchefstroom and the Orange
Free State there were individuals who opposed the Act on the ground
that it would infringe the autonomy of the university, and that this
infringement threatened whites as well as non-whites.[6]

Table 35 gives the number of non-whites at universities in South
Africa for 1954.

1. *Report of the Commission of Enquiry . . . 1953-54,* op. cit., p. 14.
2. E. G. Malherbe, 'The University of Natal and the Separate University Legislation', *Apartheid and the World's Universities,* report of a meeting held in London, November 1957.
3. 12 December 1956.
4. 14 December 1956.
5. For their argument see: *The Open Universities in South Africa,* published on behalf of the Confer-ence of Representatives of the University of Cape Town and the University of the Witwatersrand, Johannesburg, held in Cape Town, 9-11 January 1957.
6. Kenneth Kirkwood, 'The South African Universities and the Separate Universities Education Bill', *Apartheid and the World's Universities,* op. cit.

TABLE 35. Attendance of non-whites at South African universities, 1954

University or college	African	Coloured	Asian
Cape Town	27	163	81
Witwatersrand	74	13	127
Natal	101	13	213
Fort Hare	314	36	30
TOTAL	516	225	451

The Extension of University Education Act, 1959, did not make it impossible for non-whites to attend the open universities, but it made attending non-white institutions for whites a criminal offence,[1] while non-whites could only attend at any university on condition that the minister granted permission, that they had qualified for entrance, and that the council of the university which they wished to attend would allow them to register.

The reasons given for the Act were as follows:

1. That the Act represented a further step in the implementation of apartheid. Separate universities would complete apartheid in education, already developed for the elementary school upwards.
2. That intellectual leaders were needed for the separate groups and that these would be best produced in university institutions geared to their own language and their own culture.
3. That the situation at the open universities could only continue side by side with social segregation since the whites there would not tolerate more than a minimum of social contact with non-whites.
4. That although these measures would necessitate some limitations on the autonomy of universities, this was on behalf of an over-riding national interest.
5. The preliminary government expenditure would be £3 million (R.6 million) with upkeep expenses of £200,000 (R.400,000) to £300,000 (R.600,000) annually, only part of this to be met by African taxation.
6. Control by the government was needed as it was necessary to prevent undesirable ideological developments—such as had disturbed the non-white institutions not directly under the charge

1. The maximum penalty is a fine of R.200 or six months' imprisonment.

of the government—and as the 'Bantu authorities' had not developed to take over this control.

7. Separate universities would open high university posts to non-whites.[1]

A 'conscience clause' is upheld by all white South African universities except Potchefstroom. It provides that no test of religious belief shall be imposed on any person as a condition of his becoming or continuing to be a student or member of the staff. One interesting omission was the conscience clause from the regulations governing the new ethnic universities.[2]

A government proclamation issued in December 1960 decided that Africans would no longer be allowed to register for the first time at an open university (other than the University of South Africa) in the departments of chemistry, physics, zoology, botany, mathematics, applied mathematics, geography, psychology, agriculture, social work, anthropology, native administration, Bantu languages, classic languages, philosophy, political science, law, divinity or education.

Table 36 gives the enrolment of non-white students in South African

TABLE 36. Enrolment of non-white students in South African universities during 1964[1]

University or college	Coloured	Asian	African
Fort Hare	...	3	274
North	—	—	307
Zululand	—	—	180
Western Cape	389	—	—
Indian	—	898	—
Cape Town	...[2]	75	7
Natal	37	457	132
Rhodes	—	6	—
Witwatersrand	14	123	11
South Africa	...[3]	275	986
TOTAL		1 837	1 897

1. *A Survey of Race Relations in South Africa, 1964*, p. 291, Johannesburg, South African Institute of Race Relations, 1965.
2. There were 327 in 1962.
3. There were 343 in 1962. It should be noted that the University of South Africa gives courses by correspondence and awards external degrees.
... = Data not available.

1. Minister of Education, *House of Assembly Debates (Hansard)*, 27-9 May 1957.
2. Horrell, op. cit., p. 131.

TABLE 37. Comparative student enrolments and numbers of degrees awarded at South African universities, 1959 (number of degrees shown in parentheses)

Subject	African		Coloured		Asian		White		Total	
Humanities	1 196	(92)	386	(27)	905	(39)	9 985	(1 878)	12 472	(2 036)
Education	70	(37)	81	(23)	67	(19)	2 095	(625)	2 313	(704)
Fine arts	—	(—)	6	(—)	16	(1)	1 295	(135)	1 317	(136)
Law	31	(3)	13	(—)	17	(—)	838	(142)	899	(145)
Social sciences	61	(—)	66	(—)	73	(5)	6 657	(610)	6 857	(615)
Natural sciences	149	(17)	123	(15)	173	(22)	5 208	(833)	5 653	(887)
Engineering	4	(—)	2	(—)	24	(—)	2 608	(192)	2 638	(192)
Medical sciences	138	(6)	74	(7)	176	(11)	2 748	(219)	3 136	(243)
Agriculture	11	(3)	—	(—)	1	(—)	1 441	(217)	1 453	(220)
Unspecified	211	(—)	71	(—)	64	(—)	2 306	(4)	2 652	(4)
TOTAL	1 871	(158)	822	(72)	1 516	(97)	35 181	(4 855)	39 390	(5 182)

Source: Unesco calculations.

universities during 1964, while Table 37 gives the comparative figures for student enrolment and degrees awarded for each racial group in 1959.

In 1959 roughly one-quarter of the non-white students were trained at Fort Hare University College. This college was founded in 1916 with funds provided mainly by the churches, and was the only existing institution which was specifically established for the higher education of the African community.

Fort Hare represented for non-Europeans, and particularly for Africans, a special place. It has trained many of the African leaders and they themselves had played a big part in its development.

By the University College of Fort Hare Transfer Act, the management and maintenance of Fort Hare was transferred from the hands of private individuals to that of the State, in order to bring Fort Hare into line with the government's policy of separate development.

'Fort Hare, as it exists at the moment, does not fit in with the plan for the development of the various national groups in South Africa as envisaged in the Extension of University Education Act and the Promotion of Bantu Self-Government Act.'[1]

The Principal, Professor H. R. Burrows, was not reappointed when the Bantu Education Department assumed control. The vice-principal Z. K. Matthews, was informed that he would be reappointed provided that he resigned from the African National Congress. He refused to accept the appointment under these conditions. Two professors were not reappointed, and two professors, a senior lecturer, a lecturer, the registrar and the librarian were retired on superannuation. Four members of the staff resigned. In October 1959, the Fort Hare students passed a resolution stating,

'The government, in its dictatorial action in dismissing our staff members without stating any reasons, has added to the atmosphere of insecurity and uncertainty that has engulfed Fort Hare during the past few years. . . . But let it be noted, once and for all, that our stand as students of Fort Hare and as the future leaders of our country, upholding the principles of education as universally accepted, remains unchanged and uncompromising. Our outright condemnation of the university apartheid legislation remains steadfast. . . .'[2]

As a result of this, eleven students were not readmitted to the college.[3]

New regulations were passed controlling the registration and behaviour of students. Students at ethnic-group colleges must apply each year for permission to report for registration, and with the application form must send a testimonial of good conduct by a minister of religion.[4]

The Minister of Bantu Education may refuse registration even if the candidate complies with all other conditions of registration. However, since the applicants are not informed as to the reason for the rejection of their applications, they cannot question the decision

1. *The Transfer of the University College of Fort Hare*, p. 7, a speech delivered in the Senate on 26 June 1959, by the Minister of Bantu Education, the Honourable Mr. W. A. Maree, M.P., issued by the Information Service of the Department of Bantu Administration and Development, 1960.
2. Quoted from the *Sunday Times*, 11 October 1959, in Horrell, op. cit., p. 137.
    'The Minister of Bantu Education was reported as having said, "I disposed of their services because I will not permit a penny of any funds of which I have control to be paid to persons who are known to be destroying the Government's policy of Apartheid".'
3. Mr. Rautenbach, *Verbatim Record of the Testimony in the South West Africa Cases—Ethiopia v. South Africa, Liberia v. South Africa*, p. 21-38, The Hague, International Court of Justice (CR.65/75.).
4. Horrell, op. cit., p. 149.

f the minister.[1] No student or person not under the jurisdiction
f the college may be upon the college grounds as a visitor without
he permission of the rector, or his duly authorized representative,
nd a special regulation forbids any Fort Hare student or group of
tudents from visiting any other institutions without the permission
f the institution concerned and then only on such conditions as may
e determined.[2]

The government has established ethnic-group colleges to provide
ducation for African, Asian and Coloured students. Since one of
he aims of these institutions was to provide 'intellectual leadership'
or these communities, as well as expanding educational opportu-
ities, one would expect that from 1959 to 1970 there would have
een an appreciable increase in the number of non-white students at
niversities and university colleges. (See Table 38.)

There had been an increase of enrolments from 1,871 in 1959 to
,897 in 1964 to 3,804 in 1968. But by far the highest percentage
ncrease had been registered in the enrolment in correspondence

TABLE 38. African university enrolments, 1968

frican university colleges	
Commerce and public administration	62
Agriculture	5
Arts	652
Education	345
Law	105
Theology	12
Sciences	249
SUB-TOTAL	——1 430
Other South African universities	
University of Cape Town	2
University of the Witwatersrand	2
University of South Africa[1]	2 236
University of Natal[2]	134
TOTAL WITH AFRICAN UNIVERSITY COLLEGES	3 804

. Correspondence courses.
. Non-white medical school.
Source: *Bantu Education Journal*, November 1968, p. 18-20.

. Rautenbach, op. cit., p. 65 ff.
. Horrell, op. cit., p. 149-50.

courses of the University of South Africa, from 986 in 1964 to 2,23
in 1968, an increase of 1,250.

University in-training had increased over the same period from
911 to 1,568.

A breakdown by subject shows that education registered th
highest increase, from 70 students in 1959 to 345 in 1968. Law in
creased from 31 to 105 and the sciences from 149 to 249.

However, medical sciences showed a slight decrease from 138 t
134, and agriculture had dropped from 11 to 5.

An analysis of the levels at which students were enrolled showed that
of the 1,430 being trained at the African colleges, 434 were bein
trained for diplomas rather than degrees, 42 were doing an honour
degree, 31 were doing a post-graduate diploma, 19 a master's degre
and 4 a doctorate.

The four doing doctorates were registered in education, 9 of thos
doing the master's degree were registered in arts, 6 in educatio
and 4 in natural science, while the 31 doing a post-graduate diplom
were all registered in education.

Training at post-graduate level then was mainly in education
while at undergraduate level relatively few were being trained a
the level of an honours degree. The bulk of the enrolment wa
for the Baccalaureus degree and for a diploma, with most of thes
(a combined total of 997) registered in arts and education. In 196
only 4 Africans were studying in the open universities (with the excep
tion of Natal, which has a segregated non-white medical school).

Neither enrolments, nor degrees awarded, justify the statemen
that establishment of ethnic-group colleges has greatly increased uni
versity facilities for non-whites.[1]

It was pointed out by those who opposed the government measure
that the cost per student would increase considerably if the govern
ment moved non-white students at the open universities to Fort Har
or to the non-white department at the University of Natal or if the
were going to establish new separate institutions.

At a conference of the open universities in 1957, the problem wa
summed up:

'If, notwithstanding the evidence that the "separate but equal" doc
trine has no place in university education, and despite the financia

---

1. The Minister of Bantu Education stated in the House of Assembly, on 11 February 1964, tha
the following numbers of Africans had obtained university degrees since 1956: 1957, 182; 1958
177; 1959, 197; 1960, 196; 1961, 182; 1962, 105.

burden and economic waste which we have demonstrated, a government in South Africa were nevertheless to provide equal, and not merely separate, facilities for non-whites, sooner or later the attempt will place an unbearable strain on it or on later administration.'[1]

The unit cost *per capita* for university education in 1967/68 was: Africans: R.1,490 (Fort Hare), R.1,096 (The North) and R.1,418 (Zululand); Coloureds, R.976; Indians, R.644; whites, R.577.

When calculating the difference between the cost *per capita* for African students and the cost *per capita* for white students, the lack of faculties for engineering and applied science in African universities must be taken into account, in spite of the high percentage of non-matriculated African students enrolled in diploma courses.

The faculties first started were letters, arts, philosophy and education (see Part II). The government claimed then that the result of a survey made on the need for instituting training for engineers at ethnic-group colleges showed that only five African students had declared their desire to study engineering—and before any serious preparations could be made for this faculty to be added to the ethnic-group colleges the five students had changed their minds.[2]

The University Amendment Act No. 67 of 1969 provided that the term 'university' in the principal Act would not include the universities serving Africans, Coloureds and Indians, thus excluding all non-white universities from the 'conscience clause' operable in white universities.

The University of the Western Cape Act No. 50 of 1969, the University of Durban-Westville Act No. 49 of 1969, the University of Fort Hare Act No. 40 of 1969, the University of the North Act No. 47 of 1969 and the University of Zululand Act No. 43 of 1969 consolidated the control of these situations exercised by the Ministers for Coloured Affairs, Indian Affairs, and 'Bantu' affairs respectively. They also changed the status from 'colleges' to fully fledged universities. However, as universities they would serve only a particular 'national unit'.[3]

1. *The Open Universities in South Africa*, op. cit. For this argument see p. 40-7.
2. Rautenbach, op. cit.
3. 'Under the University of Fort Hare Act (Act No. 40 of 1969), it is enacted that as from the fixed date, determined by Proclamation No. R. 313 of 1969 to be the 1st of January of the year 1970, the University College of Fort Hare, with its seat at Alice in the Cape Province of the Cape of Good Hope, shall be a university known as the University of Fort Hare and that this University shall serve the Xhosa national unit. Signed 30th May 1970.'—*Bantu* (Pretoria), September 1970, p. 22.

There is a non-white advisory council and a white council at each of these institutions.

The minister appoints the rector and vice-chancellor.

The council consists of the rector, not less than eight persons appointed by the state president and two members of the senate elected by the senate.

All members of the advisory council are appointed by the state president.

The senate consists of the rector as chairman, two members of the council elected by the council and such members of the teaching staff of the university as the council may decide. Professors from other universities may be appointed to the senate by the council after consultation with the minister and the other university concerned.

The senate controls the curricula and examinations.

The minister determines staff establishment after consultation with the council. The council controls appointments, promotions and staff dismissals subject to the approval of the minister. If serious allegations are made against a member of staff the minister may take action, but he must report on this to Parliament. This marks some decentralization in the control of the universities. It is not complete decentralization. Decisions of the council need the minister's approval, while the minister only 'consults' the council on decisions which he might take.

It does not mark decentralization to African or Indian or Coloured control. The council is white, it is the advisory council that is non-white.

Nor does it free the university from political control. At least ten members of the council (including the rector and the vice-chancellor) are government appointees.

The position of the State as far as African higher education was concerned was summed up by the Minister of Bantu Education, Mr. W. A. Maree, in 1959:

'Where one has to deal with under-developed peoples, where the State has planned a process of development for those peoples, and where a university can play a decisive role in the process and directions of that development, it must surely be clear to everyone that the State alone is competent to exercise the powers of guardianship in this field. . . .'[1]

1. *The Transfer of the University College of Fort Hare*, op. cit.

Whites

There are nine residential universities for white students in South Africa. They are administered under the Universities Act No. 61 of 1955 and its amendments of 1959, 1961 and 1969. By this Act, these universities and the University of South Africa (giving mainly extramural courses) fall under the jurisdiction of the Ministry of Education, Arts and Science. The minister appoints a University Advisory Committee to advise him on general matters arising out of the provisions of the Act. So far this advice has been mainly on financial matters. The Committee of University Principals—also constituted by the Act—advises on matters related to the admission of students, period of attendance, etc.

There is no representation from non-white colleges on this committee. The universities themselves decide who should fill vacant posts and the admittance of any particular student.

It would seem, from what is now known as the 'Mafeje affair', that a white university may not appoint a non-white lecturer except in a department of African studies or African languages. In 1968 the council of the University of Cape Town decided to appoint an African, Mr. Archie Mafeje, as senior lecturer in the Department of Social Anthropology. This decision was rescinded after the council received a letter from the Minister of National Education in which he asked the council not to proceed with the appointment of a non-white person. The government reserved the right to take such steps as necessary if South Africa's 'traditional outlook' was not observed.[1] This would seem to suggest that, while in theory white universities may appoint staff, in practice the government may block such appointments where these run counter to the philosophy of apartheid.[2]

In 1969, there were 51,992 university students with another 16,557 enrolled for correspondence degree courses at the University of South Africa. (See Table 39.)

---

1. Reported here from *A Survey of Race Relations . . . 1968*, p. 283. See also Unit on Apartheid, Department of Political and Security Council Affairs, *Notes and Documents No. 7/69*, p. 2, 3, New York, United Nations, 23 April 1969.
2. This point was made by one of the professors who resigned in protest: 'Now it is quite clear . . . that everybody who does a job here has it with the tacit or explicit approval of the Government.'— Unit on Apartheid, *Papers*, No. 16/70, p. 18, New York, United Nations, May 1970.

TABLE 39. Comparative figures: enrolment at universities and university colleges

University or university college	Africans	Coloureds	Asians	Whites
Universities				
Cape Town	2	282	126	7 218
Natal	175	44	328	5 538
Orange Free State	—	—	—	3 858
Port Elizabeth	—	—	—	962
Potchefstroom	—	—	—	3 701
Pretoria	—	—	—	11 900
Rand Afrikaans	—	—	—	916
Rhodes	—	—	44	1 791
Stellenbosch	—	—	—	7 526
South Africa[1]	2 144	478	996	16 557
Witwatersrand	5	20	239	8 583
University colleges				
Western Cape	—	774	—	—
Durban	—	—	1 621	—
Fort Hare	486	—	—	—
The North	671	—	—	—
Zululand	428	—	—	—
	3 911	1 598	3 354	68 550

1. Correspondence courses only. Of the total, 1,058 are from outside South Africa.
Source: A Survey of Race Relations in South Africa, 1969, p. 210, Johannesburg, South African Institute of Race Relations, 1970.

Students' organizations

Whites. Students, councils are elected by the students themselves and are permitted to draw up their own constitutions. These councils are affiliated to the National Union of South African Students (NUSAS; English-speaking) and the Afrikaanse Studentebond (ASB; Afrikaans-speaking). The two organizations disagree on contacts with non-whites, the ASB declining invitations to discussions with NUSAS if non-white students attend.[1] ASB favours contact at an official level. This was explained by the president, Mr. Johan Fick, as contact 'in a spirit of segregation' and only on specific issues. NUSAS on the other hand has, since the 1950s, been involved in

1. African students may be individual members of NUSAS.

TABLE 40. Comparative figures, university education 1969 examinations[1]

Group	Degrees		Diplomas	
	Post-graduate	Bachelors	Post-graduate	Non-graduate
Africans				
University examinations	46	172	32	27
College examinations	—	—	—	86
Coloureds				
University examinations	12	85	16	8
College examinations	—	—	—	20
Asians				
University examinations	50	208	48	20
College examinations	—	—	—	13
Whites	2 296	6 245	931	1 268

1. Students of the university colleges taking degree and certain diploma courses sit examinations conducted by the University of South Africa.
Source: *A Survey of Race Relations in South Africa, 1969*, p. 211, Johannesburg, South African Institute of Race Relations, 1970.

active opposition to apartheid. The governing bodies of the open universities had opposed academic segregation on racial grounds, but had not opposed the practice of social segregation on their own campuses. Their protest against the extension of the University Education Act of 1959 was based on the principle of university autonomy. From the early sixties, however, NUSAS and the Students' Representative Councils of Cape Town and Witwatersrand rejected this dichotomy. In 1965 students at Cape Town University decided to hold no more dances until the university administration allowed all students of all races to attend. In 1967, the NUSAS Assembly called upon all affiliated universities to do all within their power to ensure that racial discrimination was abolished from their campuses. The stand of NUSAS on race inevitably brought them into open conflict with the National Government. In July 1964 several students were arrested under the ninety-day detention law,[1] while Mr. Ian Robertson, NUSAS president 1965-66, was banned on 11 May 1966. Mr. Duncan Innes, president of NUSAS in 1968, was refused a passport to take up a two-months' bursary. The resi-

1. For a detailed account of this see Unit on Apartheid, *Papers*, No. 16/70, op. cit.

dence privileges of Mr. Andrew Murray, NUSAS vice-president, were withdrawn, and a former vice-president of NUSAS, Mr. Rogers Ragaven, was placed under house arrest until granted a one-way exit permit. John Daniel, a former president of NUSAS, was refused a passport to leave South Africa to study abroad, and deprived of South African citizenship when he travelled on a British passport.

The University Christian Movement (UCM) groups together Methodist, Catholic, Anglican, Presbyterian and Congregational faculty members, students and chaplains. It was formed in 1967 and includes among its university membership the University of Botswana, Lesotho and Swaziland. It is multi-racial and at its second conference, in July 1968, non-whites, joining as individuals, out-numbered whites. In spite of its being banned as an organization from African universities in the Republic, its present president is an African. The Reverend Basil Moore, who was first president and chaplain at Rhodes University, has had his passport withdrawn, and the first issue of UCM's *One for the Road* has been banned.

In 1967, the chairman of the NUSAS advisory board, Dr. Raymond Hoffenberg, was banned. He was a senior lecturer and researcher at the University of Cape Town. His banning orders specifically prevented him from continuing to teach after the end of the academic semester.[1]

The government harassment of NUSAS has not, however, stopped protest. Conflicts have increased with the government's enforcement of apartheid laws. In 1968, students at Cape Town University (together with some faculty members) staged a 24-hour strike in protest against the Mafeje affair,[2] while in 1970 students protested against the detention orders served against Mrs. Winnie Mandela and others after they had been acquitted by the courts where they had been charged under the terrorism act of 1967.

Africans. NUSAS and UCM are banned from African university campuses.

Student councils may be elected by the students. At Fort Hare University, however, students had refused to appoint a student representative council for some time since the leaders of the council there had been often expelled or refused readmittance by the university

1. He has since left South Africa and now lives in England.
2. See above, p. 111.

authorities at the end of the university year. The students have pre-ferred to communicate with the university authorities through depu-tations.

Fort Hare has not escaped student protest in spite of the pre-cautions taken by the authorities. In 1968 the ceremony that marked the installation of the new rector of the college was boycotted by the vast majority of students, slogans appeared on the walls and as a result of the action taken by the rector and security police[1] a sit-in was staged.

The South African case in African education may be briefly stated as follows:
1. South Africa is rapidly expanding African education.
2. Africans are being trained to 'take over' in the 'Bantu homelands'.
3. Separate development in education, as in every other sphere, pro-motes rather than hinders good race relations.

There is no doubt that African education has expanded at the primary level and the Africans themselves have largely financed this expan-sion. At secondary and university levels, the situation is different. Here African education has not developed much. That Africans are being trained to 'take over' in the reserves cannot be supported either by the numbers who graduate, and so can hold official positions afterwards, or by the degree of administrative responsibility which is at present permitted to them. That they are not being trained to play their part in a total South African society is explicitly stated by the South African Government itself. A key question in modern industrialized states is the number of nationals who are being trained for high-level scientific and technical posts. Here the situation is clear: Africans who are being trained at university level are being trained to be teachers (mainly in the humanities) and social workers. They are not being trained to participate at any meaningful level in scientific research.

Nor can it be said that separate development in education promotes good race relations. The inequalities inherent in the educational system would in themselves be damaging to racial harmony. But one of the aims of the educational system, set out in policy statements of both the government and influential groups in the white sectors of

---

1. Seventeen students were held by the administration to be directly or indirectly responsible for the painting on the walls. Some of these were questioned by the police and their rooms searched. See Unit on Apartheid, *Papers*, No. 16/70, op. cit., p. 21-4.

society, is group nationalism. This is translated into the slant of text-books and has real implications for the co-existence of English and Afrikaners in the same society, as well as implications for the continued harmonious co-existence of Africans, Asians, Coloureds and whites. In fact, the effects of apartheid on education go far beyond the racial discrimination that the facts and figures of this report demonstrate. The most deplorable effect is on the South African child, whatever his colour and whatever the degree of intellectual capacity developed in him, who, in all cases, is educated within the restrictions of an ideology unacceptable to the world of today.

II. Science

'1. Everyone has the right freely to participate in the cultural life of the community, to enjoy the arts and to share in scientific advancement and its benefits.

'2. Everyone has the right to the protection of the moral and material interests resulting from any scientific, literary and artistic production of which he is the author.'

Article 27 of the Universal Declaration of Human Rights

1   Definition of scope

In this part the term 'science' is taken to include the social and the natural sciences as well as applications of science to engineering, medicine and agriculture.

The specific topics investigated in this survey include the effect of apartheid on:

1. The employment of non-white scientific and technical personnel after training and the supply of high-level manpower.
2. The effect of apartheid on scientific organizations.
3. The influence of apartheid on social field research.
4. International scientific and technical co-operation.

In some of these cases it is possible to draw specific conclusions. In others, however, this is more difficult because several factors other than the effect of the apartheid policy have been operative and a much closer investigation would be needed to assess the relative importance of the various factors. Nevertheless, even in these cases it may be useful to formulate the questions and suggest the direction in which further study is needed.

In Part I, problems of access to education including access to technical and vocational training and university training have been discussed. Their implication for the training of scientific personnel in South Africa is obvious. The small number of non-white pupils who complete secondary school, the small percentage of these who take science and mathematics as a subject, determine to some extent the number of non-white students who can proceed to science training, either at university level or at the level of technical college. The Minister of Bantu Education, in reply to a question in the House of Assembly, stated that, in 1964, 77 African students had attained the standard required for admission to a degree course in science.[1] But

---

1. *House of Assembly Debates (Hansard)*, 4 June 1965, Cols. 7173-4.

here there is another block. Access to science faculties at universitie is severely limited. Of the 103 Africans who obtained degrees in 1964 only 1 qualified in civil engineering and 14 in medicine. Of the 15 Asian graduates, 22 received medical degrees and 2 degrees in archi tecture. Of the 4 Africans enrolled in 'Bantu University Colleges for doctorates in 1968 none were in the natural sciences. In th master degree 4 were in the natural sciences, in the honours degre 11 were in natural sciences. None were recorded as being enrollec in civil engineering or architecture.[1]

2   Patterns of technical employment and problems of manpower supply

Laws were enacted in South Africa as early as 1911 providing that certain skilled jobs in the mining industry be reserved for whites only.[2]

Under the Industrial Conciliation Act, 1956, and its amendment of 1959, the government may prohibit the replacement of employees of one race by those of another race, may reserve certain types of jobs to persons of a specified race, or may fix the number or percent- age of persons of a particular race to be employed in particular industries.[3]

---

1. See some interesting statistical facts about 'Bantu' education by A. N. P. Lubbe, Assistant Educa- tion Planner, Department of Bantu Education, in *Bantu Education Journal*, December 1968, p. 24, 25.
2. Mines and Works Act, 1911 (amendments 1926 and 1956).
3. For a list of job reservations see *A Survey of Race Relations in South Africa, 1964*, p. 242, Johan- nesburg, South African Institute of Race Relations, 1965. For a comprehensive survey of trade- union practice see Muriel Horrell, *South African Trade Unionism*, p. 13 ff., Johannesburg, 1961. Africans are not allowed to form registered trade unions: *The Tomlinson Report: Summary of the*

The government, in introducing this legislation, indicated that it as intended to protect the white labour force against the infiltration f non-whites into skilled labour.[1]

However, legislation is not the only method of ensuring job discrimination in South Africa. The trade unions, for example, often ee their role as protecting the white worker against competition of he black worker. As a result the trade unions have become one of he strongest supporters of a job reservation policy, and its corollary white supremacy' in the social and economic spheres.[2]

Discrimination in jobs, partly supported by legislation, partly by ade-union pressure, is also supported by custom, making it difficult or non-whites to obtain employment in technical and certain professional categories.

Thus not only is there 'inequality of opportunity for people of ifferences races to obtain the level of general education necessary or access to all technical or higher training',[3] not only has the technical or higher training to be carried out in institutions of inferior cademic status, but progress after the training period is equally ifficult because of the very limited opportunities for employment. his lack of suitable employment opportunities undoubtedly dampens he enthusiasm of many a potential non-white scientist and may ead to mediocre performance and lack of interest in scientific training.

Report of the Commission for the Socio-economic Development of the Bantu Areas within the Union of South Africa, p. 17, Pretoria, n.d. See also : Leo Marquard, *The Peoples and Policies of South Africa*, 3rd ed., p. 50, London, Cape Town and New York, Oxford University Press, 1962; *Infringement of Trade Union Rights in Southern Africa*, report submitted to the Economic and Social Council by the *Ad Hoc* Working Group, and the *Sixth Special Report of the Director-General on the Application of the Declaration Concerning the Policy of 'Apartheid' of the Republic of South Africa*, International Labour Conference, thirty-fourth session, Geneva, 1970 (published by the International Labour Organisation (ILO), Geneva). Up to the end of 1969, ILO reported that twenty-five job reservation determinations had been made under the Industrial Conciliation Act, 1956 (as amended in 1959) and that 2.99 per cent of the total labour force were potentially affected by those. In fact, the acute shortage of skilled labour has forced the government to grant exemptions from its job reservation determinations.

House of Assembly Debates (Hansard), Vol. 18, 7 June 1955, Col. 7156. Here quoted from ILO *Declaration . . . Concerning the Policy of Apartheid of the Republic of South Africa and ILO Programme for the Elimination of 'Apartheid' in Labour Matters in the Republic of South Africa*, Geneva, ILO, 1964, p. 10, footnote 1.

Quoted from ILO, *Declaration . . .* op. cit., p. 8; see also Part I of this report.

The Trade Union Council of South Africa (TUCSA) at its fifteenth annual conference in February 1969 altered its constitution so as to limit membership to trade unions registered, or eligible for membership, under the Industrial Conciliation Act, thus excluding African unions. This was done under both government pressure and because of opposition from certain trade unions.

Nearly fifty unions have offered to bargain for better wages for Africans. Some trade unionists are concerned about the dangers inherent in the lack of effective African unionization, while other unions, represented by the white unions affiliated to the South African Confederation of Labour, support the government's racial policies and believe that the interests of their own members can be best safeguarded by job reservation and other restrictive practices.—*Sixth Special Report of the Director-General . . .*, op. cit., p. 11, 12.

Opportunities do exist in the areas of the so-called 'Bantu homeland
In the declared non-white areas there has been an increasing demar
for non-white teachers, social workers and librarians. However, the
is little training in engineering or in agriculture, where the need f
non-white specialists is probably greatest. A faculty of agricultu
was only recently established at Fort Hare University.

In February 1967 the Minister of Bantu Administration and Ban
Education stated the government policy in African technical trainin

'It would be an incorrect principle to begin with the training
Bantu engineers and other technologists for the most advanc
service while there are insufficient numbers of technicians and trade
men on the lower level of the pyramid. . . . I have laid it dov
as a principle that efforts should more specifically be made in tl
direction of expansion . . . by means of diploma (rather than degre
courses . . . to meet immediate requirements.'[1]

In addition to the engineers, 5 Indian and 1 Coloured pharmacis
are reported to have qualified in 1965, while in 1964 an Africa
who had earlier gone to the United States of America to stud
obtained a B.Sc. in agronomy at the University of North Carolin
In medicine at the end of 1968, 10 Africans, 19 Coloureds and ?
Asians had qualified with degrees of M.B., Ch.B.[2]

Some of the disabilities suffered by highly qualified non-Europea
medical specialists are illustrated by the following two inciden
referred to in *A Survey of Race Relations in South Africa*. In 196
an Indian, Dr. Dorasamy Chetty, a graduate of the University of tl
Witwatersrand and the London School of Hygiene and Tropic:
Medicine, with many years of experience on malaria eradicatio
programmes in the Far East with the World Health Organizatio
was unable to obtain a post in South Africa where he could practis
and teach preventive medicine, while in 1962

'in terms of Government policy, a highly qualified African doctc
was refused an appointment to the Livingstone Hospital for not
Whites in Port Elizabeth because in his post he would have ha
several Whites working under him.'[4]

1. *House of Assembly Debates (Hansard)*, Vol. 3, 10 February 1967, Col. 1083.
2. Acting Minister of National Education, *House of Assembly Debates (Hansard)*, Vol. 10,
June 1969, Col. 1954.
3. *A Survey of Race Relations . . . 1961*, p. 221.
4. *A Survey of Race Relations . . . 1962*, p. 171.

ιe late Professor Edward Roux, the much-respected Professor of
ιtany at the University of the Witwatersrand until he was banned in
64 under the Suppression of Communism Act and prohibited from
ιtering his department, has illustrated the difficulties non-white
ιentists experience in finding a suitable outlet. In a letter written
ιortly before his death on 2 March 1966 in reply to a request for
ιformation relative to this survey he described the case of Joseph
ιotsokoane:

ι Suto, born in the Orange Free State, he took his B.Sc. in botany
ιd zoology at Fort Hare. He taught in schools for some time, saved
ιoney and came to Witwatersrand in 1950 to do an honours course
ι botany. We gave him a fair training in plant physiology, in grassland
ιology and he spent part of his year doing a botanical analysis of
ιstures in a Native Reserve in the Ciskei. When he had completed
ι e degree the question of employment arose and I communicated
ιith the Agricultural Section of the Department of Native Affairs.
ιhey were embarrassed because they had never had a post for a
ιientifically trained African. The only posts available for Africans
ιere those of agricultural demonstrators, non-matriculants, who
ιorked under white district officers. Clearly Kotsokoane could not
ι made a district officer in a Reserve, because he would then be senior
ι certain white employees and might even have to give orders to a
ιhite typist. An official of the Department wrote to me saying that
ι s policy was "to develop from the ground up, not from the bottom
ιown". Finally they created some sort of job for Kotsokoane in which
ι would be under the supervision of a white officer and in which he
ιould have no white subordinates. The salary offered was £400 a
ιear. Fortunately for him he was offered and accepted a job in
ιasutoland where he became one of four agricultural district officers,
ιe other three being whites. All four had equal status. The salary at
ιe time was £800 per year with a free house and other facilities. Joe
ι now principal of Basutoland's agricultural college.'

ι 1969 two African specialists, Drs. M. J. Mphahlele and P. Mokhoko
ιnd a Coloured man Dr. E. Johnson left South Africa to take up
ιenior posts in other countries because of the difficulty that, if appoin-
ι d to such posts in the Republic, they might be allowed to give
ιstructions to white members of staff.[1] After obtaining a master's
ιegree in nuclear physics at a Canadian university, Mr. Alfred

Msezane applied unsuccessfully for a post with the Atomic Energy Board in South Africa. He could only find employment as a teacher with a salary of R.55 a month. He decided to take up a scholarship overseas.[1]

Difficulties of finding suitable employment, despite the need and the small numbers concerned, do not apply only to graduates. They apply equally to non-whites who have matriculated but are not able to proceed to a university course. These are the people who should become skilled technicians. Sheila Van der Horst[2] writes:

'It is noteworthy that more difficulty is experienced by the Johannesburg Municipal Juvenile Employment Department in placing the handful of matriculated African youths in suitable employment than in placing any other category. Of 66 African boys who left school in 1961 after Standard VI, VIII or X, in mid-1962, 38 were in employment (mostly as labourers or clerical or office workers), 4 were continuing their studies and 24 were still seeking work. Of 73 girls 15 were working, 3 were studying and 55 still seeking employment.'

A similar survey of unemployment among the more educated African youths in the little country township of Graaff-Reinet in 1962 showed that two-thirds were still unemployed after six months.

'In many cases their frustration is extreme. There is no way up the economic ladder for them; no hope; no way out. Some sink into a cynical apathy, living a parasitic life on relations and friends, losing all self-respect, all sense of morality and obligation. Others, desiring above all else to justify their manhood by work, become rebels.'

The practice of apartheid and racial discrimination in employment is likely to discourage non-whites from undergoing training for skilled or professional work in science and technology, even if they were able to attain the educational requirements necessary for them to obtain admission to the available courses.

Another problem affecting African professionals is that of office space in urban areas.[3]

---

1. *A Survey of Race Relations . . . 1969*, p. 114.
2. 'The Effects of Industrialization on Race Relations in South Africa', in: Guy Hunter (ed.), *Industrialization and Race Relations: a Symposium*, p. 134, Institute of Race Relations (United Kingdom) London and New York, Oxford University Press, 1965.
3. See also Part III, Chapter 2, 'The Peoples of South Africa', below.

A circular from the Secretary for Bantu Administration and Development, A12/1, 15 July 1969, said:

It has come to the notice of the Department that certain local authorities, in conflict with policy, grant consulting room and office facilities in urban Bantu residential areas to non-European medical practitioners and other non-European professional persons. It is, therefore, necessary to set out the policy of the Department in this regard.

'It should be borne in mind that urban Bantu residential areas, although set aside for the purpose of occupation by Bantu, are situated in White areas, and taking into consideration the application of the principles of the policy of separate development, it follows that each national unit should be served by its own people in its respective homeland. It is therefore imperative that non-European medical practitioners and other Bantu who pursue professions should practise amongst their own people.

'Local authorities are, therefore, requested to ensure that non-Europeans who render professional services are not granted consulting room and office accommodation in urban Bantu residential areas. The Bantu should be persuaded to offer their services in the Bantu homelands where an acute shortage exists in the field of professional services and where, as a result of industrial and other development including the provision of hospitals and clinics, excellent opportunities for their establishment exist.

'Professional services in urban Bantu residential areas should be rendered by Whites in terms of the provisions of section 42(g) of Act No. 25 of 1945.

'Bantu who are at present legally exercising such rights may be permitted to continue to do so but should, by way of persuasion, be activated to establish themselves amongst their own people in the homelands.

'Your co-operation in this matter will be appreciated.'

The circular was sent to all urban local authorities.

Commenting on this circular the Director of the Institute of Race Relations asked if the millions of Africans in urban areas, were not their own people'; how, with the shortage of trained manpower, were white professional men to provide adequate services for urban Africans and what would happen in cases of emergency at night with no resident doctors on call in townships.[1]

. *A Survey of Race Relations . . . 1969*, p. 114.

The pattern of employment is clear. The menial, unskilled jobs are occupied by Africans, the highly skilled jobs, professional, technical and administrative as well as most of the other white-collar jobs, by whites. The most striking feature of all is perhaps the very small proportion of Africans employed in skilled and semi-skilled industrial jobs. It is in this middle range of occupations that the various restrictions, either enacted by legislation or arising from the social colour bar, have combined to exclude the African. As pointed out by Muir and Tumner:[1]

'In other societies large numbers of brighter children from the lowest classes would set their sights on technical and craft jobs. But this middle range of occupations is virtually closed to the African through legislation and through the social custom and tradition of the white population. In the African occupational structure there is a virtual hiatus between the professional and clerical occupations and the semi- and unskilled jobs.'

The Asians make an appreciable contribution to the labour force employed in clerical work and sales while both the Asians and the Coloureds contribute a sizeable proportion of skilled industrial workers.

The over-all picture of the pattern of employment is a dearth of workers engaged in professional, managerial and clerical occupations in comparison with the situation in developed countries, while for the white population alone the distribution is very similar to that for other developed countries. A barrier exists between skilled and unskilled employment across which it is difficult for the non-white and in particular the African to pass.

In 1968 it was estimated that while 12 pupils graduated as engineers per 100,000 in Canada, in South Africa only 2 people graduated as engineers per 100,000. Yet the two countries are comparable as far as industrialization is concerned.

It is not surprising in the light of Tables 41 and 42 that South Africa faces a shortage of skilled manpower of quite daunting magnitude.

In his paper *The Human Resources of the Republic of South Africa and their Development*,[2] Dr. S. Biesheuvel reported the results of a precise survey carried out by the South African Institute of Physics

1. *Comparative Education*, Vol. 9, No. 3, 1965, p. 303.
2. Published by Witwatersrand University Press, 1963.

TABLE 41. Economically active population by occupation group: percentage distribution, 1960

Occupation group[1]	Country				
	Canada[2]	Netherlands	New Zealand[2]	Norway	South Africa
(a) Professional, technical and administrative	10.6[3]	12.2	15.1	11.2	4.65
(b) Clerical and sales	27.5[3]	21.8	21.0	14.5	8.35
(c) Industrial	35.8	42.8	41.7	44.9	34.2
(d) Agriculture	11.7	10.8	14.5	19.4	30.4
(e) Service and others	14.4	12.4	7.7	10.0	22.4

1. ISCO classification:
   (a) 0,1—professional, technical, administrative, executive, managerial.
   (b) 2, 3—clerical and sales.
   (c) 5,6,7,8—miners, quarrymen, workers in transport and communication, craftsmen, production process workers.
   (d) 4—farmers, fishermen, hunters, loggers.
   (e) 9, X, others—service, sport and recreation, not classifiable, and members of the armed forces.
2. 1961.
3. Administrative, executive, etc., are included with clerical and sales.
Source: United Nations Demographic Yearbook 1964, table 10.

TABLE 42. Economically active population: percentage distribution of population groups by occupation, 1960

Occupation group	All races		African	Asian	Coloured	White
	Number employed	Distribution				
Professional, technical and administrative	277	5.0	1.4	6.4	2.7	16.6
Clerical and sales	477	8.3	1.2	24.0	3.5	33.2
Skilled and semi-skilled industrial	422	7.4	0.6	20.9	20.3	22.5
Unskilled industrial	1 521	26.7	33.1	14.2	18.8	10.4
Agriculture	1 736	30.2	38.2	8.0	22.8	10.2
Service and others	1 280	22.4	25.5	26.5	31.9	7.1
TOTAL	5 713	100.0	100.0	100.0	100.0	100.0

in collaboration with the South African Mathematical Association and the Council for Scientific and Industrial Research on the available number of physicists and mathematicians with at least an M.Sc degree and the estimated need in the immediate future. In the 46 organizations that participated in the survey, 40 per cent of the 295 posts for these two categories of scientists were vacant. The report regarded this estimate of the shortage as conservative as it was based on existing posts not truly reflecting the country's needs

In the field of medicine the shortages are very large. The numbers of doctors per head of population in 1960 was 1 in 1,800 in South Africa, compared with 1 in 1,000 in the United Kingdom and 1 in 750 in the United States of America[1] and the Minister of Education. Arts and Science forecast a shortage of 1,500 doctors in 1965. This over-all rate does not, however, present the whole picture. The shortage is acute in African areas. It was estimated that there were 25 private practitioners for the 600,000 residents of the African township of Soweto, Johannesburg, and another 36 work daily at municipal clinics there.[2]

The reason for the shortage is clear when it is recalled that in 1960 there were 130 non-white doctors only. Indeed, a very much larger number than the 1,500 doctors mentioned by the minister would be needed to bring the number of doctors per head of the African population up to white standards. A considerable increase in the number of Africans receiving medical training would be needed to redress the shortage.

The Nursing Act (1957) provided that the Nursing Council, which deals with registration, training and discipline of nurses and midwives, should consist of white persons only. Separate registers for nurses and midwives of different population groups must be kept, and only in a case of emergency may a white nurse be employed under the control or supervision of a non-white nurse.

Government spokesmen have suggested that the manpower needs can be satisfied by a better use of white manpower co-ordinated with a vigorous overseas drive to recruit new immigrants.

Table 43 gives the number of immigrants arriving in the Republic, the number of emigrants and the gain or loss by migration over the years 1948-68.

1. *A Survey of Race Relations . . . 1963*, p. 252.
2. *Star* (Johannesburg), 26 July 1966.

TABLE 43. Number of immigrants arriving in the Republic of South Africa, the number of emigrants and the gain or loss by migration over the years 1948-68

Year	Number of immigrants	Number of emigrants	Gain or loss
1948	35 631	7 534	+ 28 097
1957	14 615	10 943	+ 3 672
1960	9 789	12 612	— 2 823
1961	16 309	14 903	+ 1 406
1962	20 916	8 945	+ 11 971
1963	37 964	7 156	+ 30 808
1964	40 865	8 092	+ 32 773
1965	38 326	9 206	+ 29 120
1966	48 048	9 888	+ 38 160
1967	38 937	10 737	+ 28 700
1968	40 548	10 589	+ 29 959

Source: State of South Africa Yearbook, 1970: Economic, Financial and Statistical Yearbook of the Republic of South Africa, p. 119, Johannesburg, 1970.

At the highest peak (1966) there was a gain of 38,160 but the normal figure would approximate 28,000 per year.

Biesheuvel[1] has discussed whether the shortage of skilled manpower could be alleviated simply through better use of white manpower resources. He concluded that more white manpower could be provided in the 'lower-professional, technical, middle-management and higher technical categories', but already difficulty was being caused by trying to employ the least capable 25 per cent of the white population in jobs beyond their capacity.

'First-line white supervisors of black labour are frequently drawn from this group; but many lack the ability to instruct or direct the work of others. . . . In every country a certain proportion of the labour force inevitably falls into this class and finds itself relegated to the bottom of the occupational pile. Here, however, the bottom of the pile is reserved for the black worker and the less effective white workers have to be kept artificially apart or above them by means of statutory and conventional restrictions.'

The difficulties of providing the necessary high-level manpower are even greater, however. This type of manpower has been defined by

1. Biesheuvel, op. cit., p. 14.

the American scholar Harbison[1] as including professional men and technologists whose work clearly requires a university degree or equivalent training and senior administrators and managers carrying considerable policy and financial responsibility. Biesheuvel[2] estimated that a modern nation needs about 4 per cent of its economically active manpower to be of this type. Even if 8 per cent of the employed white manpower were employed in high-level posts this would still amount to only 1½ per cent of the total employed manpower. Advanced modern States find it difficult to provide 4 per cent of employed manpower for such posts. It is unlikely that South Africa could find three times or more than that proportion of white South Africans to fill such posts without a serious deterioration in efficiency. Indeed Biesheuvel[3] reports the results of a survey carried out by the South African National Institute for Personnel Research which led to the conclusion that there was 'little hope to meet from within the white group, the growing need for high-level personnel that now confronts South Africa'.

In an article on manpower training and educational requirements for economic expansion, the South African scholar E. G. Malherbe[4] discusses the requirements not only of the very-high-level manpower but also of the lower level of technicians, teachers, junior administrators, managers and supervisors, etc. He quotes an address made in 1960 by Dr. F. Meyer, president of the National Development Foundation of South Africa:

'Why cannot we increase productivity and bring down the cost of living? Why cannot we modernise our factories? Why cannot we improve or expand our marketing and selling? and hundreds of similar questions you may ask. The answers are all the same, namely: because we do not have the trained managerial executive and technical manpower to plan, organize and administer these things. The opportunities are there. We can get the money, the materials and the equipment but we cannot lay our hands on the trained manpower to turn ideas into action.'

The problem of the shortage of manpower has become more acute over the past three years. At a meeting of the Afrikaans Business

1. 'High-level Manpower for Nigeria's Future' in *The Ashby Report on Higher Education in Nigeria*.
2. *South African Journal of Science*, Vol. 49, 1952, p. 120.
3. Biesheuvel, op. cit., p. 12.
4. E. G. Malherbe, 'Manpower Training: Educational Requirements for Economic Expansion', *South African Journal of Economics*, Vol. 33, No. 1, 1965.

Institute in May 1970, Mr. A. J. van Wyk pointed out that—allowing for a growth rate of 6 per cent—there would be a shortage of 65,000 white workers and a surplus of 98,000 non-white workers unless the labour policy was changed.[1]

There was a marked reduction in the output of several mines. Tom Muller, reviewing the lowered production of Stilfontein's gold mine, blamed the situation partly on the shortage of European miners and artisans.[2] Mr. Dick Cooke, president of the Chamber of Mines, estimated that the shortage of white labour amounted to between 1,500 and 1,700 men. He was quoted as saying that the shortage was acute and likely to grow; there were not enough men to go around.[3]

Harry Oppenheimer, Chairman of the Anglo-American Corporation warned of the effect on gold production and on South Africa's economy of the attitude to non-white labour.[4]

Professor J. J. Stadler of Pretoria University estimated that by 1973 the number of vacancies for skilled men would be 40,000 even if 30,000 immigrants arrived each year until then.[5]

The government-owned Iron and Steel Company (ISCOR) faced a shortage of 3,000 workers. A recruiting team was sent to Germany and to the United Kingdom. They offered posts to 663 workers of whom 300 were expected to accept.[6]

Mr. J. F. Oberholzer, Member of the Provincial Council, Johannesburg City Council, was quoted as saying: 'In the professional fields such as civil engineering and architecture we simply cannot provide the services we should. As a result we have to turn to outside consultants, at three times the cost.'[7]

The Johannesburg *Star* claimed[6] that the shortage of engineers could well prohibit planned development. Of 129 engineering graduates, 85 were bursary holders, 26 of the remaining intended to study further, and only 18 new engineers were available for the market.

The shortage of manpower is likely to be increased by a new government ruling on 7 August 1970 under the terms of the Industrial Conciliation Act which provides for job reservation according

1. *Guardian* (London), 5 May 1970.
2. *Sunday Times* (Johannesburg), 12 April 1970. Part of the drop in production was also due to an over-all drop in African labour recruited from neighbouring territories.
3. *Cape Times*, 3 January 1970.
4. *Cape Argus*, 29 December 1969.
5. *Cape Times*, 3 January 1970.
6. *Star* (Johannesburg), 16 December 1969.
7. *Sunday Times* (Johannesburg), 23 November 1969.

to race. Africans may now be barred from being typists, receptionists in doctors' consulting rooms and telephone operators outside the reserves and areas defined as 'Bantu' residential areas in Section 1 of the Bantu (Urban Areas) Consolidation Act No. 25 of 1945, except in certain specified cases and then only in a separate office or room, or outside working hours and under supervision.[1]

It is clear that there is no solution to the requirements of high-level manpower other than by providing the training on the necessary vast scale that would enable sufficient members of the non-white population to contribute their share to the filling of technical, professional, administrative and managerial posts according to their ability.

A key role to scientific research and development is played by the technician. Depending on the type of work, from two to five or six technicians may be needed for each professional officer. Several people have drawn attention to the severe shortage of technicians in laboratories in South Africa. For example, Malherbe writes:[2]

'in South Africa the technicians appear to be in as short supply as professional engineers, if not more so, with the result that many professional officers of necessity dissipate their energies on non-professional work'.

In some very limited ways it is possible to make use of non-white technical staff, if they are available, but the educational system does not produce them. If they were available and one did use them, there would be social difficulties involved in providing separate facilities.

Even in Western European laboratories adequate technical help is not always available, for financial reasons, and generally speaking South African universities are poorly provided for financially by standards in Western Europe and the United States of America. However, technical assistants are usually drawn from the class of highly skilled manual workers in which, as has been shown above, non-white workers are almost completely excluded. It appears, there-

1. Press Statement by the Honourable M. C. Botha, M.P., Minister of Bantu Administration and Development of Bantu Education, 7 August 1970. See also: 'Government Notice: Employment of Bantu in Certain Classes of Work: . . . except in a number of exceptional cases *inter alia* where Bantu persons serve non-whites as defined hereunder, Bantu persons may not be employed or continue to be employed in the following capacities: (a) shop assistant or salesman in a shop or factory; (b) reception clerk in an accommodation establishment or professional undertaking; (c) telephonist in a shop, office, accommodation establishment or factory; (d) typist in a shop, office, accommodation establishment or factory; (e) cashier in a shop, office, accommodation establishment or factory, (f) Clerk in a shop, office, accommodation establishment or factory. 'It should be clearly understood that this is not the final prohibition but only a further and amended notice of intention to restrict.'
2. Malherbe, op. cit.

fore, that the difficulties created by lack of technological assistance in South African laboratories can be attributed to racial discrimination.

3 Effects of apartheid on scientific organization in South Africa

The main official organization responsible for research in South Africa is the Council for Scientific and Industrial Research (CSIR) which carries out research in the laboratories of its own institutes, gives grants of about £250,000 per annum to universities and museums for specified research projects, sponsors medical research projects jointly with the Committee for Research in the Medical Sciences, university medical schools, etc., promotes co-operative research by industry through the formation of industrial-research associations and universities and undertakes sponsored projects for industrial firms on a contract basis. Total expenditure of CSIR is approximately R.80 million, an increase by a factor of 2.5 in the past decade. CSIR is responsible for about half of expenditure on basic and applied research in South Africa. The budget for 1968-69 included R.1.34 million for university research: chromatography (Pretoria), cosmic rays (Potchefstroom), geochemistry (Cape Town), marine research (Durban), natural products (Cape Town), oceanography (Cape Town), palynology (Bloemfontein), polyenes (Stellenbosch).

One aspect of its work has been to support the holding of research conferences and symposia in South Africa and to encourage its researchers to travel overseas, a policy to compensate for the geographical and increasing political isolation of South Africa. The

Medical Research Council also explicitly encourages travel overseas,[1] as do universities.

Government-sponsored research is carried out also in the laboratories of the Atomic Energy Board and of a number of government departments of the national and provincial governments.

More than thirty private industrial organizations have substantial research laboratories. During 1969 a Scientific Advisory Council was formed. This will advise the Prime Minister and the Minister of Planning and government departments with an interest in scientific research, and can be expected to gear scientific research more closely to government plans.

The centres of scientific research are all at 'white' universities and almost all the scientific and technical posts are held by Europeans. A few departments in the universities employ as technicians some Africans, Indians or Coloured persons (this is more frequently the case for the English-medium rather than the Afrikaans-medium universities). In the government research laboratories, on the other hand, the laboratory assistants, except in the very lowest categories, are always white.

CSIR is a member of the International Council of Scientific Unions (ICSU) and its affiliated unions. In 1971 CSIR was concerned with the management of South African national programmes linked with global programmes under the auspices of ICSU's Scientific Committee for Antarctic Research, Oceanographic Research and the International Biological Programme.

In addition, CSIR organized the second international symposium on Gondwana stratigraphy and palaeontology under the auspices of the International Union of Geological Sciences.[2]

During 1962 the South African Government began to put pressure on scientific associations to introduce racial segregation. Speaking at a conference of the Library Association in November of that year the Minister of Education, Arts and Science criticized the association for permitting non-whites to become members and said that the government expected these bodies to follow the pattern of apartheid and to immediately form separate associations for whites and non-whites. The Library Association decided to comply, to accept no further non-white members and to allow the existing eleven non-

---

1. See *Nature* (London), Vol. 228, No. 5269, 24 October 1970, p. 12-31.
2. *A Survey of Race Relations . . . 1963*, p. 78.

whites to retain membership only until their own societies had been established.[1]

A few weeks later a letter was sent by the minister to fourteen scientific bodies that receive government subsidies (of between £40 and £400 per annum) in the following terms:

'i. It has been decided with reference to scientific and professional societies, no mixed membership is allowed and where this exists a separation must be effected immediately. Where, in a certain area, a non-White group consists of small numbers, they should be included in a larger geographical area.

'ii. With reference to separate scientific and professional societies the same procedure should be followed as has been announced for sport societies by the authorities some time ago. According to this, non-White societies should be combined by way of affiliation in national societies, which can appoint one or two representatives to attend periodically certain executive meetings of the national societies for whites. In this way channels can be created, not only for interchange of ideas, but also to pass on to non-white scientists the knowledge which has crystallised out in congresses and conferences of White scientists.

'iii. From the above-mentioned it is clear that if your constitution makes provision for membership of non-Whites, it will be necessary to modify it appropriately to ensure that your society shall qualify for financial support from the Government.

'iv. Speedy information would be appreciated on what the position of your society is, with reference to non-White membership.'

The minister's letter caused a good deal of criticism and ridicule. The *Rand Daily Mail* (16 February 1963) commented editorially:

'A council member of the Associated Scientific and Technical Societies has revealed that there are only eight non-Whites among the 12,000 members of the 13 societies. Half of them are Chinese; none of them are voting members and none are active. . . . A sensible attitude would have been to leave the eight non-active, non-White scientists as an example of enlightenment under apartheid—in due course to be lauded by the South Africa Foundation. But the Minister cannot leave well alone. He demands a separate body for them.

'Could anything be more absurd? Or more likely to bring odium on South Africa's name in a field where so far it is unsullied?'

1. *South African Digest*, 9 July 1971, p. 5 (issued by the Department of Information, Pretoria).

Apparently the societies did not respond, and early in 1964 the minister took the matter up again. At that time, seven of the societies decided not to change their constitution to exclude non-white membership, one decided not to reapply for a government subvention, and the remaining six were adopting a 'wait and see' attitude.

The attitude of some of the societies is illustrated by the answers to a questionnaire sent out recently by the Secretariat for the purpose of compiling this section of the report and addressed to fifteen societies or professional organizations.

The questions put to these organizations were as follows:

1. Do you admit to membership all suitably qualified people, irrespective of race?
2. What is the total membership of your organization?
3. How many persons of the (a) African; (b) Coloured; (c) Indian racial groups are members of your organization?
4. Do you have separate categories of membership for people of different racial groups?
5. Is your policy in these matters determined by government regulation?
6. Has your policy in relation to these questions had any effect on relations of your organization with similar organizations in other countries?

Six of the organizations failed to reply, one refused to answer the questions. The answers of the remainder are summarized in Table 44.

The imposition of segregation in professional organizations would be equivalent to depriving non-white members of the right of discussion with their white colleagues in congresses and meetings. Such lack of discussion would greatly decrease the opportunities for the development of non-white members as competent scientists.

The policy of racial segregation in scientific societies is likely to cause unfavourable reactions against South African science where international relations are concerned. The important international scientific congresses are organized by ICSU. On 4 October 1958, at its Eighth General Assembly in Washington, a resolution was passed on its policy of political non-discrimination which contains the following paragraphs :

'1. To ensure the uniform observance of its policy of political non-discrimination, the ICSU affirms the right of the scientists of any country or territory to adhere to or to associate with international

TABLE 44. Answers to questions about attitude towards racial segregation in scientific organizations, 1966

ame of organization	Answers to questions					
	1	2	3	4	5	6
ssociated Scientific nd Technical Societies South Africa	Yes	12 410	Not known[1]	No	No	No
outh African stitute of Physics[2]	Yes	227	(a) 2 (b) 0 (c) 1	No	No	No
edical Association South Africa	Yes	6 104	Not known[3]	No	No	No
ental Association South Africa	Yes	1 080	(a) 0 (b) 0 (c) 8	No	—[4]	No
outh African sychological ssociation[5]	Yes	210	(a) 2 (b) 0 (c) 4	No	No	No[6]
outh African enetic Society	Yes	80	None	No	—[7]	No
oyal Society f South Africa	Yes[8]	273[9]	None	No	No	No
he Institute for the tudy of Man in Africa, o Medical School, ospital Street, ohannesburg	Yes	350	None	No, no members, but speakers recruited from all ethnic groups	—	No

1. Said: 'None of our constituent societies keep statistics about the race of their members.'
2. Said: 'It has been decided that in the interest of professional etiquette and in the interest of the traditional free flow of information between scientists in different countries, the information requested by you should be made available.'
3. Said: 'In accordance with medical principles we do not differentiate or keep records of colour, race, sex or creed.'
4. Said: 'Our policy is not determined by government regulation at present. It is understood, however, that when sufficient members in other racial groups qualify to justify a separate organization for such groups, they will be required, in terms of government policy, to join their own associations.'
5. Said: 'In 1961 a split occurred in the South African Psychological Association on the question of admission of non-Whites. Those who favoured their exclusion seceded and formed the Psychological Institute of the Republic of South Africa, which admits only Whites to membership.'
6. Said: 'The constitution and policy of this association are in accordance with that of the International Union of Psychological Sciences, of which the South African Psychological Association is a member.'
7. Said: 'Since the question of a prospective non-European member has never arisen, we have formulated no policy in this regard. The university facilities usually used for meetings and congresses would presumably not be made available to us for mixed racial gatherings.'
8. Said: 'There has not yet been a case in which a coloured or African has applied for membership.'
9. Said: '89 fellows and 184 ordinary members.'

scientific activity without regard to race, religion or political philosophy.

. . . .

'4. Meetings or assemblies of ICSU or its dependent organisms such as its special committees and its joint commissions should be held in countries which permit participation of the representatives of every national member of ICSU or of the dependent organisms of ICSU concerned, and allow free and prompt dissemination of information related to such meetings.'

The official policy of racial segregation, if practised by scientific societies, would make it difficult for them to satisfy the conditions, thus preventing them from acting as host organization on their territory for conferences organized under the auspices of ICSU. If this was seriously applied it would increase the growing isolation of South African science. It is doubtful whether any scientific organization can maintain an anti-segregationist policy. This is only possible where few non-whites have qualified for admission to these organizations.

4 The influence of apartheid on social field research

Field-work in social sciences in South Africa faces problems arising from the policy of apartheid. In order to carry out research in a 'Bantu' reserve or in an African area any person who does not belong to the African group entitled to live in these 'homelands' requires a permit which may be withdrawn at any time without any reason being given. There is often very full co-operation from Bantu

Affairs commissioners when doing field-work. However, there have been cases where an anthropologist has been refused permission to do field-work in a particular area or an investigator has been asked to leave the field for security reasons. A white investigator is not permitted to lodge with Africans in the field. More usually a white sociologist would be required to live in a police station or a recognized mission station. Sociological studies in the native townships, as distinct from the reserves, may be badly hampered by the fact that the white research worker cannot live among the people he is studying. It may be possible to receive permission to live in a caravan, but not in an African hut or a homestead which would be much cheaper and more convenient. The research worker can get only a permit to go in daily, and to employ an African field officer who is permitted to live in the community studied.

White field-workers going among African or Coloured people feel that they are under the surveillance of the police the whole time. They work with the fear that they may forfeit their permits to work in specified areas or, if foreigners, lose their permits to reside in South Africa.

An even more serious obstacle to investigation is the suspicion and hostility exhibited by informants (or possible informants). Even where there is no open hostility there may be a reluctance to talk. Many of the Africans may only know a white investigator as a possible local official or Special Branch man. Using an African, Indian or Coloured assistant may be little more helpful, as he or she may be seen as a possible spy or 'sell-out'. Moreover, the imprisonment of so many people for political offences and the degree of tension between racial groups in the country make any kind of field-work difficult.

Since permits from the Department of Bantu Affairs are necessary if material in the African reserves or other African areas is to be gathered or published, there is no guarantee that the department, having initially permitted field-work, will, after all, authorize the use of the material. In addition, the requirements for access to African areas make certain studies, e.g. a study of native law or native custom, difficult to pursue in South Africa.

In view of these conditions, the anthropologist Professor Monica Wilson in an analysis of an African suburb of Cape Town[1] omitted

1. Monica Wilson and Archie Mafeje, *Langa: A Study of Social Groups in an African Township*, p. 11, London and New York, Oxford University Press, 1963.

altogether investigation of political organizations and trade unions Professor Wilson explains the situation as follows:

'We did not investigate political organizations or trade unions. Questions were not asked about them early in the investigation because that would have aroused suspicion, and during the course of the study the two main political organizations, the African National Congress and the Pan-Africanist Congress, were banned. Furthermore, two cases occurred in which journalists were imprisoned for refusing to reveal to the police their sources of information on political matters. A very large number of the people of Langa take a lively interest in politics, and readers must make allowance for this fact.'

Since some South African social scientists believe that apartheid is a practical solution to the local problems, it is not surprising that their research would be directed to questions arising out of this belief; research into the selection or training of rural African labourers for work in 'border industries', for example.[1] However, it is done with the intention of developing border industries and is thus directed to reinforcing an apartheid social and economic situation.

There is a general tendency to concentrate on non-controversial issues, e.g. the mass of ethnographical studies of 'tribal' systems in contrast with the relative dearth of studies of the dynamics of social-economic change arising through urbanization and industrialization. One special field of research, for example, which has so far been inadequately explored and for which South Africa presents a unique opportunity in view of the existence side by side of populations of different cultural, dietary and genetic histories, is the effect of these parameters on human growth, illness and health. Similarly, little is known of the psychological effects of malnutrition.

Certain lines of research are made virtually impossible by the particular socio-political environment to be found there, e.g. an investigation into cross-racial sexual relations, or an investigation (especially by a European) of non-European political attitudes.

Given the policy of the South African Government, and the steps it has taken to ensure the implementation of this policy, it may be

1. Border industries are industries being established on white territory near to the 'reserves'—particularly near to the Transkei. In this way the 'reserves' act as a direct reservoir of African labour, which is not subject to prevailing urban rates of pay, and the Africans can theoretically return to the 'reserves' at the end of the day.

questioned whether the National Council for Social Research (NCSR), which provides funds for research in the social sciences and which is directly administered by the Ministry of Education, Arts and Science, would hesitate or not to support research projects that might appear ideologically suspect, and whether projects sponsored by universities, which would be less likely to raise fundamental issues of racial policy, would not be given preference. This suspicion is certainly entertained by some social scientists who are either working in South Africa or who have had recent experience of South Africa. By its nature, however, it is almost impossible to obtain direct evidence of discrimination of this kind.

An important moral dilemma also faces the social scientist who does not believe in apartheid but whose work into African customs may be used to further government policy.

An official book censorship[1] has also had great impact on social sciences. Books like Dollard's *Caste and Class in a Southern Town*, Richmond's *The Colour Problem*, Kuper's *Passive Resistance in South Africa*, and many of the Unesco series *The Race Question in Modern Science* are banned.

5 Effects of apartheid on national defence and scientific research

The South African Government's policy of apartheid has led to the United Nations passing the resolutions quoted in the preface of this report as well as arousing the hostility of many Member States.

1. See Part IV.

Speaking in the Senate in 1962,[1] the Minister of Defence asserted that military action against South Africa was being secretly planned by some Afro-Asian countries and declared that it would therefore be necessary for South Africa to build up its own forces.

The defence budget for 1969-70 was R.271,600,000, R.17,469,000 more than the previous year, and R.231,600,000 more than it was in 1959. In 1969-70 it represented 2.5 per cent of the total national product.[2]

This large and rapid increase in defence expenditure has been accompanied by the setting up in 1963, under the CSIR in Pretoria of the National Institute for Defence Research with sections dealing with physics, chemistry and electronics. In announcing the establishment of the new institute, Professor L. J. le Roux,[3] vice-president of CSIR, said that it was developing a rocket-propelled ground-to-air missile. He also indicated that a Naval Research Institute would soon be established. At about the same time, it was announced[4] that CSIR was recruiting highly qualified scientists to be sent overseas for the necessary training to conduct research into the construction of rockets. On 7 November 1963, Professor le Roux stated that the South African Defence Research Council had set up a specialist group of scientists to study the further development of poison gases like Tuban, Soman and Sarin. He said that

'these poisons are capable of being delivered in vast quantity by aircraft or long-range missile and they can have a destructive effect similar to that of a nuclear bomb of 20 megatons. These gases are ten times more poisonous than any other substance you can name.'[5]

He also reported that the new institute was working closely with the Institute for Aviation Medicine of the South African Defence Force and the National Institute for Personnel Research. In 1959 the South African Atomic Energy Board was launched, and by 21 July 1970 had developed a unique method of processing South African uranium to a form more advanced than uranium concentrate.[6] Mr. Vorster announced that South Africa would launch a 'vaste programme d'énergie nucléaire de l'ordre de 20,000 mégawatts'.[7]

1. *House of Assembly Debates (Hansard)*, Vol. 8, 12 March 1962, Cols. 1836-46.
2. ibid., Vol. 13, 5 May 1969, Col. 5289.
3. *South African Digest*, 31 October 1963.
4. *South African Digest*, 5 September 1963.
5. Reuter, 7 November 1963.
6. *International Herald Tribune* (Paris), 22 July 1970.
7. *Le Monde* (Paris), 24 July 1970.

In August 1968 the Armaments Development and Manufacturing Corporation of South Africa Limited (ARMCOR) was set up to make South Africa less dependent on overseas countries for its defence requirements as soon as possible and to rationalize the armaments industry of the country. Its policy is to exploit South Africa's own scientific and industrial capacity as soon as possible.[1]

Though exact figures are not available as regards that part of the scientific research in South Africa which has recently been directed towards defence, it nevertheless remains clear that the effect of the apartheid policy is to divert a certain proportion of the total available resources for scientific research from research geared towards pacific and civilian aims.

Not all of South Africa's research is geared to defence. There is a high level of research in other areas: for example, in extraction of petroleum from low-grade oil deposits[2] (still in its initial stages) and in surgery, where South Africa has done the world's first heart graft. South African research had perfected inexpensive plant and animal protein foods to a point where, at the cost of only a few cents daily, people can remain healthy on specially enriched foods.[3] The practical application of some of this research, on, for example, bilharzia, malnutrition and typhus fever, would appear to be limited by the political, social and economic situation of non-white South Africans. Bilharzia had been successfully wiped out in the white population but it was estimated that 90 per cent of all African children in the Transvaal suffered from it.[4] The extent of kwashiorkor or marashura was greater than the official figures, based on notification, suggested. Notification was stopped in 1966, but a partial questionnaire done by 200 doctors for the National Nutrition Research Institute of CSIR found that the incidence of kwashiorkor was probably four times higher than notification.

South Africa is certainly not the only country in the world in which there is a high incidence of malnutrition or diseases connected with poverty. What is unique is that this is within the context of a highly industrialized economy, with outstanding contributions in advanced fields of scientific and medical research and that poverty is supported by the discriminatory nature of the social structure.

1. *State of South Africa Yearbook*, 1970: *Economic, Financial and Statistical Yearbook of the Republic of South Africa*, p. 51, Johannesburg, 1970.
2. Oil in large quantities has not been found in the Republic, which remains dependent on foreign sources.
3. *Bantu* (Pretoria), January 1969, p. 15.
4. *Express*, 9 November 1969.

6 Effects of apartheid on South African international scientific and technical co-operation

Abhorrence of apartheid has resulted in the exclusion or resignation of South Africa from the following international organizations:
Commission for Technical Co-operation in Africa South of the Sahara (1962).[1]
Food and Agriculture Organization (FAO) (1963).
Council for Science in Africa (1963).
Economic Commission for Africa (ECA) (1963).
International Labour Organisation (ILO) (1964).
The Commonwealth Medical Association (1970).
South Africa has been excluded from the Assembly of the World Health Organization (WHO).

South Africa withdrew from Unesco in 1955 (see 'Preface to the First Edition').

Dr. G. C. Lawrie of the South African Institute of International Affairs commented[2] that although South Africa's technical and scientific achievements in many fields were outstanding the country was, for political reasons, unable to make the international contribution these achievements justified.

The Minister of Foreign Affairs announced in 1963,[3] that as a result of various adverse moves made by international organizations, the Onderstepoort Veterinary Research Institute would no longer serve as a world reference centre on behalf of FAO for certain diseases. South Africa would withdraw from various FAO panels of experts and study groups. No further technical assistance would be provided through FAO. South Africa would, however, extend and

1. The last time a South African delegate attended a meeting of the Commission for Technical Co-operation in Africa South of the Sahara was in December 1961, as a result of the attitude of African States towards any co-operation with South Africa as long as apartheid exists. South Africa withdrew from the organization in 1962.
2. *The Republic of South Africa and the External World*, Johannesburg, South African Institute of Race Relations, 1961 (RR.212).
3. *South African Digest*, 26 December 1963.

develop collaboration in the scientific and technical fields with individual States on a direct bilateral basis.

7 Effects of apartheid on the emigration of scientists from and the recruitment of scientists to work in South Africa

The extension of the principle of separate development to higher education has serious repercussions in the universities. In 1961 it was reported that twenty-five members of staff from Cape Town had left, Natal had lost thirty-five, and that at the University of the Witwatersrand eight professorships, nine senior lectureships and nine lectureships were vacant. Since that time losses have continued on a considerable scale. Some of the scientists who have left had played a senior part in the intellectual life of the country.

Government circles have appeared indifferent to the loss of such a large number of academics. In 1965 they refused to give a passport to Professor K. Danziger, head of the Psychology Department at the University of Cape Town, but instead issued him with a one-way exit permit, thus precluding his return to South Africa. Dr. Duminy, the principal of Cape Town University, referring to this incident said:

'It is grievous for a university to sustain a loss such as this at any time but at a time like the present when highly academically qualified men are not easily come by, it is a setback of a particularly crippling and distressing kind. . . . The reasons for the decision are therefore completely obscure.'[1]

1. Cape Town, 10 December 1965.

Several African students who had been offered scholarships overseas have similarly been issued with one-way exit permits in lieu of passports, thus preventing their return to South Africa. For example, Mr. Reginald Boleu, an African from the University of the North, who, after a brilliant college record, had been offered a scholarship to study nuclear physics at the University of Uppsala, and Mr. G. L. Mongoaela, an ex-lecturer at Stellenbosch and Natal Universities, who had been offered a post-graduate scholarship at Wisconsin University, both left during 1965.[1]

It would be incorrect to attribute all loss of staff from South Africa to the introduction of apartheid in higher education. The salaries in South African universities are low and the facilities for research often less than those offered abroad, so that even in the absence of an apartheid policy a turnover of staff could be expected. But in very many cases the introduction of apartheid seems to have been partly or wholly to blame. The losses occurred mainly from the English-medium universities.

The introduction of apartheid has also had the effect of restricting the recruitment of staff, particularly from the United Kingdom. Dr. Duminy stated recently that difficulty had been experienced in recent years in attracting staff members from abroad owing to the country's academic isolation, the inadequacy of its research facilities, inferior salary scales and the prevailing political climate.

Reports of the social and political climate in South Africa resulting from the apartheid policy can hardly be considered to be encouraging for the prospective academic immigrant. More direct opinion about the official racial policies being applied in South African universities was expressed by 500 staff members of British universities (of 2,000 approached) who signed a declaration in November 1965 with a pledge not to apply for or to accept academic posts in South African universities which practise racial discrimination. This declaration caused some consternation and discouragement in liberal academic circles in South Africa. It was pointed out that the presence in South Africa 'of liberal minds from Britain or from any part of Western Europe is vital, or at least helpful to the survival of liberal ideas in this limbo of apartheid'.[2]

The effect would be particularly serious in the social sciences.

---

1. *A Survey of Race Relations . . . 1965.*
2. Winifred M. Roux, wife of the banned Professor Edward Roux, in the *Guardian* (London), 31 December 1965.

Although a number of leading university personnel have left South Africa, over all there is still a large excess of immigrants over emigrants, including professionally qualified people. The Deputy Secretary for Immigration, Piet Werderman, estimated that South Africa gained about R.150-million-worth of professional and technical skills a year through its immigration drive. This was the amount it would have cost the country to train more than 3,000 qualified professional men and 7,000 artisans.[1]

Overseas funds for research fellowships have diminished. The withdrawal of South Africa from the British Commonwealth as a result of her racial policies has meant that her students no longer qualify for many scholarships and fellowships formerly available (Nuffield Travelling Fellowships, Commonwealth Fellowships, scholarships of the British Council of Universities interchange scheme, or bursaries awarded for post-graduate study by the Royal Society).

The Secretary of the Royal Society of South Africa pointed out recently:

'Within my own very limited experience the main effect of apartheid on scientific institutions has been a decrease in the numbers of overseas visitors who want to come and work here (very noticeable since 1960). This decreased contact means that it is more difficult to place advanced students in suitable overseas institutions, though, as yet, no real hardship in this direction has been felt.'

There may also be a reluctance to emigrate to South Africa at a lower level than that of university-trained staff. It is difficult to assess the extent to which skilled labour has refused to emigrate to South Africa because of its political and racial policies. But there are indications that this may well be so and that some trade unions discourage their members from emigrating.

The Trades Union Congress of the United Kingdom passed a resolution on 28 May 1969 which declared its total opposition to the system of apartheid, and urged all affiliated unions to discourage their members from taking jobs in South Africa.[2] The effect of even a partial boycott at this level could be a serious impediment to South Africa's technical and scientific progress and to her economic growth.

1. Unit on Apartheid, *Papers*, No. 12/70, p. 20, New York, United Nations, April 1970.
2. The sponsor of the resolution was the Draughtsmen's and Allied Technicians' Association.

We live in an age which, if it is not to be an age of the technocrat divorced from the rest of the population, must provide broadly based access to scientific knowledge.

Any discussion on the effect of apartheid on science, therefore, must be concerned not only with the training of a scientific élite, although this is important in any industrialized society, but also with the ways used to ensure that the non-élite understand, to some extent, the type of development which is going on around them. This sort of information is given both at school level and by the mass media. Here the effect of apartheid on science is clear.

With restricted science facilities in non-white schools (see Part I, Chapter 5 above), restricted mass media (see Part IV below), as well as the restrictions placed on non-white participation in scientific creation, the non-white population is almost completely deprived of taking part in the scientific developments of today's world.

III. Culture

Article 13(1)
'Everyone has the right to freedom of movement and residence within the borders of each State.'

Article 16(1)
'Men and women of full age, without any limitation due to race, nationality or religion, have the right to marry and to found a family. . . .'

Article 27(1)
'Everyone has the right freely to participate in the cultural life of the community, to enjoy the arts. . . .

'Everyone has the right to the protection of the moral and material interests resulting from any scientific, literary or artistic production of which he is the author.'

The Universal Declaration of Human Rights

'That the wide diffusion of culture, and the education of humanity for justice and liberty and peace are indispensable to the dignity of man and constitute a sacred duty which all the nations must fulfil in a spirit of mutual assistance and concern.'

Preamble to the Constitution of Unesco

'In their rich variety and diversity, and in the reciprocal influences they exert on one another, all cultures form part of the common heritage belonging to all mankind.'

Article 1(3), Unesco General Conference,
fourteenth session:
Principles of International Cultural Co-operation

Definition of scope

To examine all the effects of apartheid on the social and cultural scene would be practically impossible. Sheila Van der Horst emphasizes that:

The policy of apartheid and its application are fundamental to an understanding of race relations in South Africa because it affects not only the politically conscious but permeates the whole country and governs the daily lives of all citizens. . . . It determines where members of each racial group are born, in what schools and manner they are educated, within what group they may marry, where they live, die and are buried. It determines the circumstances in which members of different racial groups meet. It is much more than an over-all policy influencing economic and social conditions. Notices reserving separate lavatories and waiting rooms, separate entrances to stations, post offices, separate buses and railway coaches are relatively new, they affront many, and particularly the more westernized, non-Whites.

'Above all, it restricts and denies economic opportunities not only to the better jobs, but, by restricting townward movement, to any jobs at all.'[1]

The field covered in this chapter has therefore been deliberately restricted. An attempt will be made to place apartheid in its social setting, and then certain aspects of culture will be specifically examined. These aspects have been chosen because of their implications not only to South African life, but because, in many cases, they sparked off far-reaching debates in other parts of the world. The religious situation in South Africa intensified the world-wide Christian debate on the responsibility of the Church in matters of race relations.

[1]. Sheila T. Van der Horst, 'The Effects of Industrialization on Race Relations in South Africa' in: Guy Hunter (ed.), *Industrialization and Race Relations: a Symposium*, Institute of Race Relations (United Kingdom), London and New York, Oxford University Press, 1965.

The decision of overseas playwrights not to have their plays performed under conditions of segregation in the Republic of South Africa raised questions as to the personal responsibility of dramatists toward the performance of their works.

Apartheid as it affects libraries raises the questions of the possibility of equal but separate facilities between population groups in the same State.

Underlying all these questions is another: is it possible or desirable for cultures to remain self-contained units, or is the borrowing between cultures fundamental to the growth of any particular culture?

2   The peoples of South Africa

Africans

European settlement and expansion upset trading relationships between tribes, reciprocal relationships and the extreme fluidity of territorial boundaries. Long-distance trade networks, where they existed, were upset either by the diversion of trade to white areas, or by European occupation of territories that formed part of the trading link. The process of consolidation and absorption of 'tribes' that had proceeded for centuries before was halted, and fission—which had always gone on—accelerated as rival chiefdoms sought 'protection' in alliances with whites.[1]

The African traditional tribal system in South Africa was partly (although not completely) destroyed by the military defeat of the African in the series of wars waged against conquest, by the

---

1. For a reconstructed account of pre-colonial southern Africa see *African Societies in Southern Africa*, edited by Leonard Thompson, London, Ibadan and Nairobi, Heinemann, 1969.

adoption by some Africans of Christianity, as well as by industrialization which demanded the acceptance of both a cash economy and
urban living. In the reserves, the 'Bantu homelands', Africans continued to maintain as much of the old ways as was possible. But the
reserves are in no way a land apart. The chiefs are ultimately responsible to the South African Parliament, land in the reserves is no longer
only owned by the paramount chief as trustee for the whole tribe.
Now, while communal tenure is still the main type of land tenure,
a considerable percentage of the land owned remains vested in the
State through the South African Native Trust.[1] Overcrowding and
poverty of the reserves continues to influence the trek of Africans
to white farms and urban districts.

The Tomlinson report stated that the urbanization of the South
African population is a consequence of economic development:
the rural areas, including the African areas, do not offer sufficient
opportunities for work or opportunities which are sufficiently remu-
nerative.[2] While in 1904 fewer than one-quarter of the total population of South Africa lived in the urban areas, in 1951 the proportion
had risen to 42.6 per cent. The Africans contributed 1,954,000 to this
increase, compared with 1,469,000 whites.[2]

In 1951, 78.4 per cent of all whites lived in towns, 77.5 per cent
of all Asians, 64.4 per cent of all Coloureds and 27.1 per cent of all
Africans.[3] The percentage increase of urban population between
1936 and 1960 was Africans 156, Asians 144, Coloureds 112, whites
81, while the percentage to urbanized population was estimated
in 1960 to be 80 per cent for whites and Asians, 62 per cent for
Coloured and 29 per cent for Africans.[4]

Approximately 35 per cent of Africans live in towns or villages,
providing, in 1962, about 54 per cent (800,000) of the total population engaged in manufacturing and construction and about 88.5
per cent (616,000) of those engaged in mining.[5]

In the towns, Africans, as well as whites, have had to adjust to

1 See the Natives, Land Act No. 27 of 1913, the Native Trust and Land Act No. 18 of 1936 and
   the Group Areas Act No. 41 of 1950.
2. *The Tomlinson Report: Summary of the Report of the Commission for the Socio-economic Development of the Bantu Areas within the Union of South Africa*, p. 27, Pretoria, n.d.
3. *State of South Africa Yearbook, 1970: Economic, Financial and Statistical Yearbook of the Republic
   of South Africa*, p. 62, Johannesburg, 1970.
4. In actual figures, between 1951 and 1960 the number of Africans considered 'urban' had jumped
   from 2,390,586 to 3,471,233, the number of whites from 2,088,551 to 2,574,651, Coloured persons
   730,577 to 1,030,858 and Asians from 284,663 to 397,023.—*Bulletin of Statistics* (Pretoria), end
   September 1967, Table A-1.
5. Van der Horst, op. cit., p. 98.

modern urban living. This adjustment has not always reached the same degree. While some Africans have almost completely accepted modern standards of living, some have attempted to retain African traditions in an urban milieu.[1] It is difficult to estimate how far apartheid has hindered the urbanization of the African. That it has affected it, there can be little doubt. The laws governing the movement of Africans qualify the number of Africans who can enter town, the Urban Areas Act segregates Africans in townships at the edge of the town, and restricts their access to places of public entertainment. Intermarriage is prohibited by law, and curfew regulations mean that no African can be in the white sector of the town between 11 p.m. and 5 a.m. without a pass, while whites may not visit a 'location'[2] without a special permit. This is not to say that non-whites are never seen in white areas. They go there to work, in the industries or as domestic servants, or to shop.[3] Culture contacts with whites are reduced to a minimum:

'One can think of two linked unequal towns, the White town owning and controlling the Black one, which it has called into being largely for its own convenience. Except for the narrowly limited relations of employment and administration—which are intrinsically unequal, and foster a sense of opposed rather than common interest—each half lives mainly in and for itself.'[4]

Even the minimal culture contact that exists is being reduced by recent government measures (see Chapters 4 and 7 below).

It is not only in the towns that the traditional African life has changed. The Tomlinson report noted the decreasing use of *lobolo*[5] even in country districts, the increase of monogamous marriages, the decrease of marriage within a preferential marriage system, and the increasing marriage outside ethnic limits.[6]

The policy of the government is to reinforce tribal traditions, turning an all-over South African nationalism into tribal nationalism.

---

1. Van der Horst, op. cit., p. 111. She suggests that the conservative, tradition-based Africans predominate in the mines, where the African labour force, except for clerical grades, is drawn almost entirely from migrant labour from the rural areas of the Republic, and from near-by African countries—Portuguese East Africa, Lesotho, etc.—while she doubts that there is a large proportion of traditionalists in the African townships of Witwatersrand.
2. African township.
3. Stores are not segregated.
4. P. Mayer, *Xhosa in Town, Townsmen and Tribesmen*, p. 43, Institute of Social and Economic Research, Rhodes University, Oxford University Press, 1961.
5. Bride price.
6. *The Tomlinson Report* . . ., op. cit., p. 15.

In the urban 'locations' the headman system was introduced. These headmen are voted for only by householders (registered tenants of municipal houses or registered occupiers of sites in the shack area), which means that the migrants have no possibility of voting. The headman was given limited judicial functions—he could hear petty cases—and was expected to be an intermediary between the location and the white administration. Mayer found that there was a distrust of headmen as being on the wrong side.[1]

The Bantu Laws Amendment Act of 1964 had for its purpose the direction of African labour and the creation of a migratory labour force, temporarily resident in urban centres, but without any permanent rights of residence, since Africans are theoretically citizens only of the reserves. This Act has important effects on the African family.

Mr. Greyling, a Nationalist Party member of the House of Assembly, explained at the reading of the Bill:

'. . . there is no such thing as "the rights of a Bantu" in the White area. The only rights he has are those which he acquires by performing certain duties. Those duties which he performs give him the right of sojourn here. The officials in these labour bureaux, in considering whether they are going to allow a Bantu to remain here, will have to give priority to the consideration as to whether that Bantu has carried out his duties as a worker, and not whether he has a supposed right which has been invented for him by members of the United Party.'[2]

Before the passage of this Bill an African could qualify to remain in an urban area if he had been born there and had resided there ever since, or had been in continuous employment for fifteen years, or had worked there continuously for the same employer for ten years. After 1964 the presence of an African in a white district for more than seventy-two hours was severely restricted. While Africans could theoretically qualify to remain in urban districts, nevertheless, any African could be endorsed out (a) if the minister had decided that the number of Africans in the area concerned exceeds its reasonable labour requirements, (b) if the African concerned comes from

---

1. 'They have to repeat to the officers of the administration everything that we say to them. This shows that they are not for the people but for the White men! We take it that they are White puppets!'—Mayer, op. cit., p. 54.
2. *House of Assembly Debates (Hansard)*, 4 March 1964, Col. 2463.

an area from which the minister has decided no more labour is to be recruited to the white area concerned, (c) if the African is deemed to be 'idle' or 'undesirable', (d) if it is deemed not to be in the interests either of the employer or the employed, or in the public interest, that the contract of service shall continue.

Wives and other dependants of Africans working in the white areas may not live with their husbands or fathers unless they have resided continuously in the same area previously. Visits without permission between husbands and wives residing in separate districts are limited to seventy-two hours.

In the House of Assembly, 18 March 1964, the Deputy Minister of Bantu Administration[1] explained the situation:

'An unmarried Bantu male qualifies to be in an urban area on the ground that he was born here or that he has been employed here for ten years by one employer or for fifteen years by different employers, and wants to marry a woman outside that urban area. The woman can only enter if she is given leave to do so. Housing is one of the factors which must be taken into account and it must be clearly understood that that means housing only in the Bantu residential areas and not housing in the backyard of the employer where that woman's husband is already employed and living in the premises. It applies only to housing in the urban Bantu residential areas and subject naturally to the regulations of that particular authority.'

A second example was the following:

'A Bantu woman who qualifies to be in an urban area wishes to marry a man employed there but not yet qualified (he is not born there, has not been employed for ten years by one employer or for fifteen years by different employers). The couple may marry. If the man ceases to work in the area, he has no longer a right to remain there. If that Bantu male cannot obtain employment he will have to go, but that is something which the Bantu woman knew from the first day; the Bantu male himself knew it; they entered into this union with their eyes open. They both knew that if he lost his employment then the last vestige of justification for his presence here would disappear. If he has to leave therefore she will have to accompany him. But there is still the possibility that the bureau may find a new job here for him. If he goes to the bureau and proves *bona fide* that

1. *House of Assembly Debates (Hansard)*, 18 March 1964, Cols. 3192 4.

e lost his employment, there is the possibility that he may get a ew job here and in that case they can remain here.'

n her study of the African township Langa, the South African socio-ɔgist Monica Wilson gives a picture of the situation of the African rban population.[1] Langa, a suburb of Cape Town, was built in the 920s as a substitute for another area set aside for African occupa-on. It was established as a 'respectable' township. The headquarters f the administration and most of the churches and a high school ere built there. Families were led to believe that they might settle ermanently. For the first twenty-five years married men and their vives made up one-third to a quarter of the population. However, ince 1954, the government has refused to allow building of further ouses for families in Langa, but additional single quarters have een built.

In Langa the proportion of men to women has risen and was in 965 over 8 : 1, the population breakdown being as follows: 18,847 African males, 2,175 African females, 4,314 African children (under 6); total (December 1965), 25,336.

In January 1966, of the 27,420 Africans living in Langa, 18,925 ived in bachelor quarters.[2] In February 1968, in the three townships erving greater Cape Town, there were 37,665 men and 15,121 women f 16 years and over. Of the men, 25,258 (or 67 per cent) were accom-nodated in bachelor quarters.[3]

Two cases may be taken as examples:[4]

Mr. Joseph Dyantyi, a resident of Hermanus since 1942, was married nd has six children between the ages of 7 and 16 years. Some time fter his wife died he wished to re-marry, to a woman working in Cape Town, but they were refused permission to set up house ogether and he was ordered to move into bachelor accommodation nd to send his children to the Transkei—where he had no land ights or close relatives to care for the children. . . .

'Mrs. Rebecca Motale, born in Cape Town and with three children, ost her right to remain there with her parents when she married a Stellenbosch man, and was refused permission to join him. She was

. Monica Wilson and Archie Mafeje, *Langa: A Study of Social Groups in an African Township*, London and New York, Oxford University Press, 1963.
. *Cape Times*, 20 June 1966, quoted in *A Survey of Race Relations . . . 1966*, p. 167.
. *House of Assembly Debates (Hansard)*, Vol. 3, 21 February 1968, Col. 1134.
. *A Survey of Race Relations . . . 1965*, p. 159-60.

convicted for being in Cape Town unlawfully. The case was, unsuc
cessfully, taken on appeal and meanwhile, according to her counsel
she disappeared to live in the bush. The counsel pointed out tha
she would have remained within the law had she elected to live i
sin, and the judge is reported to have stated that she was now existin,
in "a legally created limbo".'

In a Memorandum on the Application of the Pass Laws and Influ:
Control, the Black Sash said in part:

'. . . the African must be a collector of documents from the da
of his birth to the day of his death. . . . For thousands of African
these laws result in broken families, in unemployment, in povert'
and malnutrition, insecurity and instability and in a state of hope
lessness. . . . Millions of rands are spent in administering these laws
and millions of man-hours are wasted in the attempt to enforc
un enforceable laws. The real cost must be counted in terms of humar
sorrow, bitterness, suffering and tragedy on a vast scale.'[1]

The present trend has not been towards a diminution of this. O
the contrary, new regulations and the implementation of old one
has emphasized the status of the African: as a migrant worker witl
few rights, in a white South Africa. It has underlined the vulner
ability of those, from urban areas, who are too old or too youn;
to find work and who no longer have ties in the 'reserves'.

A new township for Africans has been established further ou
from Cape Town.

Monica Wilson makes the following general observations:

'There has been much greater security of life and property in Lang;
than in the townships of Johannesburg, but with growing restriction;
on entry, and the increase in the disproportion between men anc
women, disorder has increased. Women are less safe, going abou
alone, than formerly, and the tension between people and police i:
growing. In 1956 an African minister said that Langa was rapidly losin;
its peaceful atmosphere. "This is due to the influx of bachelors from
Windermere and similar slums. These men are now quartered in th
flats and barracks and zones so that it is now unsafe to go beyond th
married quarters after dark. Several assaults have been reportec
recently." Nowadays (1961), the police go to the zones or barrack

1. *A Survey of Race Relations . . . 1966*, p. 168-9.

ɔnly in a large group and there must be White police, who are armed, among them.'

The government policy of discouraging families from living in urban townships in favour of migrant male workers was reflected in the provision of housing over the past four years. Housing for Africans in some urban areas is deteriorating alarmingly. It was reported that in Grahamstown at the end of 1968, 9,000 Africans were living in the 1,260 shacks, and that 2,220 municipal and private dwellings were accommodating 16,000 people. No new houses for Africans had been built since 1963-64 in spite of the fact that the medical officer of health had drawn attention to the number of shacks that were springing up. In 1967 the city council applied to the government for permission to raise a loan to build 100 new houses. The government refused on the grounds that Grahamstown was classified as a 'border' area and future housing for African families would have to be provided in the homelands. Only hostels for 'single' workers might be built.[1]

The Deputy Minister of Bantu Administration stated the policy of the government when questioned about conditions in the townships around Middelburg (no houses had been built since 1938). He corrected the impression that housing loans would no longer be granted for African housing. They could—but for hostel accommodation only, and these only in the areas that would not eventually become 'Coloured' settlements.[2]

The housing situation is aggravated by the number of peasant farmers forced off the land in times of drought, and labour tenants displaced from white farms. The result is a serious problem of squatters in some areas, building their shanties from any available material on the borders of the reserves or on white-owned land. When evicted they leave to set up a new shack settlement elsewhere. One newspaper estimated that there might be 500,000 squatters in Natal province —150,000 in the Port Natal Area alone.[3]

The drift from farmland to squatting on the border of the reserves in the hope that some work is likely to be found in white industrial areas is likely to be intensified as machinery displaces African labour on white farms.[4]

1. *A Survey of Race Relations . . . 1969*, p. 175, 176.
2. *House of Assembly Debates (Hansard)*, Vol. 10, 19 June 1969, Cols. 8644-8, 8757-8.
3. *Natal Mercury*, and 9 April 1968. Here quoted from *A Survey of Race Relations 1969*, p. 178.
4. The number of Africans on white-owned farms declined by 10,000 (867,797 to 857,994) between

The Bantu Homelands Citizenship Act No. 26 of 1970 emphasized and consolidated the effect of the Bantu Laws Amendment Act of 1964. This Act provides that every African in the Republic who is not a citizen of a 'self-governing Bantu territory' in the Republic nor a prohibited immigrant will be a 'citizen' of one or other territorial authority area. Only in this area will he be able to exercise franchise rights, enjoy rights and privileges and be subject to duties and privileges granted or imposed on him by the law. The Minister of Bantu Administration and Development, during the second reading of the debate, explained the scope of African citizenship rights under the new Act:

'Under our policy all so-called rights which could lead to equality with whites . . . on a basis of integration: in all the various spheres . . . will in due course be removed by us.'[1]

The government publication *Bantu*[2] explained the purpose of the Bill:

'The Bill therefore reinforced the basis upon which also the political aspect of the government's policy rested in respect of the Bantu in white areas, namely, that they belonged to their own specific nations and that they could not integrate with the whites into one nation.'

The difficulty of deciding who belongs to which territory is underlined in the definition of who will be citizens of what: citizens of a particular territorial authority will be Africans born in the area and/or domiciled there; Africans in the Republic speaking any Bantu language or dialect thereof used by the African population of the area; and Africans in the Republic who are related to any member of the African population of the area, or who have identified themselves with any part of such population by virtue of their cultural or racial background.

The Bill does not withdraw 'citizenship' of the Republic, but establishes for Africans a dual citizenship in line with the argument that the Republic is made up of several nations and is in the process of

---

1955 and 1966 although agricultural production increased by 28 per cent. In mining there was an increase of nearly one-third in the volume of production, accompanied by a 32 per cent drop in the total labour force, the drop in African labour being about the same.—*Bantu* (Pretoria), August 1969, p. 20.
1. Here quoted from *A Survey of Race Relations . . . 1970*, p. 29
2. *Bantu* (Pretoria), April 1970, p. 6.

becoming a commonwealth of self-governing nations. It was the forerunner of a personal passport.[1] The 'certificate of citizenship' must bear a photograph of the holder. In addition it would seem that a set of fingerprints of each applicant for a certificate is taken and filed in the Bantu Reference Bureau. The Act has not yet been put into operation since the administrative machinery for its enforcement is yet to be set up.

The immediate effect of the Act will be to strengthen the legal basis for considering Africans in white areas as alien migrant labour.[2] In fact, only 38 per cent of the Africans affected by this legislation live within the territorial boundaries of their so-called homelands.[3] The files of fingerprints will also help police surveillance of Africans.

The 'certificate of citizenship' which will be issued under this law will also increase the number of documents that an African will be called upon to possess. The 'certificate' will not have to be produced on demand as are reference books. Nevertheless it will be required and an authorized official of the government has the right to request of an African that he produce his 'certificate'.

Commenting on the Bill the Institute of Race Relations pointed out that it was difficult to see what purpose it would fulfil other than to symbolize in a new document that the government regarded all Africans as aliens in 'white' areas.

It was self-evident that a large section of the 3.5 million urban Africans, many of whom had contracted ethnically mixed marriages, and many of whom were fluent in a number of Bantu languages, would qualify for multiple citizenship. These Africans feared that the Act was part of a wider plan to deprive them of urban residential rights.[4]

There have been statements made by the government and by members of the government that give support to their fears.

A General Circular of the Department of Bantu Administration, 12 December 1967, explained the government policy:

'It is accepted government policy that the Bantu are only temporarily resident in the European areas of the Republic for as long as they offer their labour there.

1. *Bantu* (Pretoria), July 1968.
2. *Star* (Johannesburg), 28 February 1970.
3. *Report of the United Nations Special Committee on the Policies of Apartheid of the Government of the Republic of South Africa*, September 1970, Addendum by the Special Rapporteur, Mr. Uddhav Deo Bhatt (S/9939/Add.1, paras. 23-7).
4. *A Survey of Race Relations . . . 1969*, p. 28.

'As soon as they become, for some reason or other, no longer fit for work or superfluous in the labour market, they are expected to return to their country of origin or the territory of the national unit where they fit ethnically if they were not born and bred in the homeland. The Bantu in the European areas who are normally regarded as non-productive and as such have to be resettled in the homelands are classified as follows:

The aged, the unfit, widows with dependent children and also families who do not qualify under the provisions of the Bantu Urban Areas Act, No. 25 of 1945 for family accommodation in the European urban areas.

Bantu on European farms who become superfluous as a result of age, disability or the application of Chapter IV of the Bantu Trust and Land Act, No. 18 of 1936, or Bantu squatters from mission stations and Black Spots[1] 32 of which are being cleared up.

Professional Bantu such as doctors, attorneys, agents, traders, industrialists, etc.

Such persons are not regarded as essential for the European labour market and as such they must also be settled in the homelands in so far as they are not essential for serving their compatriots in the European areas.'[2]

The Deputy Minister of Justice, Mines and Planning, Mr. G. F. van Froneman gave the 'repatriation of 3,800,000 appendages' (dependants of African bread-winners) as priority number one.[3]

In line with its resettlement policy, Africans have been resettled in townships at Dientjie, Morsgat, Kuruman and Limehill. Those resettled there were from the 'Black Spots', while in Mexesha, Ilinga, and Sada in the Eastern Cape there are resettlement townships mainly of women and children and the aged—the reserves cannot absorb them.

The extension of the white areas has meant that farms bought by Africans before 1936 have in some cases become surrounded by white-owned land. These also have been termed 'Black Spots'. At the end of 1967, there were 267 African-owned 'Black Spots' amounting to 102,233 morgen (approximately 222,400,000 acres) of land.[4]

There has been an intensification of the drive to eliminate these. A section of the General Law Amendment Act No. 70 of 1968

---

1. Small African areas which had become surrounded by white areas.
2. *Sunday Times* (Johannesburg), 1 December 1968. Also *Guardian* (London), 3 March 1970.
3. *Sunday Times* (Johannesburg), 30 March 1969.
4. *House of Assembly Debates (Hansard)*, Vol. 2, 20 February 1970, Col. 833; Vol. 7, Cols. 2655-6 6747-8. See also the *Guardian* (London), 3 March 1970.

simplified the procedure for serving notices of expropriation on Africans living in 'Black Spot' areas. Henceforth, if the land is communally owned, notice is considered given if the Bantu Affairs Commissioner calls a public meeting and explains the matter. If the land is individually owned and the proprietor cannot be easily found, a notice of expropriation posted in a conspicuous place is considered sufficient notice.

Africans from these 'Black Spots' were to be resettled on new sites. The government agreed to pay Africans a fair market price for the value of the land and the improvements plus 20 per cent above this as a compensation for the inconvenience caused. They were to be allocated land of equal agricultural and pastoral value.

The new sites were to be planned in advance, with the Bantu Trust providing water, sanitation, schools and clinics.

No one was to be forcibly removed.[1] In fact, it was difficult to allocate economic units for farming given the land available for African settlement. Some African families were being settled in closer settlement areas of 50 by 50 yards, in which, while paying a nominal one Rand a year for services, they were nevertheless required to dispose of all livestock except chickens. There seemed to be no provision for the next generation, and young men who could not find employment when they reached the age of 18 would have no legal home and would technically become squatters.[2]

The new settlement areas were also to absorb Africans who were endorsed out of the towns and for whom there was no space in the overcrowded reserves.

While in some cases the government made some effort to plan the new villages, in others few efforts had been made.

At Limehill when settlement started, roads were not finished, the school was not ready. There was little water—and that not pipe-borne—no sanitation and no firewood. Families were housed in tents and had to dig their own latrines. They were expected eventually to build their own houses although most of the menfolk were away working out of the area.

There were no supplies of meat, bread, milk and vegetables—one general dealer was two miles away from the settlement, and another fives miles away—but the government had provided supplies of

1. *Bantu* (Pretoria), August 1968, p. 9-15.
2. *A Survey of Race Relations* . . *1968*, p. 124-5.

mealie meal and salt, and eventually milk powder and soup powder.[1]

Similar conditions existed in Stinkwater, another resettlement area.[2]

In the resettlement villages at Sada and Mingquesha, visitors claimed that there was 'grinding poverty' and a high incidence of tuberculosis. These and other resettlement villages were inhabited mainly by old people, women and children who had no ties with a reserve, and had been endorsed out of urban areas and forced to leave white farming areas.[3]

There was some provision by the government, e.g. blankets, truck-borne water, some pensions, but this would seem to be wholly inadequate. Some idea of what these 'resettlement' camps were like can be seen from eye-witness reports of Limehill and Morsgat.

A medical report from Limehill established by four doctors doing voluntary medical work in a near-by clinic gave an account of the health conditions among Africans who were moved there the year before. It confirmed reports from other voluntary workers of the insufficiency or total lack of social facilities in the area. This had resulted in the incidence of typhoid (five cases confirmed in three weeks, nine others in four weeks, in a community of no more than 10,000), the high incidence of gastro-enteritis, especially among young children, and the presence of nutritional diseases.

Maternity facilities seemed non-existent, and there was no vaccine to provide immunizations.

They pointed out in their report that even when Limehill was compared with other African areas like Vendaland or the Northern Transvaal, the incidence of typhoid at Limehill was greater than in the Transvaal—where it was endemic—and kwashiorkor was higher than in Vendaland.

From this they drew the conclusion that the water and waste disposal facilities were inadequate.[4]

In November 1969, the *Rand Daily Mail* published the results of

---

1. *Star* (Johannesburg), 17 February 1968; *Rand Daily Mail* (Johannesburg), 3 February 1968.
2. *A Survey of Race Relations . . . 1968*, p. 135.
3. *A Survey of Race Relations . . . 1967*, p. 177-81.
4. *Rand Daily Mail* (Johannesburg) '31 January 1969.
   It was reported that the families to be moved were uncertain as to where they were being moved, and that for every working day for three weeks food rations had been supplied to them, while others claimed that the ration consisted of a small supply of mealie meal. No sanitary pits had been dug before the families arrived. Even with a mild winter they had been cold in the tents.

an investigation into Morsgat,[1] another resettlement area. The three *Rand Daily Mail* reporters found a makeshift site with no prepared sanitary facilities, a single water tank supplying the entire community with water—it had a layer of green slime floating on the surface— and no health clinic. People complained of the manner in which they had been carted away in trucks, from the hillside villages where they had lived for almost twenty-five years, to the tent settlement of Morsgat.

Denis Hurley, Archbishop of Durban, on behalf of a five-denominational committee protested on the removal of 4,000 Africans from the Dundee area; there were no houses built in the resettlement camp and people would have to live in tents.[2] Twelve thousand Africans were scheduled to be resettled from Dundee in North Natal.

An analysis of the effects of apartheid on African culture must take into account the income available to the African household. On this depends the African ability to buy books, records and periodicals or to attend theatres and cinemas. Wealth or poverty may well determine the cultural forms he uses[3] and their content.[4] This income varies considerably[5] and is higher in the urban townships than in agricultural areas. Africans in the professions could afford to set aside more for cultural activities than those who were not. But they represent a small fraction of the African population. One hint at the effect that income could have on culture in the townships is shown by the percentage of African families who were receiving an income lower than the estimated minimum living cost. In 1969 the Johannesburg Municipality estimated this to be 68 per cent in the urban township of Soweto.[6]

The urban areas have been a meeting ground for members of various tribal groups and urbanized Africans have been, in the main, less

---

1. The Deputy Chairman of the Bantu Affairs had stated that every family removed from 'Black Spots' was supplied a free food ration for three days.
2. 'We cannot oppose the removal itself, since it is provided for by law. What we are campaigning for is that the law be carried out with more consideration for the people it affects. There are no houses built and the people will have to live in tents. There is one school up to window level and we have gained no clear information about medical and food supplies. . . . Before God how can you bear the responsibility?'—*Star* (Johannesburg), 29 January 1968; *Sunday Times* (Johannesburg) 20 January 1968.
3. For an interpretation of the function of South African jazz, see M. E. Mphahlele, 'Negro Culture in a Multi-Racial Society in Africa' in: *Second Congress of Negro Writers and Artists, Rome, 26 March to 1 April 1959*, Paris, Présence Africaine, May 1959.
4. See Chapter 4, 'Literature', below.
5. See 'Introduction', Tables 3-5, page 27-28, for some comparative figures for monthly cash income.
6. *A Survey of Race Relations . . . 1969*, p. 82-3.

conservative than those who live on the reserves. But even in these 'Bantu homelands' the government's policy of 'separate development' poses important problems. It is based on the assumption that a government-backed chief, salaried by the government and easily dismissed by the government, will necessarily ensure that government policy is applied, and that the system of 'chiefs' will guarantee traditionalism and separate development and ensure white superiority.[1] There are certain trends to support this idea. The reaction in some African quarters to white rule has been to emphasize the traditional aspects (including chiefdom) of African life as opposed to the culture of the whites, and to withdraw from a white world which rejects the African into African traditional society. But there are also other trends in the system which may, in the long run, prove to be more important. Even under the system of salaried government-appointed chiefs, a chief may well find that, in putting into force unpopular government decrees, he forfeits the trust of his own people. On the other hand, the government may find a popular chief with a strong following difficult to dislodge. Neither are 'chiefs' a guarantee of traditionalism, nor is the system a guarantee against a more comprehensive African nationalism.[2]

White South Africans

'At an early date, the European, so far removed from his maternal culture, constructed a defensive wall around his intimate life, and from that time to this he had tried to ensure his own survival in these alien and unknown surroundings.'[3]

The white population is not an integrated group. Afrikaners are mainly of Dutch ancestry with some Huguenot stock. English-speaking South Africans are mainly of British origin. There has been

---

1. 'However, as the Bantu are introduced into non-Bantu areas and become more and more detribalized and Westernized, the European will be confronted with greater problems in regard to the maintenance of his position of authority.—*The Tomlinson Report* . . ., op. cit., p. 17.
2. In 1963, of the three most prominent chiefs in the Transkei, Chief Matanzima, who supports the government's apartheid policy, was reported in the press as having said that the 'Britishers' knew that the white man had no claim to the land between the Fish River and Zululand.
     Paramount Chief Victor Poto, also of the Transkei, opposed the system whereby chiefs would automatically become members of the Legislative Assembly and wished all members of the Transkei Assembly to be elected on a democratic basis. Paramount Chief Sabata Dalindyebo was quoted as saying that (we) 'seek freedom from laws which separate us from our fellow South Africans. We seek a State in which the colour of a man's skin plays no part in his civic rights . . . in which White and Black can live and work together in mutual respect'.—*A Survey of Race Relations 1963*, p. 90, 91.
3. *The Tomlinson Report* . . ., op. cit., p. 116.

a history of conflict between these two groups, erupting in the Great Trek[1] and more recently in the Boer War (the British appellation) or Die Engelse Oorlog (The English War, the Afrikaans term).

In 1904, half the white population lived in rural areas; by 1960, 84 per cent of the white population was classified as urban.[2] The most important pull of whites to the towns was caused, as in the case of the Africans, by the industries, and particularly mining, which offered more lucrative conditions than agriculture, as well as by the increase of commercial farming which made it more economic to employ African labour-tenants than whites. The mining industry was mainly financed by overseas British capital, and the need for skilled labour was mainly met by immigration of overseas miners from Britain, and was supplemented by local South African whites. Unskilled labour was provided by Africans both from within South Africa and from neighbouring territories.

The poor whites, coming from rural districts were, like the non-whites, unskilled. Some of them from the more remote areas were unaccustomed to cash wages and illiterate. They were therefore unable to compete with the skilled white labour and were forced to accept unskilled work, which they considered 'Kaffir' work.[3] A high percentage of these unskilled white workers coming in from the rural countryside were Afrikaners, and competition with Africans on the labour market intensified their desire to maintain their traditional social distance from the Africans, whom they now met, not within the semi-feudal relationship of the farms, but in urban industrialized conditions.

The Natives' Land Act of 1913 had been the reaction of whites to the land problem. It guaranteed white supremacy in land ownership. Apartheid is partly the reaction of whites to the problems of urbanization and industrialization.

'The policy of apartheid ... is a direct reaction to the new conditions arising from industrialization. It was industrialization, the growth of towns associated with it and the movement of Africans to meet the

1. Something like 10,000 men, women and children (mainly Afrikaners) trekked northwards from Cape Colony during the decade 1836 to 1846 as a protest against British rule, the suppression of their language and institutions, and the liberation of the slaves.—Leo Marquard, *The Peoples and Policies of South Africa*, p. 10, London, Cape Town and New York, Oxford University Press, 1962. However, the Voortrekkers only represented a small fraction of the Afrikaner people, a large number stayed behind.—T. R. H. Davenport, *The Afrikaner Bond, 1880-1911*, p. 1, Cape Town, London and New York, Oxford University Press, 1966.
2. Van der Horst, op. cit., p. 108, 109.
3. 'Kaffir': derogatory term for African.

labour needs of the expanding towns and industries, which led to the enunciation of this policy as a political doctrine and to the attempt to impose separation between White and Black in all spheres.'[1]

There is one aspect of Afrikaner society which needs further explanation: the stress placed on the preservation of the Afrikaner's cultural heritage. The British had dominated not only the economic scene but the cultural and political situation. By 1870 the use of Dutch in secondary schools had practically disappeared. In the Cape, English had become the medium for church services even in the Groote Kerk. English had been substituted for Dutch in the legislative councils, in the civil service and the courts. Moreover the Afrikaner as early as 1880 saw the possibility of an extension of the franchise to include non-whites as working in the interests of British influence since the Coloureds and the Africans who could vote had voted against Afrikaner candidates in elections. In 1881 the newspaper *Port Elizabeth Telegraph* stated:

'We have continually expressed our conviction that if the Afrikaner Bond is to be well beaten it will have to be done by the assistance of the Black vote.'[2]

The non-white vote therefore was suspected of being the political key for the maintenance of British influence in a country where the Afrikaners outnumbered the British two to one.

The problems of industrialization on the one hand, and the determination of the Afrikaner to obtain political dominance on the other became a struggle both against the British and against the Africans. The cultural nationalism of Afrikaner society was fed by both. Apparent in 1868, it was to become a real political force by the present day.

And yet it needs to be emphasized that the Afrikaner nationalists were sometimes also liberals, according to the definition given to that

1. Van der Horst, op. cit., p. 102.
   The Natives' Land Act No. 27 of 1913 was the first law embodying the principle of territorial segregation and segregation between Africans and whites. It listed a number of 'Native Areas' and prohibited whites, without permission from the Governor-General, from acquiring land in these areas. It also prohibited Africans without consent from the Governor-General from acquiring land or interest in land outside the scheduled 'Native Areas'. By the Native Trust and Land Act, 1936, additional land was 'released' to Africans, and the South African Native Trust was set up which could acquire land in African areas.
2. Davenport, op. cit., p. 120.

erm in their age. Among them was Hofmeeyer, who had described
as an Afrikaner

everyone who, having settled in this country, wants to stay here
to help to promote our common interests, and associate with the
inhabitants as members of one family. That is surely wide enough;
it is neither narrow nor exclusive.'[1]

Within the white group, the Afrikaner society was, until the recent
emergence of *verligte* and *verkrampte* groups, considered by outsiders
as a closely knit monolithic society. Power was shared by the Church,
the Broederbond,[2] the Federation of Afrikaner Cultural Societies and
the intellectuals, and politically expressed by the National Party.

The Broederbond, founded in 1918, aims at the 'attainment of
a healthy and progressive unanimity amongst Afrikaners who strive
for the welfare of the Afrikaner people'. Their activities include the
study of the attitudes of whites towards non-whites, and the study
of 'practical action to propagate good relations between the Whites
and the non-Whites'.

The Broederbond is an organization of consultative groups
spread over the country with a limited membership, selected to ensure
that all sectors of activities are represented. Membership is restricted
to Afrikaans-speaking white males over the age of 25 years who are
professing members of one of the three Afrikaner Churches. The
new candidate is reminded at his initiation that 'the members of the
Afrikaner-Broederbond are mission-conscious Afrikaners who desire
to represent and serve the best that is in one nation'; the names
of members and all proceedings of the Bond are strictly confidential.[3]

In 1964, a commission of the Nederduitsch Hervormde Kerk
declared that the Broederbond believe that the Afrikaner people
were a race chosen by God, that the Broederbond strove to arouse
national consciousness in the Afrikaner and to promote their interests by ensuring that the Afrikaners were given preference in the
economic and professional life of the country.[4]

1. ibid., p. 327.
2. This should not be confused with the Afrikaner Bond, the political party which was a forerunner
   of the National Party.
3. South African Government, *Report of the Commission of Enquiry into Secret Organizations,
   1965* (R.P. No. 20). This commission was set up by the government to inquire into the Bond and
   other secret organizations and found the Bond not guilty of any conduct mentioned in the committee's terms of reference. The membership of the Bond was 6,768 in November 1964.
4. *A Survey of Race Relations . . . 1964*, op. cit., p. 21.

While the Broederbond is an élite originating from many spheres, the South African Bureau of Racial Affairs (SABRA) represents Afrikaner intellectual thinking on racial relations only. Founded in 1948, it was a body for the study of race relations in line with the principles of the programme of the Broederbond. Its aim was to encourage and promote separate development of the white and non-white communities in South Africa and to safeguard the interests of both.[1] Some of its members have developed the most complete and radical doctrine of 'total apartheid'. For these it would be immoral to accept Africans as permanent residents in white areas by refusing them political and social rights. Therefore a national home for the Africans must be found; thus SABRA in the past has suggested that the native reserves should be joined with Lesotho, Swaziland and Botswana—the African share of the total area would be 45 per cent. Moreover the division of land between African and European should be treated as a 'Southern African' problem.[2]

Some of the SABRA intellectuals have criticized heavily the implementation of official policy, either because of specific measures taken against the non-white population, or because of what they consider to be the whittling away of apartheid in favour of a policy of convenience which permits the recruitment of Africans into white South Africa because their labour is needed.

Afrikaner intellectuals do not all support official policy and among those who do there are some who consider apartheid as being compatible with a just sharing of South Africa's wealth between the various ethnic groups. Afrikaners from the southern provinces of South Africa do not necessarily agree with the more conservative northern Afrikaner. In spite of these contradictions, Afrikaners are united by a strong emotional bond.

The English-speaking South Africans are a less coherent group than the Afrikaners. Like the Afrikaners their roots are in South Africa, but they are more divided politically—some supporting the National Party, some the United Party, some the Progressive Party and others

---

1. *World of Learning, 1965-66*, London, Europa Publications, 1965, cf. *A Survey of Race Relations . . . 1961*, p. 79 ff. and *A Survey of Race Relations . . . 1964*, p. 11, 19.
2. 'SABRA: Integration or Separate Development', here quoted from Gwendolen M. Carter, *The Politics of Inequality in South Africa since 1948*, 2nd ed., p. 269, London, Thames & Hudson, 1959. 'The Bureau . . . adopted a course which was directly opposed to trends of thought which denied the respective Bantu peoples of Southern Africa their own national character and right of existence in their respective national territories.'—*Bantu* (Pretoria), May 1969, p. 21.

had supported the Liberal Party before it dissolved. They control the industrial capital of the country to a larger extent than the Afrikaner, and are more fully urbanized. Liberal and radical movements, which do exist in the Afrikaner society, have always existed to a more pronounced extent among English-speaking South Africans.

But there are also conservative elements which are close to orthodox Afrikaner thought on questions of race and support the government's policy of apartheid.[1] The liberal strand in English-speaking South Africans is illustrated at present by the Black Sash—originally an organization of women voters—which in 1963 opened its membership to all women in South Africa, regardless of race. It then issued a statement that 'a white electorate bears the guilt for the discriminatory laws passed in their name'.[2] It has demonstrated repeatedly against aspects of the government's policy.

With the Institute of Race Relations it runs an advice office at Athlone, Cape Town, staffed by voluntary workers to help Africans who fall victims to the numerous apartheid laws and regulations.

The English group is considered as 'British' in heritage but it includes immigrants who may not be of English parentage, but who are English-speaking and urbanized and who find themselves more easily acceptable among the 'English' group than among the more tightly knit Afrikaners. The size and importance of the immigrant section is growing with the government's policy of increasing white immigration. As it grows the traditional image of the liberal, economically secure industrialist as the typical white English South African is also changing. The new immigrant may come from Britain, or the British Commonwealth, he is now as likely to come from Southern Europe, to be Catholic, to come from a poorer background than the longer-established South African families. He may be an immigrant coming from other African countries, from the Portuguese colonies, from the Congo and occasionally from Rhodesia. The influence of white South Africans who are 'refugees' from countries that have recently become independent should not be underestimated. To white South Africans they serve as a symbol of what they feel could happen under black rule. Their presence serves to justify apartheid as the only hope of preserving order as contrasted to the imagined disorder of independence.

1. It was estimated that about one-sixth of the Nationalist Party's members in Natal were, in 1965, English-speaking.—*A Survey of Race Relations . . . 1965*, p. 3.
2. *A Survey of Race Relations . . . 1963*, p. 10.

They are an effective counter to the liberal English-speaking South Africans. These find themselves isolated at home, unable to influence policy matters—even in 'petty' apartheid—by traditional ways of dissent.

Coloureds

The Coloureds make up approximately 10 per cent of the total South African population, numbering in 1965 about 1,742,000. The group has been formed by a mixture of white, African (mainly Hottentot) and Asian (mainly Malay) elements. Although they are part of the non-white group, their relationship with the whites has been almost completely confined to the towns and never went as far in the subservience and dependence which is part of the African life on the farms.[1]

In 1960, 68 per cent of the Coloureds lived in urban districts, compared with 84 per cent of the whites and 32 per cent of the Africans.[2] They occupied an intermediate position between Europeans and Africans. Trade unions which had Coloured and white or Asian and white membership were recognized for the purpose of collective bargaining, unlike African trade unions. The Coloureds supplied some of the skilled artisan labour and held many of the clerical jobs, and they were not barred from intermarriage with whites until the Mixed Marriages Act of 1949. Their culture was hardly distinctive from the whites' and was close to the Afrikaners'. The highest percentage of Coloureds belonging to a Christian religion belong to the Dutch Reformed Church. Most of them speak Afrikaans; some had 'passed' into the white group; they had no homelands to which they could retire,[3] and no traditional systems to which they could withdraw. Psychologically, the present government policy of more rigid separation hit the Coloureds particularly.

'With all the love of which I am capable as a Christian [wrote Adam Small, the Coloured writer] and of which my fellow Afrikaners should be capable (yes, I say my fellow Afrikaners) I must permit myself to repeat . . . that the brown people are not merely concerned about bread and butter affairs, and that note must be

---

1. Van der Horst, op. cit., p. 125.
2. ibid., p. 209.
3. There are Coloured reservations and mission stations, scattered areas on the Northern and Western Cape, but the population there is only 31,106.

:aken, because Christ demands it of us, of the diabolical humiliations
ɔf this spirit which these people of ours have to endure.'[1]

The dissatisfaction about the situation of the Coloureds, even in
Afrikaner circles, is characterized by the editorial reply in *Die Burger*:

'No, Mr. Small, dry your tears, let me and my children weep for we
shall have to pluck the bitter fruit of these things . . . it is we who
supply the fuel that stokes the cauldron of the Coloured peoples'
aspirations and then our Government comes along and sits on the
lid.'[2]

The present policy of the government, as far as the territorial separation of Coloureds from whites is concerned, is to promote, and re-
plan where necessary, Coloured reserves, to set up Coloured villages in
white farming areas in an endeavour to promote the use of Coloured
rather than of African labour in the farms of the Western Cape[3]
and to move Coloureds from the centre of urban districts to the
outskirts. Eventually, the Coloureds were to be separate from the
whites, the Asians and the Africans, the latter themselves divided
into tribal groups.

The Prohibition of Improper Interference Act, the Separate Representation of Voters Amendment Act and the Coloured Persons
Representative Council Amendment Act removed Coloured representation in the House of Assembly and the Cape Provincial Council.

The first of these, the Prohibition of Improper Interference Act,
prohibited 'mixed' political parties. Henceforth political parties were
to be racially based, nor were parties holding the same views but
racially separate to be deliberately created. The effect of this was to
remove the possibility of a Coloured base for the Liberal and Progressive Parties.[4]

The Separate Representation of Voters Amendment Act and the
Coloured Persons Representative Council Amendment Act No. 52
of 1958 were designed to remove Coloured voters from the common
roll.

Instead, a 'Coloured Persons Representative Council' was instituted. It consists of forty elected members and twenty nominated

1. *Die Burger*, 11 July 1961.
2. ibid., 12 July 1961.
3. *A Survey of Race Relations . . . 1963*, p. 152, 153.
4. The Liberal Party dissolved itself as a result of this: more than half of its 2,500 members were
   non-white. The Progressive Party decided with protest to confine its membership to whites.

members, and the chairman of the council's excutive is designated by the State President, the other four members of the executive being elected.

No proposed law may be introduced except with the approval of the Minister of Coloured Affairs after consultation with the Minister of Finance. The council may prepare estimates of expenditure, but these require the approval of the Minister of Coloured Affairs in consultation with the Minister of Finance.

To what extent the Coloured group could choose their own representatives was illustrated after the first election. In this the Labour Party led by Mr. D. Arendse won a clear majority.[1] The Labour Party stands for one-man-one-vote and direct parliamentary representation for all South Africans regardless of race. The Coloured Persons Representative Council Act had, however, made provision for twenty members to be nominated by the government. Thirteen of these were nominated from among the Federal Coloured People's Party candidates defeated at the polls.

The Federal Party endorses separate development, and co-operation with the South African Government, although they also ask for eventual equality with whites. They had gained only eleven seats, the nominations brought their number to twenty-four, of which thirteen had been rejected in the election by the Coloured community.

To these twenty-four should be added the seat won by the Republican Party and that won by the Nationalist Party, both of which support some degree of 'parallel development'. Even without the votes of the seven other nominated members, the Government had ensured at least parity between Coloured representatives supporting its policy and those opposed to it. This is in direct contradiction to the wishes of the Coloureds as shown by the voting results.

In order to create some territorial base for the Coloured group a series of measures were taken. The influx of African labour to the Western Cape was stopped. Africans were to be displaced by Coloureds.

In addition many areas have been declared Coloured under the Group Areas Act, and certain Coloured municipalities in the Transvaal (Johannesburg, Klerksdorp and Roodeport) were reported to be enforcing a residential permit system in Coloured townships and charging a fee of registration. In order to exercise control the townships were sometimes raided by night.[2] This would seem to be partly for

1. Twenty-six of the forty elected seats.
2. *A Survey of Race Relations . . . 1968*, p. 195.

he purpose of ensuring that Africans were not living in Coloured ownships.[1]

Coloured people in the Transvaal were to be resettled on a regional basis, and where Coloured areas exist outside of the areas set aside or Coloured settlement, development there was to be discontinued and the Coloured communities encouraged to settle at Klerksdorp, Potchefstroom, Middelburg, Witbank and Standerton.

In 1967 there were 26,700 Coloured families on waiting lists for housing.[2]

One of the results of the defects in Coloured education has been he number of untrained Coloureds. In 1967 the government passed he Training Centres for Coloured Cadets Act. This was designed to cope with the unemployment situation among Coloureds under 20 and, while most of them were not guilty of an offence, to prevent hem from 'lapsing into delinquency'.[3]

The Act provided for compulsory registration of Coloured youths in their eighteenth year, exemptions being given to those who were studying or doing productive work. The 'cadets' would be trained for any kind of employment' and during the 'training' could be called upon to perform any kind of work. Strict disciplinary provisions are included. A cadet who fails to comply with regulations may be brought by his principal before a magistrate's court and fined, imprisoned or confined to a training camp. There was a fear in some quarters that the reason for the Act was an attempt to substitute Coloured for African unskilled or semi-skilled labour in the Western Cape and was an attempt to exercise discipline through the use of criminal sanctions.[4]

Some of the provisions of the Act would seem to support this fear: classification for training by aptitude tests, apprenticeship to an 'appropriate employer', training of cadets who had not been streamed in scholastic training or who had failed to satisfy their employer, so as to perform 'useful labour' such as construction work.

1. 'More than 100 policemen, reservists and officials of the Bantu Administration moved in on the Coloured shanty town, Jafta's Farm, near Muizenberg in a pre-dawn raid yesterday and detained the entire African community including women and children . . . 77 Africans were eventually detained.'—*Cape Argus*, 16 June 1969.
2. *House of Assembly Debates (Hansard)*, Vol. 2, 31 January 1967, Cols. 377-8, quoted here from *A Survey of Race Relations . . . 1967*, p. 195-6.
3. *House of Assembly Debates (Hansard)*, Vol. 5, Cols. 1553-8; Vol. 7, Cols. 2550-8, 2594, 2618, 2638, 2691-2.
4. See the report of the press statement given by the Director of the Institute of Race Relations quoted in *A Survey of Race Relations . . . 1967*, (RR.43/67).

Indians

Indians were also granted their own council, separate from the Coloureds.

The South African Indian Council Act No. 31 of 1968 provided for the creation of a statutory council of not more than twenty-five Indians appointed by the Minister of Indian Affairs. There were no elected members although it was promised that the council would be elected in the future. The minister explained that electoral rolls were at present difficult to compile until resettlement in Group Areas had reached a more advanced stage.[1]

Group Areas have been proclaimed for Indians. In Johannesburg Lenasia, with an Indian population estimated at 30,000, was to be the only Indian Group Area, although another area is under consideration. Lenasia is twenty miles away from central Johannesburg—and the Indians are a trading community. Transport costs R.6 per month and for the poorer members of the community would represent a high proportion of their income. Moreover the only hospital they could go to was twenty-five miles away and schools were overcrowded even without the influx from other areas.

The proclamation of Lenasia as an 'Indian Area' accompanied the proclamation of Johannesburg's Diagonal Street as a white area. This was an area of 310 Indian businesses, which would have to be absorbed in Lenasia, or the Indians would lose their livelihoods. In Cato Minor the Indians were also forced to move.

The resettlement of Indians meant that there was compulsory selling of their businesses. These were sold to individual whites or white companies at lower than market prices and resold at a considerable profit.[2]

By mid-1966 it was estimated that 6,146 Indian families, consisting of about 41,000 people who were previously living in proclaimed or controlled areas, had been resettled in municipal housing schemes, another 13,000 families (86,000 people) were living in 'incorrect'

---

1. *House of Assembly Debates (Hansard)*, Vol. 4, 26 February 1968, Cols. 1124-9; *Star* (Johannesburg), 2 March 1968; *Sunday Times* (Johannesburg), 7 and 21 April 1968; *Progress* (Johannesburg), August 1967.
2. In one case the Indian selling price was R.73,000 in 1966, resale by the white company was R.453,000 in 1968.—*Sunday Times* (Johannesburg), 15 December 1968.
   See also profits on resale of properties in Rustenburg: *Sunday Times* (Johannesburg), 22 December 1968, and *Star* (Johannesburg), 22 December 1968.

Group Areas, and approximately 60,000 people were living in areas which had not yet been allocated to a racial group.[1]

3   Religion

Seventy-two per cent of all South Africans and 94 per cent of all white South Africans are Christians. While other religions will be mentioned in this chapter, the role which the Christian Church plays under the system of apartheid will be specifically examined.[2]

The doctrinal approach of the Dutch Reformed Churches in South Africa to race relations was that the Dutch Reformed Church 'could not associate itself unreservedly with the general cry for equality and unity in the world today. . . . It is mostly a surrogate unity and brotherhood, that men seek to realize without Christ in a world disrupted by sin. . . . The unity of man already exists in Christ, and is a supernatural organic unity. . . . One of the factors causing the imperfect realization of the existing unity in Christ is racial contrasts and racial tensions, in South Africa as in the rest of the world'.[3]

In April 1950 a conference of Dutch Reformed Churches was held at Bloemfontein. The conference was an attempt to define the Church's policy towards the African. The basic principle being discussed was apartheid, which was defined as a way which seeks to lead each section of the people in the clearest and quickest way to its own destination

1. *A Survey of Race Relations . . . 1967*, p. 205.
2. See Lesley Cawood, *The Churches and Race Relations in South Africa*, p. 6-7, Johannesburg, South African Institute of Race Relations, 1964.
3. Dutch Reformed Churches of South Africa, *Statement on Race Relations*, No. 1, November 1960, p. 7-8, Transvaal, Natal, Johannesburg, Information Bureau of the Dutch Reformed Church.

under the gracious providence of God.[1] The only way in which the permanent subordination of one group to another could be avoided was by total separation; the native reserves were to be converted into true 'Bantu homelands' with full opportunity for development and self-government and the replacing of the African in the European industrial system.[2]

After the riots at Sharpeville and Langa in March 1960, nine leading ministers of the Nederduitse Gereformeerde Kerk issued a statement, which, after protesting at the 'continuous besmirching of our country, people and Church by untrue and slanted information', and declaring that the condemnations of South Africa 'do not always spring from Christian responsibility but show signs of social humanism and of the hysterical efforts of the West to overbid the East for the favour of the non-Whites of Africa for the sake of the ideological slogan of self-determination', went on to say:

'The Nederduitse Gereformeerde Kerk has made it clear by its policy and by synod statements in the past that it can approve of independent, distinctive development, provided that it is carried out in a just and honourable way, without impairing or offending human dignity. The Church has also accepted that this policy, especially in its initial stages, would necessarily cause a certain amount of disruption and personal hardship, for example, in connection with the clearing of slums. The whole pass system must be seen in this light.'[3]

The nine ministers issuing this statement then approved of the principles of the policy of apartheid, but they also called for an improvement of the wage structure for Africans, and asked that non-whites be treated by whites in a more dignified manner so as not to reap a harvest of hate and that 'responsible and law-abiding' non-whites should not be 'misled by the false promises of agitators who are not concerned about the utmost good of the non-Whites . . .'.[4]

---

1. Here quoted from Dr. W. A. Visser'T Hooft, *Visit to the S.A. Churches: A report to the Central Committee of the World Council of Churches on a Visit to the S.A. Churches in April and May 1952*, p. 17.
2. ibid.
3. Statement on the Riots in South Africa. Signed by the Revs. Dr. A. J. van der Merve, P. S. Z. Coetzee, A. M. Meiring, C. B. Brink, A. G. E. van Velden, Dr. J. D. Vorster, W. A. Landman, Dr. F. E. O'B Geldenhuys and S. B. Loots. In: Dutch Reformed Churches of South Africa, *Statement on Race Relations*, No. 1, November 1960, p. 12-14. Transvaal, Natal, Johannesburg, Information Bureau of the Dutch Reformed Church, 1960.
4. ibid.

In December 1960, as result of an initiative on the part of the Anglican Archbishop of Cape Town—who had publicly repudiated compulsory segregation—the World Council of Churches sent a six-man delegation to consult with representatives of its eight member Churches[1] at the Cottesloe residence of the University of the Witwatersrand. Five of the Churches sent interracial delegations.[2] A statement reflecting the consensus of opinion was drawn up, each paragraph was voted on separately and an 80 per cent vote in favour was required before a paragraph was accepted—thus ensuring that the paragraph in question was passed by some members of each language and racial group.[3]

The report, known as the Cottesloe Consultation Report, stated that while being united in rejecting all unjust discrimination, widely divergent views were held on the basic issues of apartheid. Nevertheless it was possible to make certain affirmations concerning human needs and justice as they affected the races of South Africa: no one who believed in Jesus Christ should be excluded from any church on the grounds of colour or race; adequate facilities should be provided for non-white people to worship in urban areas as well as in segregated townships, there should be more effective consultation between the government and the leaders accepted by the non-white people, there were no scriptural grounds for the prohibition of mixed marriages, although certain legal, social and cultural factors might make such marriages inadvisable. It was pointed out that migrant labour had a disintegrating effect on African family life, that the vast majority of non-white people received wages which were below the generally accepted minimum standard for healthy living, that the job reservation system should give way to a more equitable method of employment, that the right to own land where one was domiciled and the right to participate in the government of the country was part of the dignity of all adult men.[4]

The Nederduitse Gereformeerde Kerk of the Transvaal and the Cape issued simultaneously another statement which said that a policy of differentiation could be defended from the Christian point of view and provided the only realistic solution to the problems of

1. Church of the Province of South Africa, the Nederduitse Gereformeerde Kerk of the Transvaal, the Methodist Church, the Presbyterian Church, the Congregational Union, the Bantu Presbyterian Church, the Nederduitse Gereformeerde Kerk of the Cape, the Nederduitsch Hervormde Kerk of Africa.
2. Cawood, op. cit., p. 131-2.
3. ibid.
4. ibid., p. 132-3.

race relations. The Nederduitsch Hervormde Kerk of Africa next day issued a press statement, in which they dissociated themselves from the resolutions passed and reaffirmed their faith in racial separation in the belief that the ideals of Christianity would best be served in that way.[1]

Opposition to the Cottesloe report continued to grow. During March 1961, the Nederduitsch Hervormde Kerk synod met and decided by 487 votes to 13 to withdraw from membership of the World Council of Churches, which it considered was hindering its work among non-whites.[2]

The Transvaal synod of the Nederduitse Gereformeerde Kerk, meeting in April 1961, also decided to withdraw from membership of the World Council of Churches, since the Cottesloe resolutions were at variance with the policy of the Church and were embarrassing to the government. In October the Cape Nederduitse Gereformeerde Kerk synod decided by a large majority to reject the Cottesloe report as 'undermining the policy of separate development'; the synod also decided to leave the World Council of Churches, but to continue to correspond with it.[3]

Individual members of the Dutch Reformed Churches continued to question South African racial attitudes. In November 1960, eleven leading theologians of the Nederduitse Gereformeerde Kerk, the Nederduitsch Hervormde Kerk and the Gereformeerde Kerk published a book, *Vertraagde Aksie*, calling for a new outlook on South African racial attitudes. This resulted in the heresy trial of Professor Geyser, one of the authors of the book, before the Synodical Commission of the Hervormde Kerk in December 1961; he was found guilty on one of three charges of heresy. He decided to contest the findings in the court of law, but an agreement was reached outside of the court (in 1963) and he was reinstated as a minister of the Church.[1]

In August 1963, the Christian Institute of Southern Africa was established. It is interracial and interdenominational. The director of the institute is the Rev. C. F. Beyers Naudé who had been elected moderator of the Southern Transvaal synod of the Nederduitse Kerk, had defended the Cottesloe resolutions and was editor of an inter-Church monthly magazine *Pro Veritate*.[5] The Christian Insti-

1. Cawood, op. cit., p. 133.
2. ibid., p. 134.
3. ibid., p. 134-5.
4. ibid., p. 135-6.
5. The editorial board of this magazine is both interdenominational and interracial.

tute came under attack from certain Dutch Reformed quarters. Professor Verhoef of Stellenbosch, for example, felt that members of the Christian Institute had made an error in judgement: the institute gave the impression that it understood the problems and the aspirations of the Africans better than the 'Boerekerk'.[1]

That apartheid is compatible with Christianity has been denied by many denominations in South Africa. The Methodist Conference in 1947 and 1948 stated clearly that every human being is entitled to fundamental human rights. In 1952 the conference rejected the policy of apartheid as being impracticable, contrary to the interests of all sections of the South African community and inconsistent with the highest Christian principles. This was reaffirmed in 1957, in 1958, in 1959 and in 1960.[2]

In 1960, the conference outlined a programme of education in race relations which included interracial study groups, pulpit exchanges and visits between Church organizations. Moreover the possibility was to be explored of setting up a pilot city-circuit scheme of a racially inclusive Church.[3]

In 1961 the conference resolved to proceed with the removal of racial demarcation from its official records and legislation. In 1963 the conference elected an African, the Rev. Seth Mokitimi, to be president.

The 1950 Provincial Synod of the Church of the Province of South Africa—a self-governing Church within the world-wide Anglican communion (the supreme legislature body within the Church) made the following statement on race relations:

'The Conference is convinced that discrimination between men on grounds of race alone is inconsistent with the principles of Christ's Religion . . . [we] believe that the effect of much recent legislation is likely to be the rigid division of the population into social classes

---

1. *Cape Times*, 9 May 1966. Professor A. D. Pont of the University of Pretoria was reported as saying in a speech to a student body: 'It is not far fetched to allege that the Christian Institute and the journal *Pro Veritate* are nothing but liberalist stepping stones from which propaganda which suits Communism admirably are carried into our churches.' In the Christian Institute's first annual report Mr. Naudé stated that certain Afrikaans-speaking members had felt obliged to resign because of pressure brought to bear on them. See *A Survey of Race Relations . . . 1964*, p. 12-13.
2. Cawood, op. cit., p. 50.
3. Methodist Church districts are divided into circuits and in South Africa these have been determined sometimes purely geographically, but sometimes racially.

with unequal rights, privileges and opportunities, and the relegation of the non-Europeans to a position of permanent inferiority, and for this reason condemns this legislation as inconsistent with the respect for human personality that should be characteristic of a Christian society. . . .'[1]

Several Anglican clergymen had made individual statements against the policy of the South African Government. Trevor Huddleston had protested particularly over the demolition of Sophia Town,[2] the Rt. Rev. Ambrose Reeves had been outspoken in his opposition to the government's policy[3] and had been deported in September 1960, the Rev. Michael Scott had been imprisoned for taking part in a non-violent campaign against segregation, had left South Africa to take the case of South-West Africa to the United Nations and was not readmitted to South Africa.[4] In addition, in 1963 several Anglican bishops in South Africa made statements condemning the apartheid policies of the government.[5] In 1963 the Minister of Foreign Affairs was reported as having said at a National Party meeting that the time had come to tell the bishops that it was not in the interests of their Church to intervene in South Africa's political issues.[6] The synod of bishops meeting in November 1963 issued this statement:

'In these circumstances, it seems necessary to the Bishops of the Church of the Province of South Africa, now meeting in Synod in Bloemfontein, to reaffirm their unanimity in proclaiming their conviction that the Church must openly and fearlessly condemn all that it believes to be evil and false in the social, political or economic life of any nation and, whenever the claims of obedience to the State and God are in conflict, it is to God that our obedience must be given.'[7]

In 1952, 1957, 1960 and 1962, the Catholic bishops of South Africa issued joint pastoral letters on the situation in South Africa. In 1957 the pastoral letter entitled 'Statement on Apartheid' condemned apartheid and went on to say:

1. Church of the Province of South Africa, *What my Church has Said.*
2. Trevor Huddleston, *Naught for Thy Comfort*, London, Macmillan, 1965.
3. See footnote 4 on page 38.
4. Michael Scott, *A Time to Speak*, London, Faber, 1958. See also Freda Troup, *In Face of Fear*, London, Faber, 1953.
5. Cawood, op. cit., p. 63.
6. Reported in the *Rand Daily Mail*, 1 November 1963. Here quoted from Cawood, op. cit., p. 63.
7. Reported in the *Rand Daily Mail*, 22 November 1963. Here quoted from Cawood, op. cit., p. 63.

'There must be a gradual change . . . but change must come, for otherwise our country faces a disastrous future. . . . This involves the elaboration of a sensible and just policy enabling any person, irrespective of race, to qualify for the enjoyment of full civil rights. . .'[1]

The pastoral letter of 1962 said in part: 'As Christian people we dare not remain silent and passive in the face of the injustices inflicted on members of the unprivileged racial groups. . . .'[2] In July 1966 the bishops, drawing conclusions from the Vatican Council's Pastoral Constitution on the Church in the Modern World, again denounced apartheid and all forms of discrimination which it engenders.[3]

In 1967 South African Lutheran pastors rejected apartheid, 'finding no support for such a teaching in the Holy Scripture'.[4]

In 1968 the debate sharpened. During that year the Rt. Rev. Edward Crowther, former Bishop of Kimberley, was deported.[5]

The Rev. Hans Haselbast, vice-rector of the Lutheran Theological College in Umpumulo, Natal, had his visa cancelled,[6] and the Rev. Basil Moore, past president of the University Christian Movement, had his passport withdrawn by the Secretary of the Interior.[6]

In 1968 the State African Council of Churches issued a 'Message to the People'. It said in parts:

'. . . In South Africa everyone is expected to believe that a man's racial identity is the most important thing about him . . . thus we are being taught that one racial identity is the final and all important determining factor in the lives of men. . . . This amounts to a denial of the central statements of the Gospel. It is opposed to the Christian understanding of the nature of men and community. It in practice severely restricts the ability of Christian brothers to serve and know each other, and even to give each other simple hospitality. It arbitrarily limits the ability of a person to obey the Gospel's command to love his neighbour as himself.'[7]

1. South African Catholic Bishops' Conference, *Statement on Apartheid*, p. 2. Issued by the plenary session of the conference, held in Pretoria, 2-6 July 1957.
2. South African Catholic Bishops' Conference, *Christ in Our World*, p. 7. Released by the General Secretariat of the Catholic Bishops' Conference, Pretoria, 1962.
3. Southern African Catholic Bishops' Conference, July 1966, released by the General Secretariat of the Catholic Bishops' Conference, Pretoria, 1966. See also *The Month at Unesco*, p. 42, Paris, International Catholic Co-ordinating Centre for Unesco, 1966.
4. *The Times* (London), 5 May 1967.
5. *Daily Express* (London), 14 January 1968.
6. *Sunday Times* (Johannesburg) 17 November 1968.
7. *Progress* (Johannesburg), October 1968. Also *Sunday Times* (Johannesburg), 22 September 1968. The Commission of the South African Council of Churches that drafted the report included members of the Church of the Province of South Africa, Presbyterian, Catholic, Methodist, Lutheran, Nederduitse Gereformeerde Kerk and the Nederduitsch Hervormde Kerk of Africa.

Not all churches supported this. All churches of the Dutch Reformed Church did not, and the Baptist Union issued a statement in which they said that much of the theological reasoning and some of the conclusions contained in the Message were inacceptable to them.[1]

By July 1971 some South African clergymen and leading laymen published an open letter to South Africa. This went considerably farther than former Church Statements: 'Making comparison between Nazi Germany and South Africa is painful for us, but such comparisons are infinitely more painful for those who suffer because they are true.'[2]

Since apartheid two great theological debates are being fought out in South Africa. The first, illustrated by the position taken by the bishops of the Church of the Province of South Africa, is an old one: the obedience which a Christian subject should give to a State which promulgates what are, in his opinion, intolerably evil laws and with it the right of his leaders to criticize these laws.

This argument was most clearly seen in the issuing of the Message and the government's reaction to it. For the writers the issue was the priority of obedience to God or obedience to the State, and in fact the Message ended with this question, while for the Prime Minister—himself a Christian—the calling of ministers of the Church 'demands of them that they preach the Gospel of Christ, the word of God and did not turn your pulpits into political platforms'.[3]

The second theological debate is primarily a debate of this century and, in its acute form, was initiated precisely by the system of apartheid in a country whose leaders were prominent Christians. It was the meaning to be given to racial equality and whether or not the doctrine of the brotherhood of all Christians presupposed a multi-racial Church. Within South Africa the lines drawn were principally between the Dutch Reformed Church, on the one hand, and the English-speaking Church, on the other. But even within these groupings the argument continued. Some theologians, including Geyser and Naudé and

1. *Star* (Johannesburg), 2 November 1968.
   The principles and substance of the Message have been endorsed by the Conference of Catholic Bishops, the Church of the Province of South Africa of the Evangelical Lutheran Church (South-Eastern Region). The Religious Society of Friends (Quakers) have endorsed the spirit in which the pamphlet has been drawn up. The Presbyterian Church of South Africa, the United Congregational Church of Southern Africa and the Methodist Church drew the attention of their ministers to the Message.—*A Survey of Race Relations . . . 1969*, p. 12.
2. *Guardian* (London), 19 July 1971.
3. In a speech made on 24 September 1968 at the opening of the Natal Congress of the Nationalist Party and again at Brakpan on 27 September. Quoted in *A Survey of Race Relations . . . 1968*, p. 22.

before them Marais and Keet,[1] within the Dutch Reformed Church, took theological positions not unlike those of the bishops of the English-speaking churches, and that in spite of the strong sanctions which could be imposed on them to conform to the main trend of thinking of the members of their congregations and of their synods. Within the English-speaking churches, too, there were some missionary leaders who advocated separatism for Africans.[2]

This debate was not confined to South Africa, it was part of the world-wide oecumenical debate of the 1950s and 1960s, although certainly by 1965 the idea of a multi-racial Church was accepted by most churches outside South Africa, and racial equality took on the meaning of multi-racialism, as opposed to racial separatism in the statements of major Christian religions.[3]

By 1970 many churches outside South Africa had moved farther than this and were considering helping directly groups discriminated against in their fight against racialism. This is illustrated by the decision of the World Council of Churches in July 1970 to give financial aid to the liberation movements of Southern Africa for assistance to refugees and for social work.

The Dutch Reformed Churches in South Africa had become increasingly isolated, not only by the withdrawal of some of their groups from the World Council of Churches, but by their theological assumptions on the question of race.

There are now nearly 2,000 recognized Christian denominations in South Africa, compared to 300 in 1925. Ninety per cent of these are 'Bantu sects', also called 'separatist' or 'independent'. The 1960 population census gives the total following of these churches as 2,188,303.[4] In Sowete the number of Africans belonging to these sects had doubled between 1962 and 1967 from 14 per cent to 28 per cent. They may be divided roughly into three types: (a) Ethiopians— churches which have seceded from white mission churches; (b)

1. Gwendolen M. Carter, *The Politics of Inequality in South Africa since 1948*, 2nd ed., p. 272-80. London, Thames & Hudson, 1959.
2. Dr. R. H. W. Shepherd of Lovedale quoted the example of the Bantu Presbyterian Church and wondered if the existence of African separatist sects did not point to needs and opportunities unmet in multi-racial churches. See B. G. M. Sundkler, *Bantu Prophets in South Africa*, 2nd ed., p. 303, London, Lutterworth Press, 1961.
3. The second Assembly of the World Council of Churches declared in part that: 'Segregation in all its forms is contrary to the Gospel, and is incompatible with the Christian doctrine of man and with the nature of the Church of Christ.' Here quoted from *The Future of South Africa: A Study by British Christians*, p. 91-2, published for the British Council of Churches by SCM Press, London, 1965.
4. 1960 population census. See also Cawood, op. cit., p. 139.

Zionist churches with an accent on healing, 'speaking with tongues and food taboos; and (c) African Messianic movements in which an African Messiah is supposed to have come to save the African people. All these groups, while holding many of the tenets of Christianity, nevertheless incorporate much of tribal African religion. Sundkler points to the importance of the Natives' Land Act of 1913 for the understanding of the growth of these separatist sects. After this, the desire for land and security produced the Zionist and Messianic myths, the theme of Moses leading his people to the promised land fitting in with the land hunger of the Africans.[1]

Under apartheid, the role of the separatist sects, with few exceptions, has been limited withdrawal from the world and accommodation to the State. The politically active African, if a Christian, is likely to be found in the other churches. There are various reasons for the political attitude of the separatists. One was the government recognition for these churches.

Church sites in urban areas may not be occupied by unrecognized churches.[2] The very atmosphere of the strong anti-white protest out of which these churches came into existence is conducive to a keeping apart from whites. Moreover chiefs have become important members of these churches, and these in return compete for the patronage of the chiefs who are themselves often part of the government system of 'Bantu homelands'.

The rise of 'separatist' churches can certainly not be considered as simply a factor of the recent policy of apartheid, but rather as an African reaction to a continuous process of discrimination going back over many years. However, under apartheid the very fact of legal apartness provides a social system in which the separatist churches are likely to flourish.

This section has not considered the effects of apartheid in other than Christian religions because of the difficulty of obtaining enough evidence as to what the situation actually is. One indication that the policy of apartheid may have a serious effect on religious practices outside of Christianity is the difficulties facing the Islamic community. Group Areas removals may rezone districts which include mosques as 'white'. But for Moslems the ground on which a mosque stands is holy and may not be used for anything but worship.

1. Sundkler, op. cit., p. 330.
2. ibid., p. 306. This order has been in effect since 31 December 1960.

4   Literature

The following are comments by South African writers on the situation of creative literature in their country.[1] First the African Ezekiel Mphahlele,[2] writing from Nairobi where he was then in exile:

I feel very gloomy about the situation as far as creative writing is concerned. . . . Our energies go into this conflict to such an extent that we don't have much left for creative work. One might ask, 'Why could this not be a spur towards creative writing". I think it is paralysing. As writers, we build up ready, stock responses which always come out in our writing. Also cultural work in South Africa is so fragmented. We are in two ghettoes, two different streams, and you can't get really dynamic art in this kind of society. You won't get a great White novel, I think, and you won't get a great Black novel until we become integrated. As soon as the White man has learned to realize that he is an African and no longer a European, he will then begin to write an African novel or an African poem. Now, he still feels as part of Europe.'[3]

1. Biographic and bibliographic data in this chapter have been collected from the following works:
   African-English Literature. A Short Survey and Anthology of Prose and Poetry up to 1965, edited by Anne Tibble, London, P. Owen, 1965.
   Das junge Afrika, Erzählungen junger afrikanischer Autoren, edited by Janheinz Jahn, Vienna, Munich and Basle, 1963.
   A Book of South African Verse, selected and introduced by Guy Butler, London, 1959.
   G. Dekker, *Afrikaanse Literatuurgeskiedenis*, 7th ed., Cape Town, 1963.
   Janheinz Jahn, *Muntu, Umrisse der neoafrikanischen Kultur*, Düsseldorf-Cologne, 1958.
   Poems from Black Africa, edited by Langston Hughes, Bloomington, Ind., Indiana University Press, 1963 (Unesco Collection of Contemporary Works).
   Schwarzer Orpheus, Moderne Dichtung afrikanischer Völker beider Hemisphären, selected poems translated into German by Janheinz Jahn, Munich, 1964.
   South African Stories, edited by David Wright, London, 1960.
2. Ezekiel Mphahlele, born in 1919 at Marabastad, an African township of Pretoria, was in his childhood a tribal herd boy. As a young man he worked on the magazine *Drum*, a picture publication devoted primarily to subjects of interest to the African population. Fleeing apartheid, Mphahlele and his wife and three children settled in East Africa, where he taught at the University of East Africa. His books include an autobiography, *Down Second Avenue* (1959), a volume of short stories, *The Living and the Dead*, and *The African Image* (1962). He now lives and teaches in the United States of America.
3. Topic No. 2, National Educational Television's African Writers Series.

Two white South African writers put across the English position in South Africa, one in prose, the other in verse. South African English poetry belongs to a 'linguistic, political and cultural minority . . .' writes Guy Butler.[1]

'Our small numbers and exposed position have prevented us from developing as strong a national sense as our cousins in other dominions. We speak a form of English which, I believe, shows fewer differences from standard English. . . . We lack cultural awareness and make a very half-hearted and ineffective contribution to political life. . . . But what market, what audience, can a scattered million be expected to provide for their writers? Our cultural capital is still London, with New York as alternative.'[2]

Anthony Delius[3] indulges more in satire than in apology:

> 'These million English are a vague communion
> Indifferent to leadership or goal,
> Their most accomplished children leave the Union.'[4]

The Afrikaner writer W. A. de Klerk[5] writes:

'What does an Afrikaans writer of the 1960s say to a fellow Afrikaans writer of the 1960s who has been isolated in his own statutory enclave? Who has reached a state of near hopelessness realizing that the more sharply defined legislation and general administrative measures become, the more nebulous things get. In fact, the whole situation . . . in South Africa bristles with ironies. . . . There was a time, not so long ago, when we, the Afrikaner, reluctantly took part in all the various festivals of the Empire. As a schoolchild I remember our receiving coronation medals and little Union Jacks to wave. These we took pleasure in destroying. After all, we were but second-class citizens of the great Anglo-Saxon world. Coloured children will be

---

1. *A Book of South African Verse*, op. cit., p. xvii ff. Guy Butler, one of the younger poets of South Africa, is professor of English at Rhodes University (Grahamstown, Cape Province).
2. In fact, literary periodicals do exist: *Contact* and *Contrast*, for example. The main periodical in the Afrikaans language, *Sestiger*, went out of print in 1965, when in an effort to avoid bankruptcy it was taken over by Voortrekker Press, whereupon the writing group refused to co-operate with the ideological demands of the new owners.
3. Anthony Delius, born in 1916 in Simonstown, South Africa, has published, *inter alia, An Unknown Border*, Cape Town, 1954.
4. From 'The Great Divide'; extracts are reproduced in *A Book of South African Verse*, op. cit., p. 135.
5. W. A. de Klerk, an Afrikaner, was born in 1917. He has published a number of dramas and novels from 1941 on. All are written in Afrikaans.

expected to take part in the *Fees*. They will have the flag and sing the *Stem*. They too will do it, largely, without enthusiasm. After all they are but second-class citizens of the great Afrikaner world.'[1]

African and Coloured writers

Three things stand out in the examination of African writing in South Africa: (a) the limited genre: almost totally the short story or the autobiography; (b) the protest nature of much of the writing; (c) the increasing tendency for South African Africans to write and to publish abroad.

How far are these three characteristics the result—direct or indirect—of the system of apartheid?

Ezekiel Mphahlele blames it on the African's environment:

'During the last twenty years the political, social climate of South Africa has been growing viciously difficult for a non-White to write in. It requires tremendous organization of one's mental and emotional faculties before one can write a poem or a novel or a play . . . [Africans] have to live from day to day. . . . The short story, therefore, serves as an urgent, immediate, intense concentrated form of unburdening yourself—and you must unburden yourself.'[2]

If one reason for the African short story is the social situation, another is the public for which the African writes. This is mainly an urban African public, only a minority of whom have had a secondary education.

If African writing draws part of its inspiration from the racy, colourful life of the urban townships, its readership is also to be found in those townships, a readership whose literary tastes are least informed, to whom excitement, romance, thrillers are the world of retreat from poverty. This audience is the audience for which *Drum*, the South African magazine deliberately aimed at Africans, catered. Short stories appearing in *Drum* were not expected to be intellectual, they were expected to be sentimental love stories, or hard-hitting detective stories. *Drum* was for a long while the most important outlet for African journalists in South Africa, and its short-story

1. *Cape Times*, 3 February 1966.
2. In: 'Post-War Literature in English by African Writers from South Africa: A Study of the Effects of Environment upon Literature', by Beruth Lindfors, published in *Phylon*, the Atlanta University review of race and culture, Vol. XXVII, spring 1966, p. 50-1.

competition encouraged short-story writing in English. In fact, one can almost speak of a '*Drum* school' of writing—and that writing would include names like Mphahlele, Modisane and Nakasa, all of whom, at some period or other, wrote for *Drum*. Short-story writing offered quick returns in terms of money, it could be combined easily with a journalistic career, there was a ready reading public, but it was a specialized public. On the whole the white periodicals (with the exception of anti-government political journals) were not anxious to publish African writers' works.

Another of the reasons for African writing was to 'unburden' oneself; the autobiography presents an acceptable method of doing so.

The biographical novels of South Africans like Jabavu, Abrahams and Modisane[1] are of particular interest; Jabavu's *Drawn in Colour* portrays the ambivalence that she felt within the African framework, her dislike and kinship with the Afrikaner, her mistrust for the English South African, her feeling of dismay at hearing that her sister had married an African she considered culturally inferior. Modisane pitilessly exposes the duality of his own manner before white South Africans, and black South Africans, the slow destruction of this personality symbolized by the destruction of Sophia Town, the acceptance of the death of part of himself as symbolized by the interment of his name, painted by mistake on his father's coffin. Biography is used, not simply as a method of re-creating a single life, but as a sharpened instrument to portray a social situation. It is this social situation which gives South African biography, and the near-biographical novels, its peculiar poignancy and its political significance. This has been summed up by Janheinz Jahn, speaking about Ezekiel Mphahlele's story *Down Second Avenue*:

'He treats his own life as a symbol of the situation in South Africa . . . because he tells the story without passion, almost without reproach, every experience becomes a paradigm, every personal oppression a general experience.'

The protest nature of much of South African writing stems as much

1. Bloke Modisane, born *c.* 1930, writer and actor, now living in England as a refugee. Noni Jabavu, African, born in South Africa in 1920, daughter of the South African linguist, the late D. D. T. Jabavu, came at 14 years of age to England for studies, later married an English film director. Several travels to South Africa, living in Uganda. Peter Abrahams, Coloured, born in Johannesburg in 1919, left South Africa in 1939, now living in Jamaica, teaches at the University of the West Indies, Kingston.

from the emotional experience of apartheid as from the publishing opportunities which this writing offers. In South Africa itself periodicals like *Fighting Talk*, *New Age* and *Africa South* (now all banned by the South African Government)[1] were primarily concerned with the political and social situation of the African under apartheid, and thus favoured literature which was critical of the social order. If *Drum* catered for the supposedly simple tastes of urban Africans, these publications catered for the political tastes of those who opposed apartheid. In addition, publishers abroad were interested mainly in African literature that was 'anti-apartheid'. Richard Rive points out that 'the only literature from the Republic which has any guarantee of selling abroad are works highly critical of the régime'.[2]

The limitations of protest writing are outlined by Lewis Nkosi:[3]

'For a black writer too much of his emotional response is absorbed into formulating his attitude towards apartheid or finding his place in the revolutionary struggle; no matter where he goes later on and no matter how bored he is with politics he cannot be free of the tragic burden of South Africa until that country has freed its 14,000,000 non-Whites. Yet there are times when a writer must suspect that his revolt against the system is too easy, even glib, predetermined rather than arrived at out of a singular personal anguish; and this revolt as far as literature is concerned, must result in the formulation of characters who are not only glib and standardized but whose only claim upon imagination is that they are caught in the apartheid mill. . . .'[4]

Some of this protest literature has been of high literary quality: one thinks immediately of Alex la Guma,[5] Denis Brutus or Richard Rive. Nevertheless, the theme of racial conflict, the problems raised by discrimination, and the theme of the effects of the philosophy and policy of apartheid narrow the creative field considerably.

There is a concern in some Afrikaner quarters that the African should produce his own literature in his own language. This is in

1. See Part IV, Chapter 2.
2. In: Lindfors, op. cit., p. 60.
3. Lewis Nkosi, born 1936 in Durban. Formerly on the editorial staff of *Drum* and of *Golden City Post* in Johannesburg. Exiled in 1960. In 1966 his collection of essays *Home and Exile* shared second prize with Ralph Ellison's *Shadow and Act* at the Dakar World Festival of the Negro Arts. He lives in London.
4. *Unesco Courier*, March 1967, p. 20, 21.
5. Alex la Guma, born *c.* 1925, Cape Town, Coloured, tried for treason in 1956.

line with the whole idea of the separate development of different peoples. The Literature Commission of the Continuation Committee of South African Churches in July 1959 invited eighty-nine writers in Bantu languages and a large number of other participants to a conference at Atteridgeville, Pretoria. The writers complained that they were forced to conceal the truth about society, to falsify attitudes and manners of speech if they were to find a publisher, in fact, the use of the vernacular confined them not only to language, but more important, to theme. It was significant that the writers represented were mainly authors of books used in schools and universities, none of them were African writers of a world reputation:

'There was scarcely a writer known to Whites, no Peter Abrahams, Ezekiel Mphahlele nor Can Temba, and the celebrated Africans that Whites have heard of—Vilakazi, Mqhayi, Mofolo, Plaatje, Jabavu —are all no more. The literary talent spotters would have been disappointed, for among the eighty-nine writers assembled, there were few whose names will ever be seen in the *London Magazine* or *Présence Africaine*.'[1]

Writers writing in African languages were faced with the fact that publishers, even when they chose to publish or not to publish on strictly economic terms, had to consider the small African reading audience, its poverty and the non-existence of a market outside South Africa. It was difficult to add to this the risk involved in publishing a controversial book which, besides catering to a small population, could be banned by the government if it was critical of the government. The injunction that African writers should produce manuscripts suitable for use in schools and should therefore deal neither with political nor with church conflicts[2] is the attitude not only of the publisher who agrees with apartheid, but also of the publisher who must be sure that he can sell the books he publishes.[3]

The widespread use of English as the language of most African South African writers and their critical attitude to mother tongue instruction within the apartheid system, which runs counter to the attitude of many linguistic groups in other countries, must be seen

1. Randolph Vigne, 'The Conference of African Writers, 1959', *South African Libraries*, Vol. 27, No. 2, October 1959, p. 33.
2. *Muntu*, English edition, translated from Janheinz Jahn, op. cit.
3. W. P. Kerr, manager, Longmans, Green and Co. Ltd., South and Central Africa, 'The British Publisher in South Africa', *South African Libraries*, Vol. 26, No. 3, January 1959, p. 78.

against the need to communicate to an audience larger than their own tribe, and in particular, their need to choose to a freer extent the subject-matter of their writings. It is difficult to see how any African writer could afford to ignore the social and political position in South Africa and still produce an adult book. Moreover, the factors which now mould African thought in South Africa, the experience from which he writes, are no longer confined to the experience of the rural countryside, nor to the historical traditions of his forefathers, but are part of a wider urban experience shared by Africans who, initially differing in tribal background, find themselves increasingly part of the same present-day situation, contemplating the same prospects for the future. Much of this situation is defined by apartheid itself, much of the common experience comes from the limitations imposed by the system of enforced separation.

Lewis Nkosi, Raymond Kueene, Ezekiel Mphahlele, Peter Abrahams, Alfred Hutchinson, Bloke Modisane—all well-known names in African writing—live outside South Africa. Alex la Guma is now in London. Denis Brutus left South Africa recently on a one-way exit permit after having been under house arrest. Richard Rive lives in South Africa, but publishes abroad. Nearly all the major works by African South African writers, writing in English, have been banned as 'indecent, objectionable, or obscene', or because they themselves have been banned.

Few new writers have emerged over the recent years, and fewer are likely to reach an international audience in the years to come. The government policy of mother-tongue instruction may leave Africans literate only in a Bantu language and the field of writing circumscribed both by language and by the political climate in the Republic.

English literature by white South Africans

In 1948, Alan Paton's[1] novel *Cry the Beloved Country* made an immediate impact and opened the way for the protest school of English-speaking writers which began to grow up in the 1950s. It also influenced African writers.

---

1. Alan Paton, born in Natal in 1903, has lived in Natal and in the Transvaal. Elected nationa chairman of the South African Liberal Party in 1956.

Professor N. P. Van Wyk Louw, the Afrikaner poet, criticized this group of writers illustrated by Nadine Gordimer[1] and Alan Paton

'The English South African writers have it easier than us Afrikaans writers. They simply touch on the race problems and offer solutions of a liberal or progressive nature keeping the door open to flit away to safety. . . .'[2]

Nadine Gordimer replied:

'During the past ten years, South Africa has lost many English-speaking writers and intellectuals generally, including the entire nucleus of the newly emergent Black African writers. . . . If I, or any other English-writing White South African, should leave my homeland, it would be for the same reason that those others have already done; not because they fear the Black man, but because they grow sick at heart with the lies, the cheatings, the intellectual sophistry . . . sick of the brutalities perpetrated by Whites in their name.'[3]

The choice as seen by the English-speaking writer who does not support apartheid, but nevertheless wants to live in South Africa, is illustrated by the positions taken by Athol Fugard[4]—the author of the play *The Blood Knot*—and by Alan Paton. In 1962, Athol Fugard explained that his plays would only be produced before non-segregated audiences, yet in 1965 *Hello and Goodbye* was presented at the Library Theatre to an all-white audience. Before each public performance there was a private viewing by a mixed audience. For this there was no publicity and no tickets sold. Three years before there were places where one could play to mixed audiences, now there was no longer a choice, permits were no longer given for mixed audiences.

'I exist in South Africa only on the basis of my profession as a playwright and in terms of what I can say. If I am silent, what am I? . . . An outsider who wants to protest can do so from a distance. I am in it here. . . . We have each to make a personal assessment of what is going to be most effective . . . speech under certain conditions or

1. Nadine Gordimer, born in Johannesburg before the war, went to Witwatersrand University. Her first novel was *The Lying Days*, published in 1953.
2. Republished in the *Sunday Times* (Johannesburg), 9 August 1964, from the literary periodical *Sestiger*.
3. *Sunday Times* (Johannesburg), 9 August 1964.
4. Athol Fugard's play *The Blood Knot* was shown in London in 1965 and enjoyed a long run in New York. In 1963 Athol Fugard founded an African theatre company in Port Elizabeth, Cape Town

silence. I believe speech is of more value. Paton has made the other choice. We respect each other. Moreover I think I have reached a stage where the horizon is tomorrow. . . . At the moment I think I can go on producing plays under segregation (even admitting some non-Whites to private readings). But eventually I may have to take a stand like Paton's. We are in a corner. And all we can do is dodge here and push there. And under it all there's a backwash of guilt.'[1]

Alan Paton, too, agreed that for a writer it was of great importance to be heard. In 1962 he was unable to attend the Edinburgh International Writers' Conference because his passport had been withdrawn by the South African Government.[2] He wrote to the conference instead, '. . . a writer, like an actor or a speaker or a musician has a passion to communicate, and that means he has a passion to be heard'.[3] However, Paton's choice was precisely to stop being heard in protest against the policy of his government.

Guy Butler reports that:

'Of the twenty-three poets who have emerged since the twenties, only four were not born in South Africa. Ten of them, however, have migrated, some in their teens, some in their twenties. Some no longer regard themselves as South Africans. Others return whenever they can.'

English South African writers, like African writers, are preoccupied with the South African situation of racial conflict. Of the two plays to reach London and New York in 1965, Athol Fugard's *The Blood Knot* and Alan Paton's *Sponono*,[4] one exploits the theme of 'passing for white' as played out by two brothers, one of whom happens to be white and the other Coloured, and the other the theme of the failure of communication or 'contact' between the two human beings who are kept divided in a double sense by the law which makes of one a delinquent, mainly by reason of his colour, and of the other an unforgiving functionary of and from a privileged group.

This is not meant to be an exhaustive survey of South African literature; not all South African writers protest and many of the problems

---

1. Interview by Lewis Sowden, *Rand Daily Mail*, 9 October 1965.
2. His passport has since been returned to him.
3. Address at a NUSAS (National Union of South African Students) Conference, University of Cape Town, published in the *Sunday Times* (Johannesburg), July 1965.
4. *Sponono* has never been played to segregated audiences in South Africa.

which face South African writers are shared to some extent with writers from other countries. For example, the preoccupation with the biographical form is not peculiarly South African. What is different in South Africa is the deliberate attempt to compartmentalize the people of South Africa. It is difficult to see how, under these conditions, the English South African writer can completely identify himself with a larger South Africa. The process by which an indigenous literature comes into being would seem to be retarded by a political process which keeps English South Africans as a group apart. This is not to say that within difficult social-political structures great art and great writing have not been produced, and certainly some of the writing coming out of South Africa draws its strength from the very nature of the South African present. A writer is part of the social situation; in South Africa he cannot remain isolated from the effects of the policy of apartheid. The restrictions of the system are bound to affect the content of the literature he produces, and partly to determine the audience for which he writes. For a dramatist the moral issues are even more immediate, for theatre is a public art, and playwrights in South Africa are faced with the choice of being heard mainly by a section of the public, racially determined by government regulation, or not to be heard at all.

Afrikaans literature

Afrikaans had become the language of the Afrikaner, different not only to the language spoken by the English, but different from the language spoken by the Dutch. It marked the Afrikaner off as a separate people, linked together not only by the saga of the trek, the tradition of the *laager*, but also by a language forged in Africa itself.

Afrikaner writers were understandably part of the upsurge of Afrikaner nationalism; it was they who framed this language into an idiom of poetic thought. They considered themselves more firmly part of the South African scene than the English-speaking writers who were still within the literary traditions of England—a view underlined by the fact that white English writers could get a reading public abroad. Afrikaner writers were restricted to the Afrikaans public in South Africa. They were far more open to the sanctions of the Afrikaner group than any other section of the writing population. They were often members of the Dutch Reformed Church. They had kinship ties in the Afrikaner community, and they sometimes shared the objectives and suppositions of the apartheid philosophy. Yet all Afrikaner writers do not submit unquestioningly to the practices of their government. There had been from the beginning a recognition of the Coloureds as part inheritors in the Afrikaner traditions. The Wolfie songs[1] of the Coloured population were acknowledged as part of the inspiration of the Afrikaner writers. Adam Small, a Coloured poet, was a respected member of their group writing in Afrikaans and for a while a member of the Sestigers Board[2] until *Sestiger* in financial difficulties was taken over by Voortrekker Press, and Adam Small was forced to resign. Rabie, another Afrikaner writer, claimed that 'the political front had been won . . . for political values but firstly, for autonomy in writing'.[3] It was the erosion of this autonomy in writing that brought protests from Afrikaner writers.

By far the most important developments among the Afrikaner writers of the sixties was a reaction to the whole structure of Afrikaner living, of which apartheid was a part. The quarrel between the Sestiger group of young writers and the older group of writers was not simply a revolt of the young over the issue of apartheid, although this, an integral part of a wider social structure, eventually became one of the issues.

'I feel in myself [wrote Etienne Leroux, a leader of the Sestigers] the rebellion against dead tradition and worn-out symbols, but I also long for a renewed sense of cosmic order and security. I realize in myself the dilemma of modern man, and I write what I feel and see and hear.'[4]

It has become increasingly obvious that the Afrikaner writer is no more willing to be dictated to as to choice of subject than his African or English-speaking colleagues. A protest by 130 South African writers and 55 painters and sculptors against the Publications and Entertainments Bill, 1963, was signed by many leading Afrikaans novelists and poets. They expressed their deep alarm for the future of creative effort in South Africa. They held:

1. Folk songs, known as the 'Wolfie songs'.
2. The Sestigers were a loose grouping of Afrikaner writers, who published the literary periodical *Sestiger* and became known by its name.
3. Address at a NUSAS (National Union of South African Students) Conference, University of Cape Town, published in the *Sunday Times* (Johannesburg), 1 July 1965.
4. Quoted in Douglas Brown, *Against the World, a Study of White South African Attitudes*, p. 173 Glasgow, Collins, 1966.

'Above all, writers who must publish inside the country are liable to be forced either into silence or superficiality with fatal consequences especially for Afrikaans literature.'

This is not to imply that the entire Afrikaner writing group is in revolt against the principle of apartheid—this is not so even among the Sestigers themselves—it is just to point out that there is an important new strand in Afrikaner writing which, by widening the subject-matter of Afrikaans writing to include social issues, has had to take into account the limitations imposed by the system of apartheid.

From 1965 to 1970 the Sestigers were faced with the more crucial question of whether or not their preoccupation with new forms and the growing influence of French existentialism could be made somehow to fit within these limitations. Until then it could be argued that the emergence of the novel in Afrikaans and the rejection by the Sestigers of much censorship in the relating of sexual episodes would in itself force a re-evaluation of Afrikaaner philosophy. Certainly some of the attacks on the Sestigers came from conservative Afrikaners who feared just this.[1] The Sestigers had, in the early sixties, made some political gestures, e.g. over Adam Small, but even when a protest was lodged, it was mainly concerned with the rights of white writers. The position of African writers in the society had been ignored. The protest against the Publications and Entertainment Bill, 1963, contained no African signatories. The existence of two major societies—one black, the other white, both apart—meant that the Sestigers had little contact with African writers while in South Africa, although they might occasionally meet them in London or in Paris. The movement for autonomy in writing did not forge the cross-racial protest that could challenge the apartheid social structure. On the contrary, it reflected this. What would seem to have worried the Sestigers was not their isolation from non-white South Africa, but the long distance from Europe and the difficulty of being translated into English or French and so 'breaking in' to the European writing world.

The Breytenbach affair, and the controversy surrounding it, changed this by sharpening the issues.

Breyten Breytenbach is an Afrikaner poet, essayist and painter living in Paris. He has won three writing awards, the last two being for the best book published in Afrikaans in 1968 and again in 1969—

---

1. The Nederduitsch Hervormde Kerk published an attack on the Sestigers after which Chris Barnard, Johannesburg author and playwright, left the Church.—*Sunday Express*, 25 February 1968.

a rare achievement. He has exhibited his paintings in France and the Netherlands and has had some of them hung in art museums in the United States, in Paris—including the Musée d'Art Moderne—and in The Hague. He is married to a Viet-Namese, who under South African regulations is classified as Coloured. The South African Government refused her a visa to accompany him to South Africa to visit his parents. This pointed to an anomaly in South African legislation which covered marriages contracted within the Republic. The Prohibition of Mixed Marriages Amendment Act No. 21 of 1968 provided that if any male person who is a South African citizen or is domiciled in the Republic enters into a marriage outside the Republic which cannot, in terms of the principal Act, be solemnized within the country (because one partner to it is white and the other non-white), such marriage shall be void and of no effect in the Republic. It was popularly known as the 'Breytenbach Amendment'.

The issue did not rest there; more difficult for the Sestigers to resolve was the political position that Breytenbach had taken on South African policy, his publication of this in various articles and radio broadcasts, and his belief that the assumed a-political nature of much Sestiger thinking may have assured them financial security in the Republic, but had resulted in a superficiality in their writing. For him the cross-fertilization that was needed if Afrikaners were to produce good literature was not to be found in increasing contact with Europe, but only within the struggle for a non-racial South African state. If any South African culture—other than the mediocre and the folkloric—was to survive, the present political structure would have to be totally demolished.[1] In a broadcast over Netherlands radio in 1968, he stated that he would prefer to be officially classified as Coloured. He came under constant attack in the South African press, and this was intensified after the broadcast.

In September 1970 a Shakespeare play that he had translated into Afrikaans was put on in South Africa. However, his name was removed from the billboards after a spate of letters in the Afrikaans press accusing him of being 'unpatriotic' and his publishers were under considerable pressure to stop the payment of royalties to him. He was not banned (no writer in Afrikaans has been to date), but this points to another problem that is particularly acute for the Afrikaner writer: the pressure that might be brought to bear on his

1. B. Breytenbach, 'Cultural Interaction', *Cultural Rights as Human Rights*, p. 39-42, 46-7, Paris, Unesco, 1970 (Studies and Documents on Cultural Policies, 3).

publisher not to advertise work, which, even though published, and even if it has no relationship with the South African internal situation, is written by someone who is known to be against government policy.

5   Public libraries[1]

South African libraries include the two national deposit libraries, the South African Library and the Library of Pretoria. Both these libraries, besides receiving a copy of every book published in South Africa, also house important collections.

South Africa has had a long tradition of library service. The periodical of the South African Library Association, *South African Libraries*, is a useful guide for library administration and methods. Its articles discuss the latest techniques in librarianship, microfilming, electronic computing, facet analysis and library research in other countries.

The libraries, with their rich book collections, with their trained staff, could be an important factor in the cultural life of South Africa. They could also be an important factor in her educational life, since they provide a method of maintaining and encouraging literacy and an avenue for self-improvement through home reading and studying.

Library service is provided separately for the different population groups. The use of libraries in urban areas is governed by the Group Areas Act, which reserves public buildings in a particular area for the

1. See also Part I, Chapter 9, 'School Libraries'. In addition to the public library service, there are university libraries open to accredited readers, and special libraries either attached to industrial firms or for special categories of people, e.g. the blind.

use of the major population group of that area. It is also governed by the Separate Amenities Act which provides that separate amenities be provided for white and non-white groups using the same service.

As a result, the major libraries remain closed to non-white South Africans. Separate reading rooms are provided in the deposit libraries. Collections of other libraries, valuable as they are, may only be used through inter-loan service. In accordance with the ideology of separate development, branches have been opened up for the different sections of the community in some areas.

In 1964 the European Library in Pietermaritzburg showed a book-stock of 63,398 books in the lending department, and 34,897 books in the reference department. The Market Square branch for non-Europeans, mainly Coloureds and Asians, showed an entire book-stock of 11,137. Additions for that year are shown in Table 45.

In Cape Town where there had been some use of public library facilities on a non-segregated basis, the Cape Provincial Administration ruled in 1963 that the council would have to make further efforts to provide separate facilities for the different population groups in accordance with the Provincial Library Ordinance of 1955. The main libraries concerned in Cape Town were the Central, Woodstock and Wynberg libraries where there was a substantial member-

TABLE 45. Library acquisitions in 1964

Additions	White library	Market Square branch	Additions	White library	Market Square branch
Lending department			*Reference stock*		
Non-fiction	1 242	179	Copyright books	1 805	2[3]
Fiction in English	1 981	270[1]	Other reference		
Fiction			books	1 141	
in Afrikaans	120		Pamphlets	1 649	
Children's books	1 570	627	Maps	142	
		98[2]	Music	153	
TOTAL	4 913	1 174	TOTAL	4 890	

1. In English and Afrikaans.
2. Vernacular books.
3. Reference books.

Source: The Natal Society, Pietermaritzburg, *Annual Report for the Financial Year ending 31 December 1964.*

ship from varying groups. As a result of this, libraries for non-whites were constructed in Woodstock and Wynberg while separate entrances to the lending libraries and separate reading rooms were established in other branches.

In 1964 there were nineteen branches of the city libraries for whites and twelve sub-branches for Coloureds. There was one travelling library for whites and two for Coloureds.

In the three African townships in Cape Town there is no library provision; one of the problems was the lack of funds and the absence of any clear-cut responsibility for financing African libraries.

'Neither the Department of Bantu Administration and Development nor the Cape Provincial Administration subsidized expenditure on library services for the Bantu. . . . It is to be hoped that the question of where the responsibility lies for the provision of libraries for the Bantu, particularly in the Cape, will soon be clearly established.'[1]

In Durban there are eleven municipal library depots and one reference library for whites, one library for Coloureds and one branch library for Africans.

Library provision for Africans in provincial rural districts varies according to place. The Transvaal Provincial Library service established in 1963 a service for Africans which is run on the same principle as that for whites. The bookstock for Africans is much smaller than the bookstock for whites, but this could be partly due to the newness of the service. In the Orange Free State there is a free library service for whites only—there is no corresponding service for Africans. In some areas there are libraries run by voluntary service and started by an individual or groups of individuals, as for instance the Bantu Service Library for the Venda people of the Northern Transvaal which was started in January 1962. The bookstock consisted of gifts from individuals and institutions. The library is housed in a private house and run on a completely voluntary basis by a teacher. That there was a demand for a library service in this area is shown by an initial reader registration of 1,000.[2]

The demand for books is always qualified by the social and economic situation of the African himself. He often grows up in a home where there are no books, he has little money to spend on books,

---

1. Cape Town City Libraries, *Annual Report 1963*, p. 4.
2. *South African Libraries*, Vol. 31, January 1964, p. 114-16.

he has often not acquired the love of reading. He is often literate only in his mother tongue, and there is little incentive to read as part of a study course when conditions for economic advancement are so low.

'The best that can be said of the non-European libraries is that they provide an opportunity for the few able to benefit from them. For the mass of the people it must be recognized that they will not use books for pleasure until there has been a considerable advance in their economic and social conditions.'[1]

South African Libraries points to poverty, the teaching in the vernacular, which means that Africans are illiterate in English and in Afrikaans while there is little literature in their 'mother tongue', and the unwillingness of municipal and provincial authorities to finance the administration of the service as reasons for the low percentage of library users among Africans.[2]

The situation with regard to school libraries has been discussed in Part I, Chapter 9. It is only necessary to reiterate here that the poverty of the bookstock in non-white public libraries makes it impossible to supplement the inadequate book provision of the libraries in non-white schools.

Audio-visual material, films, records and pictures are becoming part of the stock of public libraries in many countries and in South Africa. One would expect these materials to be of particular use to partly literate groups; in fact, their use would seem to be restricted mainly to white libraries, although Cape Town libraries reported the use of both films and story-reading for non-European audiences.

In Cape Province films were provided to library users as part of the library provision in 1959. Then, 2,319 film shows were given for Europeans and 180 to non-Europeans.[3]

In 1958, 1,295 films were shown to 59,594 adult Europeans and 49,508 European children. During the same period 67 films were shown to 5,999 non-European adults and 11,264 non-European children. The average attendance per film was 77 Europeans and 227 non-Europeans. In 1951, 2,319 film shows were held for Europeans and 180 for non-Europeans.[4] Of the total art prints purchased by the

1. 'Libraries and the Non-European in South Africa', *South African Libraries*, Vol. 25, No. 2, October 1957, p. 43.
2. Editorial, *South African Libraries*, Vol. 25, No. 2, October 1957.
3. *South African Libraries*, Vol. 28, No. 1, July 1960, p. 18.
4. Province of the Cape of Good Hope, *Report of the Director of Library Services for the Years 1958 and 1959*, p. 2.

Audio-visual Section of the Cape Provincial Libraries—7,227 by the end of 1959—only 636 were for non-European libraries.[1]

Staffing and staff training for librarians is important in any discussion of library provision. The importance of trained librarians in any library cannot be underestimated, but it is particularly important where poor bookstocks must be exploited to their fullest capacity.

Training for white librarians could be obtained until 1965 at seven centres: the South African Library Association, the universities of Pretoria, Cape Town, South Africa, Potchefstroom, Stellenbosch and the Witwatersrand. However, the South African Library Association examinations were due to end in 1965, in conformity with the trend to train librarians at universities. Only the University of South Africa and the South African Library Association offered courses in librarianship through correspondence courses to non-whites.

'The demand for such training is not great owing to the fewer libraries for non-Whites and consequently fewer employment possibilities.'[2]

In the University College of the Western Cape for Coloureds, a senior lecturer in library science has been appointed, but library training had not been established (1960) in the other non-white colleges. The decision of the South African Government that the principle of separate development be applied to learned societies[3] received the support of the South African Library Association, which decided to help in the formation of library associations for Africans, for Coloureds and for Indians.[4] The number of non-white staff employed by public libraries remains very small.

The staffing arrangements for the Johannesburg public library in 1963-64 showed 21 librarians, 21 assistant librarians and 42 library assistants who were white. There were no librarians and no assistant librarians among non-whites, but there were 12 non-white library assistants.[5] In 1969, with 15 non-white service points, 6 exclusively for African use, there were 229 white staff members to 36 non-

1. Province of the Cape of Good Hope, *Report of the Director of Library Services for the Years 1958 and 1959*, p. 2.
2. *South African Libraries*, Vol. 28, No. 1, July 1960, p. 18.
3. See also page 134..
4. National Conference of the South African Library Association, one-day conference held at Pretoria, 7 November 1962.
5. *Johannesburg Public Libraries Report*, 1963-64, p. 2?.

white.[1] The staff of the Port Elizabeth Public Library included two non-whites: a Coloured head-caretaker and two African cleaners.[2]

The number of hours that branch libraries remained open varied with the population groups. In Johannesburg the branch libraries for the white population were open normally for forty-six hours per week.[3]

The separation of facilities under the apartheid system makes it unlikely or at least very doubtful that adequate library services can be made available to all sections of the South African public. The provision of separate bookstocks would make book provision in any event extremely expensive: the price of reference books, the initial cost of building up reference stocks for each population group, the upkeep of these, would seem prohibitive. While, in theory, books may be borrowed by post through an inter-loan system, choosing from a catalogue is hardly comparable to the open access to shelves available to the white population.

The difference in methods of financing and the uncertainty as to which authority would have eventually the financial responsibility for non-white libraries must make for poor library services while the maintenance of separate library systems must lead to cumbersome administration.

1. *Johannesburg Public Libraries Report, 1968-69.*
2. *Port Elizabeth Public Library Annual Report for the Year Ending December 1963.*
3. See library schedules in *Johannesburg Public Library Annual Report 1962-63.*

6   Entertainment

The Group Areas Act, 1950,[1] empowered the President to issue proclamations concerning the 'occupation of premises' according to population groups. By Proclamation No. 164 of 1958, 'occupation' was made to include attendance at cinemas: non-whites may not be allowed to attend cinema shows in a white district unless a special permit by the competent minister is given, nor are whites permitted to attend cinema performances in a Coloured, Asian or African area.

Proclamation R.26 of 12 February 1965 defined the concept of 'occupation', as declared in the Group Areas Act, as including the occupation (of a seat) at 'any place of public entertainment'.

The Entertainment (Censorship Act), 1931, empowered the Minister of Education to prohibit the giving of a public entertainment until the Board of Censors appointed under the Act had investigated the matter. This Act was replaced by the Publication and Entertainment Act, 1963. Under Section 12, the Publications Control Board has the power to prohibit the giving of a public entertainment if the Board is satisfied that the entertainment concerned: (a) may have the effect of (i) giving offence to religious convictions or feelings of any section of the inhabitants of the Republic, or (ii) bringing any section of the inhabitants of the Republic into ridicule or contempt; or (b) is contrary to the public interest or is indecent or obscene or offensive or harmful to public morale.

The possible effect of Group Area Proclamations on traditional festivities is illustrated by the story of District Six and Coon Carnival. District Six was the main residential centre of the Coloured population of Cape Town, although there were small numbers of Indians, Malays and Africans also living there. It is predominantly a slum area and is regarded by whites as 'dangerous'. It is in this district that the only

---

1. See also the Introduction.

well-organized Mardi Gras (Coon Carnival) in South Africa takes place. It is prepared with much care long in advance and ends at the Sports Arena with troupes competing. While the participants are Coloured, the onlookers belong to every race.

District Six has now been proclaimed a white area;[1] the Coloured occupants will be moved to the outskirts of Cape Town. If the carnival is organized at all, it will be in the new area—and Cape Town will have lost one of its gayest and oldest multi-racial spectacles.

Public participation in cultural activities belongs to a very strong African tradition. The tradition of the story-teller, of dancing and music that was part of the ritual of tribal life, was translated in the urban districts into jazz and song sessions in which large groups of people participated, often around the *shebeen* drinking quarters of the African townships. While jazz was and remained principally an African cultural pastime, whites and Coloureds joined in these jazz sessions. Laws which prevented interracial mixing (Proclamation R.26), the demolition of urban townships and the regulations governing political activities affected these meetings. Not only did it make it difficult for white South Africans to join with the Africans in jazz parties, but the narrow boundary between satire and political activities greatly restricted the possible content of popular tunes. Moreover, the continual swoop of the police on African areas, in the search for Africans who had contravened one regulation or another, created a situation of insecurity under which public cultural gatherings could not exist freely. While audiences outside South Africa were applauding the jazz plays put on by the interracial Union Artists Dorkay House, Johannesburg, and plays by the African Music and Drama Association like *King-Kong* or *Township Jazz*, jazz was being crippled within South Africa itself. How effective this crippling was, was seen in the Dollar Brand case. In March 1965, the Minister of Community Development banned non-white audiences from Selbourne Hall, part of the Johannesburg City Hall. As a result, the South African tour by the famous jazz musician Dollar Brand was cancelled. Dollar Brand (Coloured) is considered one of the best exponents of modern South African jazz. A spokesman for Union Artists who were to sponsor the tour explained that it would not pay to bring Dollar Brand out for an all-white audience in the Johannesburg auditorium.[2]

1. February 1966.
2. *Star* (Johannesburg), 7 March 1965.

The Luxurama Theatre is situated in a Coloured area in Cape Town. Traditionally the audiences have been multi-racial. The Minister of Community Development explained that while it had been previously lawful for whites to attend cinemas in the Coloured area, they could no longer do so unless authorized by permit.[1] On 13 February 1965, the last multi-racial audience was held while the owners prepared themselves for the new régime of 'mixed shows by permit'.[2]

The audiences at symphony concerts given by the municipal orchestra in the Cape Town City Hall were multi-racial and unsegregated. The government first requested the City Council to provide that, at multi-racial shows, there should be separate booking offices, entrances, exits, seating and toilet facilities. The City Council at first refused. However, a Government Proclamation of 11 June 1965 declared the whole of the central city of Cape Town a white area, and the provision of separate amenities is now enforceable.

International reactions

Athol Fugard had written an open letter to playwrights in 1962 on the occasion of the opening of The Parthenon on Braamfontein Hill, the new civic theatre in Johannesburg:

'This theatre was built with the labour of hundreds of non-Whites . . . but not one of these labourers, not one non-White actor, singer or writer will be able to see a performance in the season of opera. Even the customary gesture of a "special performance for non-Whites" has gone by the board.

'It is yet again for Whites only.

'Is this—the presentation of your plays as the exclusive property or our self-indulgent White theatre—the result of ignorance or indifference on your part?'[3]

Playwrights in co-operation with the Anti-Apartheid movement in the United Kingdom, United States of America, France and Ireland, instructed their agents 'to insert a clause in all future contracts auto-

---

1. *A Survey of Race Relations . . . 1965*, p. 303 ff.
2. *Star* (Johannesburg), 13 February 1965.
3. *Forward*, September 1962.

matically refusing performing rights in any theatre where discrimination is made among audiences on grounds of colour'.[1]

John Arden gave his reasons for not permitting his plays to be shown in South Africa:

'I think I would not do so if my works were novels or poetry: and indeed I have never withdrawn my published plays for anywhere. But the theatre is nothing if it is not a public art, presented before an audience. If that audience is forcibly confined to one section of a community at the expense of another, the play performed is not public. Its very performance is a declaration of support for whatever laws or customs or prejudices have prevented certain groups or individuals from attending.'[2]

It became practically impossible to put on any of the modern English plays. John Whiteley, a South African actor, in a letter to the British actress Vanessa Redgrave, who had been one of the organizers of the ban in England, claimed that 'the banning tides . . . threaten death to theatre in South Africa . . . the immediate result of this ban is to destroy the hopes and living of English-language theatre in this country'.[3] To John Whiteley the ban meant death to English theatre, it would mean a step towards the establishment of the supremacy at a cultural level of the Afrikaner Volk.

Brian Brooks, in a tour abroad in an effort to get new plays for his theatre, managed to get only two—and one of these, *Barefoot in the Park* by Neil Simon, only when he had persuaded Simon to allow the production on condition that part of the proceeds would be given to non-white theatre.

The South African Association of Theatrical Managements appealed to the Minister of the Interior, Mr. de Klerk, to appreciate the serious threat to South African theatre that had resulted from the ban. Alan Paton, declining to appeal to overseas theatre leaders to lift their culture ban on South Africa, refuted the allegation being made in some quarters that the overseas ban was bringing politics into the theatre:

1. (a) 'We Say "No" to Apartheid', a declaration of American Artists circulated by the American Committee on Africa; (b) Declaration of 54 playwrights, 5 June 1963, Anti-Apartheid movement, United Kingdom; (c) Declaration of Irish playwrights, 22 September 1964.
    Playwrights who signed these declarations include Shelagh Delaney, Daphne du Maurier, Graham Greene, Iris Murdoch, Sean O'Casey, J. B. Priestley, John Osborne, Jean-Paul Sartre, C. P. Snow, Arnold Wesker, Conrad Aiken, Patrick Calvin, John McCann, Arthur Miller.
2. *The Times* (London), 16 May 1965.
3. *Sunday Times* (Johannesburg), 14 March 1965.

'We must face a hard fact if we want a colour bar, whether it is called apartheid or separate development, we must expect to pay a price for it. Cultural isolation is one of the prices. It was clearly the Government (by a great section of the electorate) that brought politics into the theatre, and we, the producers, the actors, the theatre-goers, must pay the price for it.'[1]

Mr. Robert Langford, chairman of the association, was reported as saying that

'all the several Johannesburg theatre managements together would not be able to scrape together enough material to fill even one theatre for one year. . . . when I started three decades ago we had the problem of no public. But that was not nearly so terrible as the situation in which we find ourselves today. Now we have a theatre-conscious public, although it is small; we have good players, we have theatres; but we have no plays, and without plays, we will have no theatre'.[2]

The ban was particularly important since South Africa was itself producing little writing in the field of drama.

South African audiences were faced with the possibility of seeing only the Restoration plays and the classics, plays that were beyond the copyright provisions.

The protest of foreign writers arose from their personal abhorrence of the evil of racism. They agreed with Paton that cultural isolation was the price that South Africa had to pay for apartheid, but their action was based on the Berne Copyright Convention, which gave artists and authors the legal right to authorize the publication and performance of their works.[3]

In 1965 a new Copyright Act was passed. During the committee stage of the Copyright Bill, a clause was inserted with the object of preventing authors from prohibiting the performance of their works in South Africa on ideological grounds. Article 50 (1) empowers the State President to make 'such regulations as he may consider necessary in regard to the circulation, presentation or exhibition of any work or production'.

Article 50 (3) of the Act also provides that:

1. *Star* (Johannesburg), 14 March 1965.
2. *Sunday Times* (Johannesburg), 7 March 1965.
3. Berne Convention, Articles 9, 11, 12, 13 and 14.

'The circulation, presentation or exhibition of any work or production in pursuance of authority granted in terms of such regulations shall not constitute an infringement of copyright in such work or production, but the author shall not thereby be deprived of his right to a reasonable remuneration, which shall in default of agreement be determined by arbitration.'

The South Africa PEN centre opposed the clause as being contrary to the Berne Convention of which South Africa is a signatory, though they condemned the decision of overseas playwrights to refuse permission for their works to be performed in South Africa. The South African delegate to the international PEN Congress claimed that the action of the playwrights was contrary to the PEN charter, but a resolution to that effect was lost after PEN heard another group of South Africans putting the case for the boycott.

In 1968, the Johannesburg Operatic and Dramatic Society (JODS) applied to the copyright tribunal for a licence to stage three American musicals without the consent of their authors, and in keeping with the 1965 Copyright Act. The licence was granted.

In April 1969, authors who had signed the 1963 statement reaffirmed their stand and new names were added to the list,[1] while some writers unable to stop performance or sales in South Africa agreed to cede royalties to the Anti-Apartheid movement.[2]

Overseas actors had also protested against apartheid. In 1956, British Equity[3] passed a resolution:

'This meeting urges the council instructing all members of the Equity not to work in any theatres in which any form of colour bar operates unless there is a clause in the contract to ensure that a definite proportion, to be decided by Equity, of the performances given under contract shall be open to all non-Europeans or if possible to persons of any colour, race or creed.'

Over the next few years Equity undertook to bargain with the South African Government on behalf of their members for a proportion of shows to be shown to non-segregated groups. This proved to be

1. The list in 1969 included Peter Weiss, Peter Shaffer, John Arden, Tony Parker, Edna O'Brien, John McGrath, David Caute, Michael Rosen, Margaretha D'Drey.
2. The authors included Jean-Paul Sartre (English editions), Samuel Beckett, Harold Pinter, Peter Shaffer, N. C. Hunter, Audrey Obey, Arnold Wesker, Henry Livings, Graham Greene.
3. British Equity is the trade union of actors and entertainers in the United Kingdom and normally arranges overseas contracts for them.

difficult to achieve; not only were they faced with the Group Areas Act, but there were local administrative procedures and there was always the possibility that where these did not apply there could be conditions written into the constitution of a sponsoring club, or in the regulations governing the use of a particular building.

In its negotiations with South African theatre management, Equity was able to register some gains. African Consolidated Theatre, the biggest cinema concern in South Africa, opened its doors for the first time to non-Europeans. The tour of the musical *My Fair Lady* proved that Equity could, if it wished, get the support of American and Australian companies to help their stand, and not to go to South Africa to perform this particular musical on terms other than the ones they were demanding.

The Dusty Springfield case, however, pointed to the difficulties of ensuring that promises made by South African agents to overseas performers that they could play before multi-racial audiences would be kept.

Before coming to South Africa, the British 'pop' singer Dusty Springfield had stated that she was determined to appear before multi-racial audiences. After her arrival in Cape Town, where she was due to appear at the Luxurama Theatre, the Department of the Interior decided to exercise the right to demand that she should have a visa, although she held a British passport. The visa would be granted on condition that she signed a declaration that she would not appear before multi-racial audiences. This she refused to do. A visa was then granted for twenty-four hours only, which meant that she had to leave South Africa the next day.[1]

In January 1965, the Minister of the Interior outlined in Parliament the government policy with regard to multi-racial audiences. Foreign artists were gladly received, but were expected to honour South Africa's customs.[2] In February, on some occasions, non-whites were advised by the authorities not to attend theatrical performances although the theatres were provided with separate seating accommodation.

The Equity resolution of 9 March 1965 stated that:

'While recognizing that there are those who honestly believe that racial intolerance can best be fought by their presence, working in

---

1. *A Survey of Race Relations . . . 1965*, p. 301 ff.
2. *House of Assembly Debates (Hansard)*, Vol. 1, 1965, Cols. 17-19.

South Africa, and while believing that a decision of conscience cannot be forced on the membership, nevertheless invites all members of Equity to sign a declaration that they endorse the Council's policy and will not perform in South Africa if they are forbidden to play before multiracial audiences.'[1]

Up to 12 May 1966, 2,876 members had signed the declaration. With or without the signature, however, the instructions, as apart from the total declaration, remained binding.

Actors' Equity Australia has in force a resolution similar to the British Equity one of 1965, and in the United States of America members of Actors' Equity have been directed not to appear in South Africa.

The British Musicians' union operates a total ban on all performances in South Africa and all its members are required to observe its instructions. The London Symphony Orchestra, for example, excluded South Africa from the itinerary of its tour arranged to coincide with the sixtieth anniversary of the orchestra.

7   Sport

There is no legislation dealing with sport specifically, although representatives of the government have threatened that special legislation might be introduced if the policy of the government is not complied

1. British Actors' Equity Association.

with. However, the Group Areas Act, the Separate Amenities Act and Proclamation R.26 all affect sporting activities.

The separation of the 'races' in the field of sport covers five different but related issues: (a) mixed teams; (b) interracial team competitions; (c) the participation of non-white players in games played on fields in all-white districts; (d) the composition of foreign teams visiting South Africa; (e) mixed audiences.

Mixed teams

The policy of the South African Government, as stated on several occasions by the Minister of the Interior, is that whites and non-whites should arrange their sporting activities separately. They should not belong to the same clubs. In sporting organizations, however, a white organization may offer affiliation status to a non-white organization, but in this 'federation' whites should represent the organization where external relations are concerned.[1]

In some overseas matches there could be separate South African 'contingents': the whites representing white South Africa, and the non-whites the non-white population in South Africa.[2]

In line with the government's policy, the South African Olympic and National Games Association (SAONGA), composed of representatives of a number of national bodies in the field of sport, has encouraged its constituent white bodies to offer affiliation to non-white bodies.

The South African Sports Association (SASA), a non-racial organization, was not prepared to accept affiliation on terms offered by SAONGA. In 1961 SASA launched a campaign 'Operation Sonreis' (Support Only Non-Racial Events In Sport), and sportsmen were urged to boycott games conducted on racial lines.[3] The South African Government in October of that year banned Denis Brutus, the secretary of SASA, from attending gatherings.[4]

---

1. *A Survey of Race Relations . . . 1961*, p. 273, and *A Survey of Race Relations . . . 1964*, p. 282.
2. *Guardian* (London), 9 June 1964.
3. See also section below, 'International Reactions', page 220 below.
4. Denis Brutus was arrested in 1963 in the offices of the White Olympic Association where he had gone to meet a Swiss journalist who was to report on his South African visit to the Olympic Committee in Lausanne. While awaiting trial he left South Africa in an attempt to reach the Baden-Baden meeting of the International Olympic Committee (IOC). He was stopped in Mozambique by the Portuguese Security Police and returned to South Africa.

    After serving 1½ years imprisonment for infringement of his banning order, he left the Republic for England where he now lives.

Interracial competition

In June 1960, the Minister of the Interior stated the government's policy:

'The Government does not favour interracial team competition within the borders of the Union and will discourage such competition taking place as being contrary to the traditional policy of the Union—as accepted by all races in the Union.'[1]

In a speech in Parliament on 11 April 1967 the Prime Minister, Mr. Vorster, further clarified the official government policy on sport. In a statement with regard to participation in the Olympic Games he said:

'I therefore want to make it quite clear that from South Africa's point of view no mixed sport between Whites and non-Whites will be practised locally, irrespective of the standard of proficiency of the participants ... the position is simply that Whites practise and administer their sport separately and that the other colour groups— the Coloureds, the Indians and the Bantu—practise their sport separately. ... Our views and our attitude are quite clear—no matter how proficient one of our people may be in his line of sport, we do not apply that as a criterion, because our policy has nothing to do with proficiency or lack of proficiency. If any person, either locally or abroad, adopts the attitude that he will enter into relations with us only if we are prepared to jettison the separate practising of sport prevailing among our own people in South Africa, then I want to make it quite clear that, no matter how important those sport relations are in my view, I am not prepared to pay that price. On that score I want no misunderstanding whatsoever. I also want to say in advance that if, after I have said on these matters what I still want to say, anybody should see in this either the thin edge of the wedge or a surrender of principles, or that it is a step in the direction of diverging from this basic principle, he would simply be mistaken. Because in respect of this principle we are not prepared to compromise, we are not prepared to negotiate, and we are not prepared to make any concessions. ...'[2]

---

1. *A Survey of Race Relations ... 1961*, p. 273.
2. Prime Minister, *House of Assembly Debates (Hansard)*, 11 April 1967, Cols. 3959-67. The Transvaal Congress of the Nationalist Party meeting in September 1969 reaffirmed this statement as the official policy of the Party.

In spite of protests from outside of the Republic and from some sportsmen within, the policy has not changed.

In 1970 Frank Waring, Minister of Sports, was reported as saying:

'The Government will in no way be intimidated by demands for integrated sport. Mixed trials locally will not be allowed, nor will White teams be permitted to compete against non-White teams in or outside the Republic.'[1]

The Prime Minister, Mr. Vorster, speaking in Salisbury, Rhodesia, after the withdrawal of the MCC[2] invitation to a South African team to tour England, emphasized that no change in policy had taken place:

'In South Africa sport has always been played separately. It is not the making of this Government or the previous Government. This is how we developed in South Africa.'[3]

These statements defining policy in sport mean in practice that a white team cannot compete against a non-white team, nor can a white sprinter run in the same race as a non-white sprinter.

In fact, in 1964 the first 'non-white' games were held in the Republic and this was followed by the second 'non-white' games in 1970.[4]

The participation of non-white players in games played on fields in all-white districts

There seems to be in South Africa some confusion as to whether or not individual non-white players could play on fields in all-white districts. Technically both the Reservation of Separate Amenities Act, 1958, and the Group Areas Act would apply, but it could be argued that all that was legally necessary was that the non-white player must be provided with 'separate amenities'. This is illustrated by the Papwa cases.

In 1963 and 1964, the Indian golfer Sewgolum Papwa was invited to play in several championships. The golf officials considered

---

1. *Guardian* (London), 28 May 1970.
2. Marylebone Cricket Club, until recently the controlling association for cricket in the United Kingdom.
3. *Observer* (London), 24 May 1970; *Sunday Express* (London), 24 May 1970.
4. *Bantu* (Pretoria), September 1970, p. 12.

that there was no need for a special permit to enable him to play, although he could not enter the club house. He and another Coloured player, playing in the open at Bloemfontein, were provided with a tent, later replaced by a caravan, as a rest room. They were not invited to an official civic reception arranged for the rest of the golfers.[1]

In 1966, the Ministry of Planning refused Papwa a permit to play in the Western Province open championship, on the grounds that, in the future, permits would only be issued to non-whites to play in tournaments in which they had previously taken part. In line with this decision, however, Papwa was issued a permit to take part in the Natal open in which he had payeld before.[2] He was refused permission to take 'part in the South African Open championship in 1970.[3]

The line between what was legally necessary and what could in fact be done has become increasingly difficult to define. This is particularly so with regard to the Coloureds, since until recently they did not suffer from the same measure of discrimination as did the Africans. Moreover, their sporting activities overlapped with both the main English-speaking South African game (cricket) and the main Afrikaner games (rugby and soccer). Informal arrangements, while often discriminatory, nevertheless gave them a wider degree of sporting choice than that available to the Africans. One of the trends during the past five years is to institute a more rigid form of apartheid vis-à-vis the Coloureds, and gradually to withdraw the 'privileges' that they had come to accept.

An example of this was in the Bloemfontein jockey discussion. Officially non-white jockeys are not regarded as jockeys and are issued with provisional one-day licences to ride only at particular meetings. In March 1970 the Bloemfontein Turf Club decided to bar non-white jockeys from riding at race meetings.[4]

This decision was presumably partly as a result of the problems surrounding the granting of a visa to the Japanese jockey Sueo Masuzawa in the previous month.[5] The result of it, however, was to remove one of the 'loopholes' under which approximately a dozen non-white jockeys could use the Bloemfontein Turf.

1. *A Survey of Race Relations . . . 1964.*
2. *Cape Times,* 8 and 10 January 1966.
3. *Star* (Johannesburg), 18 January 1970.
4. *Sunday Times* (Johannesburg), 8 March 1970.
5. *A Survey of Race Relations . . . 1970,* p. 277.

The government was prepared to enforce its separateness in sport, as far as South African teams were concerned, outside of the borders of the Republic and in neighbouring African territories.

In 1969 the government used its passport powers to veto a multi-racial soccer game in Swaziland in which two South African teams were carded to play each other: Highlands Park (white) and Orlando Pirates (African).

The Minister of the Interior, Mr. S. L. Muller, said through the *Transvaler*—official organ of the Nationalist Party of the Transvaal—that he could not allow two South African teams to cross the border to play a game that would not be allowed in South Africa.[1]

South African boxers were stopped from taking part in an inter-racial tournament that was to have been held in Swaziland in September 1969 as part of the independence celebrations.[2]

Composition of foreign teams visiting South Africa

The South African Government's policy of apartheid was to be enforced not only with regard to South African teams inside or outside South Africa, it was also to be imposed on foreign teams visiting South Africa. The New Zealand All Blacks rugby team was due to visit South Africa in 1967, as part of a series of rugby matches between the countries that had gone on over some years. New Zealand proposed to include in its team two Maoris, one a representative of the Maori Advisory Board on the New Zealand Rugby Council, and the other a member of the All Blacks team which had toured the United Kingdom. There was some speculation that South Africa would accept the New Zealand proposal that Maoris should be included in the visiting team, either by ignoring the fact, or by declaring the Maoris white for the occasion.[3]

However, Dr. Verwoerd made a public statement:

'Like we subject ourselves to their customs, we expect that when other countries visit us they will respect ours and they will adapt themselves to ours.'[4]

---

1. *Star* (Johannesburg), 23 August 1969; *Sunday Times* (Johannesburg), 24 August 1969.
2. *Sunday Times* (London), 24 August 1969.
3. *The Times* (London), 4 September 1965; *Guardian* (London), 2 April 1965.
4. *The Times* (London), 7 September 1965; *Guardian* (London), 7 September 1965; *Star* (Johannesburg), 6 September 1965.

The All Blacks decided that they would not tour South Africa in 1967. In 1959, the Santos (Brazil) football team, also interracial, refused to visit South Africa when informed that its black members would not be allowed on playing grounds. A revision of policy was made, however, in 1969 for the New Zealand team of 1970 which included part-Maoris.

In 1971, however, the South Africans accepted a French rugby team which included Roger Bourgarel, a Guyanese (Coloured) of French nationality. This would seem to be a concession both to French public opinion and to a mounting opposition to the government's policies on sport within the Republic.

Mixed audiences

Proclamation R.26 of 12 February 1965 made special permits necessary in any public game for permitting audiences of other racial groups. In addition, the Minister of Community Development said in March 1963 that if a sports stadium is situated in a predominantly white area, it should in general be used by whites only. Exceptions might be made, by permit, for non-whites to attend provincial or international matches, provided that separate seating entrances and toilet facilities were available. Permits might be granted for Coloureds and Asians to attend matches below the provincial level at grounds so situated that white residents of the area would not be disturbed. The Minister of Community Development and the Minister of Planning handle permits for Coloureds and Asians, while the Minister of Bantu Administration and Development handles applications for Africans.

In reply to Mrs. Helen Suzman's (Progressive Party) questions in the Assembly, the Minister of Community Development gave the following details on applications for permits:

Department of Community Development, 12 February to 9 April 1965: 207 granted, 192 refused or outstanding.

Department of Planning, 12 February to 4 May: 150 granted, 16 refused, number outstanding not stated.

Department of Bantu Administration and Development, 12 February to 18 June: 104 applications received, 63 granted, 36 refused, 5 outstanding.[1]

1. *House of Assembly Debates (Hansard)*, Vol. 14, 30 March 1965, Cols. 3659-60; Vol. 14, 9 April 1965, Col. 4348; Vol. 14, 4 May 1965, Cols. 5267-711; Vol. 15, 18 June 1965, Col. 8600.

There seemed to be no clear idea, even in government circles, as to how Proclamation R.26 was to be interpreted. There was no indication as to what was to be considered a 'place of public entertainment' and less as to which of the population groups in a given area would be racially qualified to attend a particular place. The Minister of Community Development favoured defining this by reference to the population group in the area. Moreover, the Ministry of Bantu Administration and Development was not granting permits for Africans to watch club matches in Cape Town, and Africans were banned from attending football matches at the Rand Stadium, Johannesburg.[1]

There could be specific bans on non-whites attending special matches. Thus the South African Government barred non-white spectators from attending the South African open golf championship in Johannesburg, in spite of the fact that Papwa was known to have a considerable non-white following.[2]

International reactions

As part of 'Operation Sonreis' (see 'Mixed Teams' above) SASA wrote to the International Olympic Committee (IOC) asking it to request that SAONGA ensure that its constituent bodies offer membership to all South Africans on a basis of equality.

At the Baden-Baden meeting in October 1963, the International Olympic Committee passed a resolution that SAONGA should be asked to make a firm declaration of its acceptance of the Olympic Code. SAONGA was asked to get from the South African Government some guarantee of a change of policy with regard to colour discrimination in sport, failing which SAONGA would be debarred from entering a team in the Olympic Games.[3] SAONGA made some attempts to comply with this regulation: it arranged for separate games for whites and for non-whites and several non-Whites were provisionally selected.

At this stage the South African Minister of the Interior made a

1. *Star* (Johannesburg), 13 and 20 March 1965; *Post* (South Africa), 16 March 1965.
2. *Guardian* (London), 15 February 1966.
3. After the South African defence at Baden-Baden, the IOC adopted the following resolution: 'The National Olympic Committee of South Africa must declare formally that it understands and submits to the spirit of the Olympic Charter and particularly articles 1 and 24. It must also obtain, from its government, a modification of its policy before December 31, 1963, failing which the South African NOC will be forced to withdraw from the Olympic Games.'

press statement reiterating the government's policy. He emphasized that the participation in international or world sports competitions by mixed teams representative of South Africa as a whole could under no circumstances be approved. SAONGA would have to satisfy the government that it had complied with the 'traditional South African custom in sport' before the government would grant permission. The President of SAONGA informed the International Olympic Committee about the situation. South Africa could not take part in the Tokyo Games of 1964.

There was some ambiguity as to whether or not the decision to bar South Africa from the Tokyo Games applied to the Olympics in general or only to the Tokyo Olympics. It would seem to have been accepted as a 'suspension' pending changes in the method of selecting teams in South Africa for play abroad, but the extent of the 'modification of its policy' mentioned in the IOC resolution of 1963 had not been spelled out.

At the 1966 Rome session, the IOC agreed to accept a South African proposal that a mixed committee would be set up composed of three white officials and three black officials, under the chairmanship of Mr. Frank Braun. This committee was to choose a multiracial team for the Mexico Olympics. The method of choice did not seem to extend to multi-racial competitions in the Republic.

The IOC at its 1967 meeting in Teheran was willing to admit South Africa to the Mexico Games following a list of concessions that Mr. Braun of the South African Olympic Committee indicated that the South African Government had made.[1]

But the final decision was left pending until a commission set up

---

1. These were:
   (a) Whereas participation in the Olympic Games previously was to have been on the basis of non-whites representing non-whites and whites representing whites, blacks and whites will in future form one team to represent South Africa.
   (b) Whereas white and non-white participants, previously, were to have travelled separately to the Olympic Games, they will, in future, travel together.
   (c) Whereas white and non-white participants previously had to be dressed differently, had to be accommodated separately and could not march under the same flag with opening ceremonies, they will now wear the same uniform, stay together and march as an integrated team under the South African flag.
   (d) Whereas, previously, South African whites and non-whites could not compete against one another at the Olympic Games or other international meetings, this will now be standard practice.
   (e) Whereas at previous Olympic Games white officials only were responsible for the selection of participants, an equal number of white and non-white officials under the chairmanship of the president of the South African National Olympic Committee will now be responsible for the selection of participants in all those Olympic sports in which different population or racial groups take part.

by the IOC to visit South Africa had reported back. The commission confirmed that South African sport was organized and played along racial lines, but it nevertheless argued for the inclusion of South Africa at the Olympics on the ground that the South African Olympic Committee was doing all that it could do given South African conditions.

Following this report the IOC passed a resolution inviting the South African National Olympic Committee to enter a team which conformed with the Fundamental Principle 1 of the Olympic Code (on racial equality in sport).[1]

This was followed by a series of withdrawals from the Mexican Games. The Supreme Council for Sport in Africa[2] announced that the whole of Africa would withdraw, some Asian countries announced their withdrawal and the U.S.S.R., supported by Italy and France, requested a special meeting of the IOC to reconsider the matter. This executive meeting decided that South Africa should be excluded from the Games as the security of its team could not be guaranteed.

The Supreme Council for Sport in Africa, meeting in Cairo in March 1970, drew up an indictment of specific charges against South Africa.[3]

These were the basis for the confrontation at the IOC meeting in Amsterdam, where nineteen African Olympic committees charged South Africa with racialism in sport. At this meeting the IOC voted to bar instead of 'suspend' South Africa from the Olympic Games.[4]

By 1970 protests against apartheid in sport had spread to virtually every international sporting body.

In March 1970 South Africa was barred from entering for the Davis Cup.[5] This decision had been preceded by the controversy

1. The vote was reported to be 37 to 28 with 6 abstentions.
2. Constituted in December 1966 as the highest authority on African sport matters.
3. The charges were: (a) that the South African National Olympic Committee (SANOC) is not in a position to resist the political pressures of its government; (b) that it has never guaranteed access by non-white sportmen to its affiliated national sporting bodies; practises racial discrimination against the non-white sportmen, failing to ensure their participation as full and equal members in all the committee's competitive and administrative activities; (c) that it does not allow multi-racial competitions and fails to guarantee the equality of training facilities and installations; (d) that it has not complied with the Baden-Baden decision; (e) that in March 1969, it organized 'South African Games' at Bloemfontein to which it invited exclusively athletes of white race; (f) that it used the Olympic emblem in conjunction with a racialist sporting festival without the authority of the IOC.
4. *The Times* (London), 18 May 1970; *Observer* (London), 17 May 1970. The vote was 35 to 28 with 3 abstentions.
5. *Guardian* (London), 24 March 1970; *Daily Telegraph* (London), 24 March 1970; *Sunday Times* (London), 29 March 1970.

surrounding the refusal of the South African Government to issue a visa to the black American player Arthur Ashe.[1]

Only the South African male tennis players were affected by the decision of 23 March 1970. South Africa participated at the Women's Federation Cup tennis tournaments in May 1970. As a result of this, Hungary, Israel and Poland withdrew their players.

The International Lawn Tennis Federation, however, at its annual meeting in Paris in July, defeated a motion to expel South Africa from world tennis by a large majority (172 against 56) and the related motion to exclude South African women players from the Federation Cup Tournament was abandoned.[2]

South Africa was not allowed to join in the world amateur-cycling championships at Leicester (United Kingdom) in August 1970.[3] She had already been banned from competing in international table tennis, weight lifting, boxing, basketball, Association football, fencing, volleyball and judo, and from competing in the 1969 world modern pentathlon championship and the 1970 world gymnastic championships.

Even where international committees had not considered a ban or were reluctant to exclude her she could be excluded by the action of governments that were hosts to international teams. The Jamaican Government, who will be host to the world's netball championships to be held in Kingston in 1971, announced that they would refuse

1. *The Times* (London), 29 January 1970; *Daily Telegraph* (London), 29 January 1970; *Guardian* (London), 29 January 1970. Ashe had requested a visa to enable him to go to South Africa to compete in the national championships at Johannesburg. In explaining why the South African Government had refused Ashe a visa, Mr. Frank Waring, Minister for Sport, stated:
   'In terms of its stated policy in respect of interstate Davis Cup competitive matches, the Government will, in the event of South Africa being the venue for such a match, provide visas for the members of the visiting teams, including Mr. Ashe in a Davis Cup team. Mr. Ashe's general antagonism towards South Africa, which is reflected in statements which he made from time to time and his reference to the fact that he was not interested in playing South Africa as a member of the American Davis Cup team, but that he wanted to compete in the South African national tennis championships as a private individual, made it clear that he is aware of the accepted practice in South Africa and that his application is, in his own words, an attempt 'to put a crack in the racist wall down there'. . . . It therefore follows that Mr. Ashe's application for a visa to compete in the South African tennis championships cannot be acceded to.'—*The Times* (London), 29 January 1970.
   Ashe's legal representative commented that his client had stated several times that he wished to go to South Africa solely to play tennis. His entry had been officially accepted by the South African Lawn Tennis Union.—*A Survey of Race Relations . . . 1969*, p. 250. See also the *Report of the Special Committee on the Policies of Apartheid of the Government of the Republic of South Africa*, New York, United Nations, 18 September 1970, p. 18, 19 (A/8022).
2. *Report of the Special Committee on the Policies of Apartheid of the Government of the Republic of South Africa*, p. 44, New York, United Nations, October 1970 (A/8022/Add.1).
3. *Sunday Telegraph* (London), 29 March 1970.

visas for South African players.[1] The Yugoslav Aero Club which was host to the tenth world parachuting championships, to be held at Bled, informed the Springbok team that the Yugoslav Government would not grant them entry visas.[2]

Even where there was a tradition of sport competition between South Africa and another country, this tradition could be reversed. New Zealand cancelled an invitation to white South African athletes, to avoid jeopardizing her application to stage the 1974 Commonwealth Games in Christchurch,[3] and the Springboks' 1970 cricket tour of the United Kingdom was cancelled. This last underlined the national and international problems countries might face in playing South Africa and the reluctance of governments to run the risk of internal protest mounting to threatened disorder, as well as the possibility of being themselves banned in international sporting events. A letter from four members of the MCC summed up the situation in Britain:

'It was on December 5, 1968, at a Special General Meeting of MCC that we drew attention to the damage to community relations that might well result from the presence here of a racially selected team. Then on May 7, 1969, at MCC's Annual General Meeting we warned of other likely consequences of the projected tour: a boycott of the matches by leading Coloured cricketers, the damage to the Commonwealth Games, the grave effect on the Commonwealth itself. . . .'[4]

The proposed tour had aroused a good deal of public resentment in cricket history. It had been preceded by the Basil d'Oliveira affair[5] and the South African Cricket Association's refusal to extend an invitation to the multi-racial international Cavaliers Club to tour South Africa if non-white members were included in the composition of the Cavalier team.[6]

The Springbok Rugby Tour in 1969 had proved how difficult and costly it could be to give protection to a South African tour in the

---

1. *Guardian* (London), 28 May 1970.
2. *Star* (Johannesburg), 18 April 1970.
3. *Daily Telegraph* (London), 10 December 1969; *The Times* (London), 10 December 1969.
4. Letter to *The Times* (London), 26 May 1970, signed by the following members of the MCC: Martin Kenyon, David Woolwich, the Rev. Woodroffe and Peter Howell.
5. In 1968 the South African Government refused to accept the MCC team which included Basil d'Oliveira (Coloured).
6. *Evening Standard* (London), 30 January 1970.

face of well-organized demonstrations[1] and there was the threat that there would be widespread withdrawals from the Commonwealth Games.[2]

As a result of this, and at the request of the British Home Secretary, Mr. Callaghan, the Cricket Council withdrew its invitation to the Springboks.[3]

The International Table Tennis Federation refused to recognize the all-white South African Table Tennis Association as the negotiating body for South African table tennis but recognized instead the South African Table Tennis Board, which, while technically non-white, permitted white players to join if they desired to do so.

South Africa was asked to leave the International Football Association.

There were also bans which followed the government's policy.

In international cricket, a West Indian team would not be able to take part in cricket in South Africa, since the West Indian cricket team has been traditionally interracial.

Dave Marais, president of the white South African Football Association, commenting on South Africa's expulsion from the 1970 Davis Cup summed up the present situation:

'The position is bound to deteriorate unless the Government changes

1. In 1969 eight anti-apartheid groups in Britain jointly formed a Stop the Seventy Tour Committee.
2. By 21 May 1970, fourteen African States, India, Jamaica, Malaysia and Pakistan, had threatened to leave the Commonwealth Games.—*The Times* (London), 21 May 1970.
3. The letter from Mr. Callaghan, Home Secretary, to Maurice Allom, Chairman of the Cricket Council stated:
   'The Government has been very carefully considering the implications of the tour, if it were to take place, in the light of the many representations that have been received from a wide variety of interests and persons. We have had particularly in mind the possible impact on relations with other Commonwealth countries, race relations in this country and the divisive effect on the community. Another matter for concern is the effect on the Commonwealth Games.
   'I have taken into account too, the position of the police; there is no doubt as to their ability to cope with any situation which might arise, but a tour of this nature would mean diverting police resources on a large scale from their essential ordinary duties.
   'The Government has come to the conclusion, after reviewing all these considerations, that on grounds of broad public policy they must request the Cricket Council to withdraw their invitation to the South African Cricket Association, and I should be grateful if you would put this request before the council.'—*Daily Telegraph* (London), 22 May 1970; *Guardian* (London), 22 May 1970; *Evening Standard* (London), 21 May 1970.
   The Cricket Council in calling off the tour stated: 'With deep regret the Council were of the opinion that they had no alternative but to accede to this request . . . the Council see no reason to repeat the arguments to which they still adhere, which led them to sustain the invitation to the South African cricketers issued four years ago. They do, however, deplore the activities of those who, by the intimidation of individual cricketers and threats of violent disruption have inflamed the whole issue.'—*The Times* (London), 22 May 1970; *Morning Star* (London), 23 May 1970; *Guardian* (London), 23 May 1970.

its attitude. Soccer was one of the first to suffer. Then it was the Olympic Games. Now it is snow-balling and no sport in South Africa can feel safe.'[1]

The trend is clear: in sport, as in drama, as in entertainment, South Africa (black and white) is becoming increasingly isolated from the rest of the world.

In fact the United Nations General Assembly in resolution 2396 (XXIII) of 2 December 1968 requests all States and organizations to 'suspend sporting exchanges with the racist régime and with organizations or institutions in South Africa which practise apartheid'.

Beaches

Racial zoning extends to beach provision.

In December 1965, the Minister of Planning, Mr. Haak, announced that the beaches of the municipal areas, Milverton, Cape Town, Simonstown, Fish Hock, the Strand and Gordon's Bay should be allocated to different population groups.

Certain beaches, traditionally used by non-whites, but which were situated opposite to areas reserved for white residential districts, were now to be used by whites only.

While the Milverton Town Council unanimously decided to comply with the minister's wishes, the Amenities and Finance Committee of the Cape Town City Council recommended that the council decline to accept Haak's decisions, contesting his powers to force local authorities to erect notice boards reserving beaches for the exclusive use of any group.

The council, moreover, did not agree that beach segregation was necessary, and if segregation became inevitable they wished 'a more equitable distribution of beaches for various races'.[2]

Dr. Oscar Wostheim, M.P.C., analysing the allocation of beaches, was reported as saying:

'Any worth-while beach allocated to non-Whites has been allocated for only a limited period. . . .'

Beaches formerly used by the Coloured group were no longer available for them, while:

1. *Star* (Johannesburg), 25 March 1970.
2. *Cape Times*, 14 January 1966.

'Starting from the best part of the beach at Muizenberg, the beaches have been arranged in a chromatic spectrum, starting with Whites and ending with Africans who have the worst beach. In between is found the Chinese (nearest the Whites), Indians, and Coloured.'[1]

The Cape Town City Council had repeatedly refused to erect notice boards at beaches within the area controlled by the council; these were eventually set up by the Cape Provincial Executive.[2] Beaches allocated for Coloured people in greater Cape Town are far from Coloured group areas while Kalk Bay with its Coloured fishing community has been reserved for whites only.

8   Assumptions and reality

The assumption behind the division of South Africa into separate cultural groups is that it is possible to define a group in which the racial always coincides with the cultural; that, furthermore, it is possible for groups to live a culturally self-contained existence; that the custom of South Africa has always been that of cultural difference and white supremacy and that this situation can continue indefinitely in the future.

To this should be added the assumption of some supporters of apartheid that it is possible under separate development to provide facilities adequate for each of the population groups of South Africa

1. *Cape Times*, 8 January 1965.
2. *Cape Times*, 23 April 1968 and *A Survey of Race Relations . . . 1968*, 294-5.

and that the division into racial, cultural and linguistic groups is likely to prevent race friction.

It is to be doubted that self-contained cultural groups have ever existed for any length of time. Certainly the areas of greatest cultural activity in the past have been areas where differing cultures have met and borrowed from each other. Nor is this borrowing foreign to South Africa.

The Afrikaans language itself has borrowed heavily—from Dutch, from Hottentot and from English.

South Africans have together shared the jazz culture of the urban districts, have participated in the same games and have shared in the creation and the enjoyment of literary and artistic events.

Governing the culture of South Africans has been not only their various traditional pasts, but the culture springing up in urban milieux and modified by access to sources of culture and information outside of the community. This action has been going on whatever the racial background of the South African concerned. Nat Nakasa expressed this:

'Who are my people? I am supposed to be a Pondo, but I don't even know the language of that tribe. I was brought up in a Zulu-speaking home, my mother being a Zulu. Yet I can no longer think in Zulu because that language cannot cope with the demands of our day. I could not, for instance, discuss negritude in Zulu. . . . I have never owned an assegai or any of the magnificent tribal shields. . . . I am more at home with an Afrikaner than with a West African. I am a South African. . . . "My people" are South Africans. Mine is the history of the Great Trek. Gandhi's passive resistance in Johannesburg, the wars of Atewayo and the dawn raids which gave us the treason trials in 1965. All these are South African things. They are a part of me. . . .'[1]

Nor can it always be truly said that the custom of South Africa has always meant a complete separation of the races. The arguments between Cape Town and the Central Government over library facilities separate for each of the population groups of South Africa prove this. As far as entertainment halls, operas and theatre facilities are concerned, this would be too expensive and uneconomical for private enterprise and would depend on the goodwill and the finance

1. Nat Nakasa, 'It's Difficult to Decide My Identity', written 20 June 1964. Reprinted in *Classic Quarterby* (Johannesburg), Vol. 2, No. 1, 1966, p. 50.

of the Central Government. In the case of libraries and of museums it would be impossible to duplicate unique items and prohibitively expensive to duplicate many books. Indeed, for reference materials, there has in fact been very little real attempt to do this.

What has 'culture' meant to the ordinary African South African? It has not meant producing great literature, which few people in any country can produce, but it has meant participating together—and sometimes with friends from other racial groups—in the jazz groups, in the *shebeen* parties, it meant reading *Drum* and indulging in the anti-governmental jibes that form part of many societies. These types of activities lend themselves less easily to assessment than certain more formalized types of activities; they are less documented, even though they are important to a larger group of people. It is these that are heaviest hit by the Urban Areas Act, which provides for removal of Africans to the urban outskirts, by Proclamation R.26, which makes interracial mixing without elaborate facilities for separating the audiences impossible, and by the political censorship which makes anti-governmental joking risky.

This report on the effects of apartheid on culture has left aside the whole problem of informal and personal contacts between people and private entertaining. That these are important in the ordinary daily living together of any people, no one will deny. The extent to which they can take place in South Africa is limited by the regulations governing eating together outside the home, staying overnight in named areas or in getting permission to visit 'locations'. It would be impossible, for example, for a racially mixed group of South Africans to have tea or coffee together in any public place in the Republic.

Besides this, the whole atmosphere of mistrust between people, the basic suppositions of the superiority and inferiority of racial groups, the difficult political problems, the suspicion that government-paid informers exist, make meaningful human relationships not only across colour groups, but within groups themselves, difficult to maintain.

As long as the present situation continues one thing is certain, South African culture (for whites and non-whites) will become increasingly less creative.

Cultural isolation is a high price to pay for separateness.

IV. Information

'Everyone has the right to freedom of opinion and expression; this right includes freedom to hold opinions without interference and to seek, receive and impart information and ideas through any media and regardless of frontiers.'

Article 19 of the Universal Declaration of Human Rights

1   The legal framework

In Article 19 of the Universal Declaration of Human Rights, freedom of information, based on freedom of opinion, is asserted under its double aspect: the freedom to inform and the freedom to be informed. The object of Part IV is to examine how and to what extent these freedoms have been affected by apartheid.

Freedom of the press is part of the constitution of the Republic of South Africa. Although not guaranteed by a specific constitutional act, the law, judicial decisions, proclamations and rules state clearly that freedom of the press is officially held and affirmed by the Government of South Africa. It should not however be forgotten that freedom of information for all citizens is linked to the possession of political rights and may only be exercised effectively by those who fully possess these rights. It may be and is, often restricted by legislation but this is only justified where any curtailment of the rights of the individual ensures the recognition of and the respect due to the rights of others, or where the just demand of the moral or public order requires it. These limits to freedom of information are readily recognized in any democratic society.

Consequently laws and regulations do not only affirm freedom of information, they may also reduce progressively the constitutive elements of liberty. In South Africa, a number of legislative acts, decisions, juridical regulations and administrative orders in fact restrain freedom of information, by denying the right to discuss certain opinions and to partake in certain types of activities, or by instituting a general control over publications. A summary analysis of this network of legal texts and procedures shows clearly that they are for the most part inspired by the desire to consolidate the practice of apartheid, or to put it into effect. Besides, the organization of the different means of information is in fact often done is such a way as to give to the policy of apartheid the support, the framework and the means necessary for its development.

Some of the present restrictions on freedom of information in South Africa were foreshadowed in the legislation and in the customs even before the National Government came to power. Examples of these can be seen in the Native Administrative Act No. 38 of 1927, which instituted a special censorship of films in the territories then reserved for Africans, and which prohibited words or acts that could encourage hostility between 'the natives' and 'Europeans'. The Entertainments (Censorship) Act No. 28 of 1931 established a censorship board for films and public entertainment, one of the duties of which was to eradicate scenes of intermingling between whites and non-whites. The powers of censorship of this board were extended by the Customs Act of 1955 to cover the import of printed publications.

After 1948 there was a considerable reinforcement of these regulations, and the enactment of others.

The first important Act was the Suppression of Communism Act No. 44 of 1950, which gave of communism such a wide definition as to endanger freedom of information.

Article 2(b) and (d) defines 'communism' as:

'(b) [any doctrine or scheme] which aims at bringing about any political, industrial, social or economic change within the Union by the promotion of disturbance or disorder, by unlawful acts or omission or by the threat of such acts or omissions or by means which include the promotion of disturbance or disorder, or such acts or omissions or threat; or . . .
'(d) which aims at the encouragement of feelings of hostility between the European and non-European races of the Union the consequences of which are calculated to further the achievement of any object referred to in paragraph (b).'

The powers which this law gives to government authorities and administrators both as far as persons are concerned and with regard to the press are extremely wide.

The government may prohibit any publication which it considers 'serves mainly as a means for expressing views or conveying information, the publication of which is calculated to further the achievements of any of the objects of communism' (as it is defined by the Act). An amendment of 1965 (Act No. 97) permits any journal or periodical to be banned, if, in the opinion of the authorities, it continues or replaces, whether or not under the same title, a publication that was formerly banned.

But the 'banning' goes further than the suppression of publications: people may be served with banning notices, and the restrictions placed on their activities affect access to or the right to disseminate, information.[1] The minister has the power under the Act to prohibit an individual from attending a particular meeting or playing any part in certain organizations or taking part in certain activities for a period of time (Section 5 modified). The minister may prohibit for a period of time any person from living in a given area, assign him to a determined residence (forbidding all communication with others or visiting) if he is convinced that such a person defends, facilitates or encourages the realization of communism (Section 10 amended). All acts deliberately done in order to defend or facilitate or encourage the realization of communism are 'criminal offences' (Section 11).

The amendment of 1965 authorizes the minister to apply Section 11 to all persons resident in the Republic who encourage in the Republic or outside of it the realization of any objective of communism, or who advise on, or engage in, activities which may facilitate this accomplishment.

The Act (Section 12) declares that a person is presumed to be a member of a banned organization if he attends one of its meetings or defends or encourages the realization of its objectives, or if he distributes any periodicals or other documents of that organization. The Minister of Justice may authorize any civil servant to inquire into any publication which the minister has reason to presume illegal, likely to be prohibited, and to give to this civil servant all powers to search, requisition and seize these documents.

By the amendment of 1962 (Act No. 76) it was made an offence, without the consent of the Minister of Justice or except for the purpose of any proceedings in a court of law, to record, reproduce, print, publish or disseminate any speech, utterance, writing or part thereof made anywhere at any time by persons who have been prohibited from attending gatherings. An amendment of 1965 extended this to speeches by members of organizations declared unlawful and to all other persons, in the Republic or elsewhere, whom the minister considers are advocating or defending the achievement of any of the

---

1. There are at least twenty-five different kinds of bans, but all banned persons are automatically prohibited from attending gatherings, from being members of thirty-five listed organizations and from having anything to do with the preparation, publication and dissemination of any book, periodical or pamphlet. Their sayings or writings may not be published. The banning orders are generally issued for periods of five years.—*A Survey of Race Relations . . . 1964.*

objectives of communism or any act or omission calculated to further the achievements of any such objective. The minister may, without notice to those concerned, declare by notice in the government *Gazette* that it has been rendered illegal for their speeches or writings to be quoted in South Africa.

The amendment of 1962 also stated that all persons who are listed or banned, or are former office-bearers, officers, members or active supporters of any organization which has been declared unlawful may be prohibited by a notice posted in the *Gazette* from becoming office-bearers, members or active supporters of any organization of a specified kind, unless with the written permission of the Minister of Justice or of a magistrate.

This was supplemented by two general notices: Government Notice No. 2130 of 1962 prohibited all persons covered by the amendment of 1962 from becoming or continuing as office-bearers in a list of thirty-five specified organizations, or any organization connected with those or any organization which in any manner propagates, defends, attacks, criticizes or discusses any form of State or any principles or policy of the government of a State, or which in any manner undermines the authority of the government of a State.

Government Notice No. 2961 of 1963 deals more directly with the press. It prohibited all persons covered by the amendment of 1962 from becoming or continuing to be office-bearers, members or active supporters of an organization which in any manner compiles, publishes or disseminates any newspaper, magazine, pamphlet, book, hand-bill or poster, or which assists in doing so.

A general system of control over the importation of publications has been established by the Customs Act No. 55 of 1955. It prohibits the importation into the Republic of South Africa of any goods which are 'indecent' or 'obscene' or objectionable on any grounds whatsoever, unless imported for research purposes by educational institutions under a permit issued by the Minister of the Interior. The final decision lies with the minister, who ought at all times to consult the Board of Censors appointed by the Entertainments (Censorship) Act No. 28 of 1931 before his decision is given.

The Publications and Entertainment Act No. 25 of 1963, incorporating the Customs Act, 1955, and the Post Office Act, 1958, introduced a method of general control over all forms of publications. This Act instituted a Publications Control Board, whose members, chairman and vice-chairman are appointed by the Minister of the

Interior. The board may, if it considers it necessary, set up a committee to examine and report to it on any publication. This committee is presided over by a member of the board and consists of at least two other persons chosen by the board. The control of the board also extends to objects, films and public entertainments.

The term 'publication' includes all newspapers which are not published by a publisher who is a member of the Newspaper Press Union of South Africa (who had drawn up a 'code of conduct'), and all books, periodicals, pamphlets, writings, typescripts, photographs, prints, records, etc., available to the public.

Publications are considered undesirable if they are indecent, obscene, offensive or harmful to public morals, blasphemous or offensive to the religious convictions or feelings of any section of the inhabitants of the Republic, if they bring any section of the inhabitants of the Republic into ridicule, or contempt, if harmful to the relations between any sections of the populations of the Republic, or if prejudicial to the safety of the State, the general welfare or to the peace and good order. The board exercises the powers of control attributed to the Minister of the Interior under Section 21 of the Customs Act. These provisions do not apply to *bona fide* judicial proceedings, to any publication of a technical, scientific or professional nature (*bona fide*) intended for the advancement of or for use in any particular profession or branch of arts, literature or science or any matter in any publication of a *bona fide* religious character (Section 4). Only booksellers with a special authorization may import paperbacks.

At the request of any person and (except in the cases of a person to whom any function has been assigned by this Act or the Customs Act, 1955) upon payment of a prescribed fee, the board may proceed to examine any publication or object and to state whether that publication or object is, in the opinion of the board, undesirable or not. The decisions of the board are published in the *Gazette*.

The board may by notice in the *Gazette* forbid the importation, except under special permit, of publications from a specified publisher, or which deal with any specified subject, if, in the opinion of the board, those publications or objects are undesirable or likely to be undesirable.

The board takes the place of the Board of Censorship established by the Entertainments (Censorship) Act of 1931, and exercises a general power of censorship over films.

No film may be shown to the public unless it has been approved.

The board may approve or reject a film unconditionally, or approve a film subject to the condition that such film shall be shown only to a particular group of persons or only to persons belonging to a particular race or class, or the board may order portions of the film to be cut.

The law forbids the approval of any film which may have the effect of disturbing the peace or good order, prejudicing the general welfare or affecting the relations between any section of the population of the Republic.

An appeal against the decision of the board may be made to the Minister of the Interior, whose decision is final.

The board may prohibit any public entertainment; an appeal to the courts may be made against the decision of the board.

It is important to underline the severity of the penalties under this Act. For the first conviction a fine of from R.300 to R.500 or imprisonment for a period not exceeding six months, or both, is imposed. For the second conviction, a fine of between R.1,000 and R.2,000 and imprisonment for a period of not less than six months.

The courts may confiscate any publication or film when an offence is committed.

The Publications and Entertainments Amendment Act No. 85 of 1969 dealt with periodicals produced in the Republic other than newspapers published by members of the Newspaper Press Union. It dealt with subsequent issues of a periodical which had been deemed undesirable either by a court of law or by the Publications Control Board. The board may now declare every subsequent issue of the periodical undesirable, if it considers that it is likely that they will be undesirable. It will then become an offence to produce, distribute or display the publication. The board may withdraw the notice at any time, and persons are given thirty days to appeal to the Supreme Court against the board's ruling under this amendment to the principal Act.

The Official Secrets Act of 1956, was amended in 1965. The present text considers it an offence, punishable by a fine of not over R.1,000 or an imprisonment for a period not exceeding seven years, or both, for any person to be in possession of, or to publish directly or indirectly, documents or information related to war material or any military or police matter, and to communicate such documents or information, if this is likely to be prejudicial to the safety or interest of the State.

This new Act has been opposed in Parliament and objected to by many newspapers. The president of the South African Society of Journalists declared that, in his opinion, this measure considerably restrains the freedom of the press.[1]

Section 10 of the 1969 General Law Amendment Act further amended the Official Secrets Act of 1956. The section of the principal Act relating to military information now became applicable to security matters as well as to military and police matters.

A 'security matter' was defined as any matter relating to the security of the Republic, including any matter dealt with or relating to the Bureau for State Security or relating to the relationship subsisting between any person and the said Bureau. The Bureau for State Security (popularly known as BOSS) was set up by Public Service Amendment Act No. 86 of 1969. The Bureau co-ordinates and complements the activities of the security branch of the police and the military intelligence division of the defence force. Its funds are provided for under the Security Services Special Account Act No. 817 of 1969. They will not be subject to treasury approval in relation to expenditures from the Consolidated Revenue fund. It is excluded from the requirements of the Public Service Act in terms of which the Minister of the Interior must present to Parliament a return of the names, salary scales and special qualifications of anybody appointed to the administrative division.

Some provisions of the Act have been condemned by the Johannesburg Bar Council, Cape Bar Council, Pretoria Bar Council and the Natal Law Society.[2] BOSS also came under attack from the Herstigte National Party, who feared that they were also subject to its investigations.

The South African Society of Journalists recorded its concern about Section 10 of the Act. They considered it the most serious curtailment of freedom yet made of the freedom of the press in South Africa.[3] The Newspaper Union was concerned about the possibility that the press might unwittingly report on matters that concerned the Bureau for State Security.

Under the Prisons Amendment Act No. 75 of 1965, it is an offence to sketch or photograph a prison or part thereof, a prisoner, or the

---

1. *Natal Mercury*, 13 April 1965.
2. *Star* (Johannesburg), 29 June 1969.
3. *A Survey of Race Relations . . . 1969*, p. 35, 36.

burial of an executed prisoner, or to cause such a sketch or photograph to be published, or to publish any false information concerning the behaviour or the life in prison of any convicted or ex-convicted person. Financial laws such as the Newspaper Imprint Act and the Sabotage Act[1] give to the Minister of Justice the right to demand a deposit of £10,000 for any publication which he considers may be banned. This sum may be confiscated if the publication is, in fact, suppressed.

Finally, freedom of the press is not mentioned in the constitutional law of the Transkei (Act No. 48 of 1963). On the contrary, Article 39 excludes from the competence of the Legislative Assembly of the Transkei every matter related to international relations, the entry of persons other than Transkeian citizens into the Transkei and postal, telegraph, telephone, radio and television services.

2   The application of the law

The *Annual Survey of South African Law, 1963* states that there were 7,500 banned publications.[2] According to the vice-president of the Publications Control Board, 466 publications were banned during the first half year of 1965.[3] It was estimated that by June 1969, 13,000 publications had been banned,[4] including those banned by the Censorship

---

1. See *Repressive Legislation of the Republic of South Africa*, New York, United Nations, 1969 (ST/PSCA/Ser.A/7, Para. 192).
2. *Annual Survey of South African Law, 1963*, p. 52.
3. *Sunday Times*, 6 September 1965.
4. Ellison Kahn, professor of law, University of the Witwatersrand, *Sunday Times*, 8 June 1969.

Board before the Publications Board was created in 1963. In 1969, 616 imported and 63 local publications were prohibited and the embargo on 9 had been lifted.[1] In 1967, 409 imported publications and 12 local publications had been prohibited, and in 1968, 419 imported publications had been prohibited. Prohibitions had been lifted on 18 during the period 1967-68.[2]

It would be unfair to attribute the banning of all these publications to the policy of apartheid. Many have been banned because they were considered pornographic, indecent or representing a threat to the public order or to the security of the State. It is in this last category, however, that it is not clear which decisions were exclusively dictated by security reasons and which by apartheid. The impression was conveyed that most of these publications could only have been banned for this last reason. Examples are the banning, under the Suppression of Communism Act, of the weekly, the *Guardian*, and its successors *Advance* and *New Age*. A clear example of censorship was the omission of fifty-two pages from the second volume of the Oxford University Press *History of South Africa*. The English edition included a chapter on African nationalism between 1912 and 1970 written by Professor Leo Kuper, formerly of South Africa, now Director of the African Studies Center, University of California.

With regard to persons, the *Gazette* dated 6 November 1964, listed the names of 303 persons banned under the same Act. A government notice, No. 296 of February 1963 published a list of journalists banned under the Suppression of Communism Act.

Muriel Horrell estimated that since the Suppression of Communism Act became law and up to 30 November 1969, 979 persons had been served with banning orders, of whom 89 had subsequently left South Africa, 17 had died, 518 orders may have been withdrawn or not renewed and 355 remained in force against persons in the Republic. She calculated that listed persons—who may not have been banned —amounted to 401, of whom 67 whites and 23 non-whites had left South Africa. Twenty-one whites and 48 non-whites, who formerly lived in the Republic, cannot be quoted within it.[3]

As a result of the banning of their main collaborators, the weeklies *Spark* and *Torch* went out of print. In 1965 *Forum* went out of print.

1. Minister of the Interior, *House of Assembly Debates (Hansard)*, 17 February 1970, Col. 1889.
2. Minister of the Interior, *House of Assembly Debates (Hansard)*, Vol. 9, 8 April 1969, Cols. 3498-501.
3. *A Survey of Race Relations . . . 1969*, p. 41-2.

Ralph Horowitz, in the last editorial published in the magazine, wrote that in the present climate of South Africa there is little place for a protest periodical.

Among the journalists who have been arrested under the ninety-day detention Act[1] are Ruth First (*New Age*), Margaret Fint (*Sunday Times*, Johannesburg) and Paul Trewhela (*Rand Daily Mail*). In 1960, Ronald Segal, editor of *Africa South*, was prohibited from participating in any meeting for five years. As a result of harassments, searching and banning, the *New African* and its collaborators decided to publish it in exile. The importation of the periodical was then forbidden under the Customs Act. In July 1965, the homes and offices of journalists of the liberal press were searched. The editor in chief of the *Rand Daily Mail*, Laurence Gandar, and one of his best-known reporters, Benjamin Pogrund, were tried and convicted after they had written articles on the conditions of life in prison. Gandar is now in England.

The case of the African journalist, Nat Nakasa, who has written for *Drum* and for the literacy review *Classic*, is well known. The South African Government refused to issue him with a passport so that he could benefit from a scholarship at Harvard. He was issued with a one-way permit and forced to go into exile. He died in the United States.

---

1. Section 17 of the General Law Amendment Act No. 37 of 1963 provides that as from 1 May 1963 a commissioned officer of the police may without warrant arrest any person whom he suspects has committed or intends to commit sabotage or any offence under the Suppression of Communism or Unlawful Organization Acts, or who in the police officer's opinion is in possession of any information relating to such an offence. A person so arrested is detained in custody until, in the opinion of the commissioner of police, he has replied satisfactorily to all questions put to him. No one may be detained for more than ninety days on any particular occasion.—*A Survey of Race Relations . . . 1964*, p. 59 ff.

3   The press

In South Africa, there are twenty-two daily newspapers, sixteen published in English with a combined daily circulation of 746,800 and six in Afrikaans with a combined daily circulation of 165,500.[1] The percentage, then, is roughly 8.8 copies per 100 inhabitants. The percentage is still considerably less for the African population, where only a very small number has access to the press. Six dailies issue special week-end editions. These have a circulation considerably higher than the dailies. Figures are even higher for the six Sunday newspapers published in the Transvaal and in the Natal Province.[2] But although two English-language Sunday newspapers and the Afrikaans Sunday papers have a nation-wide circulation, this circulation is unequally distributed between the various population groups.

As far as the press designed for African readers is concerned, *World Communications* reports: 'The number of Bantu papers is constantly growing, and there has been a significant increase in the number of vernacular editions of established English-language periodicals. Some are published in several vernaculars.'[3] A daily, launched in Johannesburg in 1962—a white-owned newspaper with an African editor and intended for African readers—had a first-day circulation of 16,000 copies.[2]

A press specially designed for Africans exists. The creation by missionaries of a newspaper in the Zulu language—*Imbo Zabantsindu*—was followed by the creation of the Bantu Press group in 1931. This press now consists of three groups: the Afrikaanse Pers Beperk which publishes *Zonk*, the magazine *Bona* (with a monthly circulation of around 83,000) and *Imbo Zabantsindu*, with a circulation of 16,000. The Post newspaper group publishes the *Weekly Post* and the

1. *World Communications, Press, Radio, Television, Film,* 2nd ed., p. 117, Paris, Unesco, 1966.
2. ibid.
3. ibid., p. 118.

monthly *Drum*, with a total circulation of 165,000. Bantu Press publishes the afternoon daily, the *World*, with a circulation, in December 1965, of 73,109.

There are two Indian and one Moslem newspapers designed mainly for the Asian group.

The Coloureds have access to either the Afrikaans-language newspapers, or the English-language newspapers.

There exists nevertheless, in spite of this increase, a clear disproportion between the circulation of English- and Afrikaans-language newspapers compared with newspapers designed for Africans, and particularly with those written in the vernacular (mother tongue). This is particularly so if the population figures for the various groups are taken into account.[1]

Important as is quantity in studying the effectiveness of the press as a channel of information, two other factors are no less important: the way the press in fact functions, and the conditions under which it functions.

Organization

As in many other countries, ownership in South Africa is strongly concentrated. The Government Commission of Inquiry into the Press, set up in 1951, was prompted by the need felt in some quarters that concentration in the English-language press should be studied. The first part of the report of this committee established that the Argus and the South African Associated Newspapers groups between them dominate the English-language daily and Sunday press in South Africa.

The main Afrikaans-language dailies are linked to the National Party, and prominent members in the present government sit on their boards.

Since 1933 the major portion of the newspaper press designed for Africans has been controlled by persons who have large interests in the South African mining industry, or by the Afrikaanse Pers Beperk.

The concentration of the press is reinforced by the monopoly of control which the South African Press Association enjoys both as to the collection and in the distribution of news.

The concentration of the press is certainly not the result of apart-

1. See Introduction, Table 2, 'Population by Racial Group'.

heid. What is important to this study, particularly with regard to the Afrikaans-language press, and the press designed for Africans, is who controls it, and what interests (as far as the policy of apartheid is concerned) they represent. The Minister of Education distributes 20,000 copies of *Bona* free of charge to African schools. A cursory glance at the numerous magazines produced for Africans shows that particular types of publications are favoured: those that, if they do not openly favour the policy of apartheid, at least do not question it.

Commercial advertising, special concessions, certain exemptions from taxation which the newspaper monopolies have access to, make it difficult for newspapers owned outside of this circle to come into existence. Again this is not the result of apartheid—but it makes the control of dissent easier.

While newspapers are still published, particularly in the English-language press, which criticize aspects of the government's policy, it is worthy of note that of all the publications existing in 1960 which could be considered hostile to the framework of discrimination and apartheid, only one survived in 1965, the bi-monthly *Contact*, founded in 1958 by Patrick Duncan. *Contact*, itself, had been subject to many harassments, including the banning of four of its editors, and the detention of one of them; it has now been discontinued.

The English-language press has, generally speaking, defended liberal principles. Certain newspapers—notably the *Rand Daily Mail* and the *Cape Times*—have opposed the methods of control, the banning measures that have been put into effect to safeguard the policy of apartheid, as well as many of the measures designed to implement certain aspects of racial zoning. A reading of these newspapers over a period of time, however, as well as an examination of both the presentation and the slant of articles, suggest that criticism is becoming blunted, or at least less outspoken.

This may be due to particular repressive measures taken against some of the journalists and to the present political climate, rather than to a change of ideological commitment.

Criticism of aspects of the government's policy has not been confined to English-language newspapers; it is appropriate to note that *Die Burger* sometimes takes a moderate or reserved position vis-à-vis government measures.

Professional activities

The policy of apartheid also affects the type of employment open to Africans in the press. There are a number of Africans in the 'Bantu' press, including the editor and senior journalists of the *World*, but they have no real say in the policy of the newspapers. What is remarkable is that so few dailies in South Africa include non-whites on their editorial staff. The various measures that affect the African population directly, the pass laws, laws governing the length of time that they may stay outside particular areas, the problems of access to particular information, the impossibility of sharing meaningful contacts with either the civil service or Members of Parliament, make it virtually impossible for an African to become a successful journalist.

The newspapers which were most willing to employ a multi-racial journalistic service have disappeared, while Nat Nakasa, who wrote for the *Classic* and the *Rand Daily Mail*, was forced into exile.

The problems of getting first-hand information about the 'homelands' affects white journalists as well as non-white, since only 'citizens' of these 'homelands' may go there without special permit.

It was mentioned earlier (Chapter 1, 'The Legal Framework', above) that certain provisions of the Publications and Entertainment Act No. 25 of 1963 are not applicable to newspapers published by a member of the Newspaper Press Union of South Africa, which had accepted a 'code of conduct.'

The code begins, as one would expect, by declarations in favour of freedom of the press and 'individual liberties'. It is to ensure these liberties that the press should maintain a high standard. The code enumerates the rules of professional behaviour. The press should avoid excesses, or the use of 'undesirable material' both in the presentation and in the diffusion of its news. This final advice is important as far as this study is concerned: if the press wishes to preserve its traditional right of criticism, its commentaries should take due cognizance of the complex racial problems of South Africa.

A board of reference ensures that this code is respected, and may investigate, after having received a written complaint, any infringement of the code and, if it considers that the code has been broken, may order a published correction. Adherence to the code and to the board's jurisdiction is voluntary, and anyone disagreeing with it may withdraw by written notice to the board.

It is interesting to note that the South African Society of Journalists has not accepted the code.[1]

A far more drastic reorganization of the press has been suggested by the Press Commission, which had been set up in 1950, and which sent in its second report to Parliament on 11 May 1964.[2]

The commission censured overseas newspapers, including *The Times* of London and the *New York Times*, for their alleged hostility to Afrikaner nationalists and claimed that many reports were written as propaganda against the white people of South Africa and with little regard to South Africa's historical background and its linguistic and racial plurality. It then went on to recommend that a statutory Press Council be established 'for the control and discipline' of the press. This Press Council would consist of representatives of proprietors and newspapermen of journals published in South Africa, representatives of the public to be elected by two electoral colleges, one Afrikaans and one English, and representatives of the government and of the main opposition party.[3] The participation of non-whites on this council is not mentioned.

The commission recommended that the council should maintain a register of approved journalists, and that only those journalists who were granted registration should have authority to cable news overseas. All press cables should be filed with the Department of Posts and Telegraphs and should be available for public inspection for forty-eight hours after their dispatch. This council should have powers to impose fines, to reprimand and to order publication of its judgements and there should be no right of appeal against its judgements.[4]

The recommendations of the council have not been put into force, but they have provoked a great deal of discussion both in South Africa and abroad.

Writing in the *Cape Argus*, S. J. Marais Steyn, M.P., argued that 'should the government accept this recommendation for a Press Council, every report emanating from South Africa to the outside world will be suspect'.[5] *Die Burger*, less outspoken in its criticism, pointed out that, if this council was set up, its powers to punish

1. The South African Society of Journalists accepts Asians and Coloureds as members, but may not accept Africans, because of the provisions of the Industrial Conciliation Act.
2. The first report was submitted in April 1962.
3. *A Survey of Race Relations . . . 1964*, p. 43-4.
4. ibid., p. 44.
5. *Cape Argus*, 15 May 1964.

infringements of a code of conduct would be 'a remarkable jurisdiction to entrust to a body of laymen'.[1]

4   Radio and cinema

It is generally agreed that the radio is of primary importance as a channel of communication both within a country, and with the outside world. This is particularly so in countries with a large percentage of illiteracy where it can be an instrument for education and for social and cultural development.

The South African Broadcasting Service is a State monopoly entrusted to the South African Broadcasting Corporation (SABC) by the Broadcasting Act No. 22 of 1936.

It is an autonomous organization placed under the management and control of a board of governors appointed by the State President, who also names the chairmen and vice-chairmen of this board.

Originally, the board was to 'frame and carry out its broadcasting programmes with due regard to the interests of both English and Afrikaans culture',[2] but by Act No. 49 of 1960, the government instituted a Bantu Programme Control Board, to be appointed by the State President, and amended Section 14 of the principal Act to read 'English, Afrikaans and Bantu Culture'.[3]

There are in South Africa 45 transmitters,[4] 1,140,000 wireless

---

1. Here quoted from 'Nationalist Viewpoint', *Cape Times*, 13 May 1964.
2. Act No. 22 of 1936, Section 14.
3. Act No. 49 of 1960, Section 13*bis*.
4. *World Communications, Press, Radio, Television, Film*, op. cit.

receivers and 10,700 wired receivers. This gives a percentage of 6.9 per 100 inhabitants.

There are three principal programmes: English, Afrikaans and commercial, to which should be added a Bantu programme and a weekly programme for Indians.

In 1952 a rediffusion service was started for Africans. In 1959 there were 12,450 subscribers[1] and in 1971 it was calculated that Radio Bantu reached 93.4 per cent of the African population.[2]

The personnel of Radio Bantu comprised 200 African technicians, white personnel only acting as 'advisers'.

The programmes deal with information and education (a school programme in five Bantu languages is intended for 250,000 children).

South Africa has considered it necessary to counteract the propaganda broadcast by countries outside of South Africa. To this effect, the South African Government has paid increasing attention to the development of its overseas broadcasts. Programmes of the Voice of South Africa are already stating South Africa's case.[3]

The centralization of radio and, above all, the creation of special programmes for Africans, is certainly one facet of the policy of apartheid. (One may mention, in that respect, that the President of the SABC as well as the Minister of Post and Telecommunications, were, in 1965, both members of the Broederbond.)

The SABC may legally constitute an autonomous public service, but it is generally agreed that it is primarily a government organ, fully supporting government policy, under tight State control.[4] A private member's bill was tabled by Mr. E. G. Malan in 1963 condemning the refusal of the government to supply Parliament with full information on the activities of the SABC and asking that a commission should be set up to inquire into, among other things, the corporation's policies, bias in news reports and political talks, the use of the radio for political propaganda and indoctrination and the work of the Bantu Programme Control Board.[5]

That the SABC favours apartheid can be seen most clearly by the slant of its programmes: *Current Affairs* is prepared by,

1. ibid.
2. *South African Digest*, 21 May 1971, p. 5.
3. *Guardian* (London), 28 November 1965.
4. See *The Times* (London), 23 October 1965, *Observer* (London), 11 November 1962, *Sunday Express* (London), 15 November 1965.
5. *House of Assembly Debates (Hansard)*, Vol. 10, 21 March, Col. 3714, here quoted from *A Survey of Race Relations in South Africa, 1963*, op. cit., p. 280.

among others, the editor of *Die Vaderland*,[1] and it refused to broadcast, as it would normally do, any commentary on the golf tournament in which Sewgolum Papwa (Indian) had taken part.[2] A spokesman of the SABC was reported as saying that in terms of the policy laid down by the SABC's board of governors, the corporation did not broadcast multi-racial sport[3] in South Africa.

A television service was one of the objectives of the SABC and provision for it was made in the Broadcasting Act of 1936, as amended (Article 12). But the government has for many years refused to implement this article.

A commission was set up to study the feasibility of introducing television. At the time of writing the content of its report and the government's reaction to it is not known.

Finally, it should be remembered that the Transkeian Constitution expressly excludes the fields of radio and television from the competence of the Legislative Council of the Transkei.

There has been an attempt to stimulate the film industry in South Africa, with financial aid from the State.[4] Some films have been produced in Afrikaans, but most of the English-language films are still imported from the United Kingdom or from the United States of America. However, documentaries are produced and distributed by the Ministry of Education, and newsreels are also produced. A new company, Film Trust (Pty.) Ltd., has been formed to produce films especially for Africans. These would use African actors and scriptwriters and would handle 'acceptable' overseas films dubbed into African languages.

World Communications mentions an audience average of 55 million[5] representing an individual attendance of 4.4 per year. Government sources report that there are more than 400 cinemas, not counting mobile and open-air cinemas.[6]

Cinemas in white areas are prohibited to non-whites. It is difficult to measure the number of cinemas actually available to Africans in the absence of precise figures. In 1968 there was only one in the Soweto township of Johannesburg and many Africans go to cinemas owned by Indians and Coloureds in the Fordsburg area. In May

---

1. *Die Vaderland* is an Afrikaans newspaper linked to the Nationalist Party.
2. See also Part III, Chapter 7, 'Sport'.
3. *A Survey of Race Relations . . . 1963.*
4. *World Communications, Press, Radio, Television, Film,* op. cit., p. 118.
5. ibid.
6. *Connaissez-vous l'Afrique du Sud?,* No. 58, December 1965.

1968 the Department of Community Development instructed the owners to provide separate facilities for Africans and to limit the number of Africans to one-tenth of the audience.[1] The construction of new cinemas is planned for 'Bantu areas'.

Films for Africans are subjected to strict censorship. In most countries there is some censorship of films, but, in the Republic of South Africa, this is used as an instrument to further 'separate development'. The Censorship Board has the power to prohibit the showing of films (otherwise authorized) before any particular class or race. On many occasions the board has decided that, while a film may be shown in a non-white cinema, children of from 4 to 16 years and Africans may not be admitted. There is a tendency to bar from the general public any films which do not present non-whites in an inferior position to whites. *Heaven's Above* with Peter Sellers was banned, because the producer had refused to cut scenes in which a non-white appeared on an equal footing with whites. *Blackboard Jungle* and *I'll Cry Tomorrow* have also been banned. A scene in *Show Boat* was cut because Ava Gardner mentioned her racial background. The films *West Side Story*, *Cleopatra* and *Spartacus* were banned for African audiences.

5   International news

It is one of the main wishes of the South African Government that international information should be slanted so as to conform with the policy of the government and particularly with its apartheid policy.

1. *A Survey of Race Relations . . . 1968*, p. 291-2.

Everything has been done to prevent the introduction into the country of overseas information, judged from this point of view as 'undesirable'.

The Customs Act and the Publications and Entertainment Act include measures to hinder the action of journalists, and to limit the penetration of overseas broadcasts.

There is a long list of newspaper correspondents who have been expelled or have been refused visas.

A more discreet system, that of the issue of 'credential cards', permits the administrative authorities to control, restrain or suppress activities of foreign journalists. An example of this is the government's action in refusing visas to the forty press and television representatives from the United States who were to accompany Robert Kennedy on his visit to South Africa. British journalists, who normally did not need a visa to work in South Africa, were requested to apply for a temporary alien's permit for the duration of their stay.[1]

The second report of the Commission of Inquiry into the Press is particularly revealing. This report was almost completely dedicated to the activities of correspondents (permanent or feature writers) of foreign press agencies.

Thus 75.95 per cent or 1,665,214 words cabled to British journals during the period of the commission's inquiry and which reported on the political and social situation of South Africa were judged as bad or very bad, giving a bad image of South Africa, as far as the racial situation was concerned.

News carried by Reuters, Associated Press, United Press International, and Agence France-Press was considered with few exceptions unfair, unobjective, angled and partisan.[2]

It is only fair to add that the commission's report contained attacks, not only on foreign journalists, but on the English-language press in South Africa, while the Nationalist press is hardly mentioned in the report.[3]

The South African Government distributes large quantities of free, well-illustrated brochures abroad to present its point of view. But it is, above all, in the area of broadcasting that its propaganda has increased over the past years.

---

1. *Star* (Johannesburg), 28 May 1966.
2. *The Times* (London), 12 May 1964, *Guardian* (London), 12 May 1964.
3. *Cape Times*, 13 and 21 May 1964.

Certain overseas radio services can broadcast at present with more powerful transmitters than the South African transmitters. And the growing number of transistor sets gives them a large audience. The world press stated that a law was being considered to forbid all aid given to radio stations considered as hostile to South Africa. The Minister of Posts and Telegraphs would be authorized to establish a list of all foreign radio stations whose broadcasts are contrary to the morals or the religion of the Republic or a section of the population of the Republic or prejudicial to the good of the Republic.[1] Above all, the government is anxious to increase considerably its own means of propaganda. To do this, four transmitters of 250 kW each have been installed at Bloomand. They broadcast in four main directions: East and Central Africa and part of the Middle East; West Africa and Western Europe; North America, Australia and New Zealand; South America, Central America, India and the Far East.

Inaugurating the first of these transmitters Dr. Verwoerd declared:

'This enterprise has become indispensable due to the propaganda attacks beamed to the African continent in twenty-three languages, of which seven are Bantu dialects. The aim of our radio message to the external world is to inform them exactly as to what happens here. . . . It is on the other hand necessary to explain that the only method of conciliation between the races rests in the process of their separate development at all levels.'[2]

1. See *La Correspondance de la Presse*, 18 August 1966.
2. Translated from *L'Afrique du Sud d'Aujourd'hui*, November 1965.

Conclusion

This report concludes most explicitly that in education, science, culture and information, apartheid violates, both in principle and in practice, the United Nations Charter, the Constitution of Unesco, the United Nations Universal Declaration of Human Rights, as well as the standards which have been set by the international community in conventions, recommendations and declarations which have been adopted within the United Nations System.

Moreover, 'separate development', as practised within the Republic of South Africa, does not mean equality between various ethnic groups in any of the spheres with which Unesco is concerned. On the contrary, it is a policy of deliberate inequality built into the educational system, expressed in scientific and cultural activities, and underlined in the regulations governing access to information.

Apartheid not only is not an admissible answer to racial and group conflict but is itself the major source of this conflict. This is most serious in relationships between whites and non-whites, but the very heightening of group awareness, which is part of the aims of the apartheid system, should *per se* intensify hostilities between Afrikaans- and English-speaking South Africa, and, by the separation of Africans into self-contained tribal units, create a tribal nationalism leading to increased intertribal rivalry.

The image of man—to whatever ethnic group he belongs or is made a part of—which results from the policy of apartheid in South Africa, is an image which is clearly opposite the one to which the community of nations is ethically and legally dedicated.

The ill effects of apartheid are not confined to the situation within South Africa: 'the practice of apartheid and all other forms of racial discrimination constitute a threat to international peace and security and are a crime against humanity', as stated in the resolution on 'Unesco's Tasks in the Light of the Resolutions Adopted by the

General Assembly of the United Nations at its Twentieth Session on Questions Relating to the Liquidation of Colonialism and Racialism', which was adopted by the General Conference at its fourteenth session (November 1966).

The Secretary-General of the United Nations emphasized in an address on 3 February 1964:

'There is the clear prospect that racial conflict, if we cannot curb and finally eliminate it, will grow into a destructive monster compared to which the religious or ideological conflicts of the past and present will seem like small family quarrels. . . . This, for the sake of all our children, whatever their race and colour, must not be permitted to happen.'

The group of experts, established by the Security Council resolution of 4 December 1963, warned that

'a race conflict starting in South Africa must affect race relations elsewhere in the world, and also, in its international repercussions, create a world danger of first magnitude.'

It is with the knowledge of such a danger, and with the full consciousness of Unesco's dedication to the dignity of man and to peace, that this report has been established.